IMAGES
of America

LA GRANGE

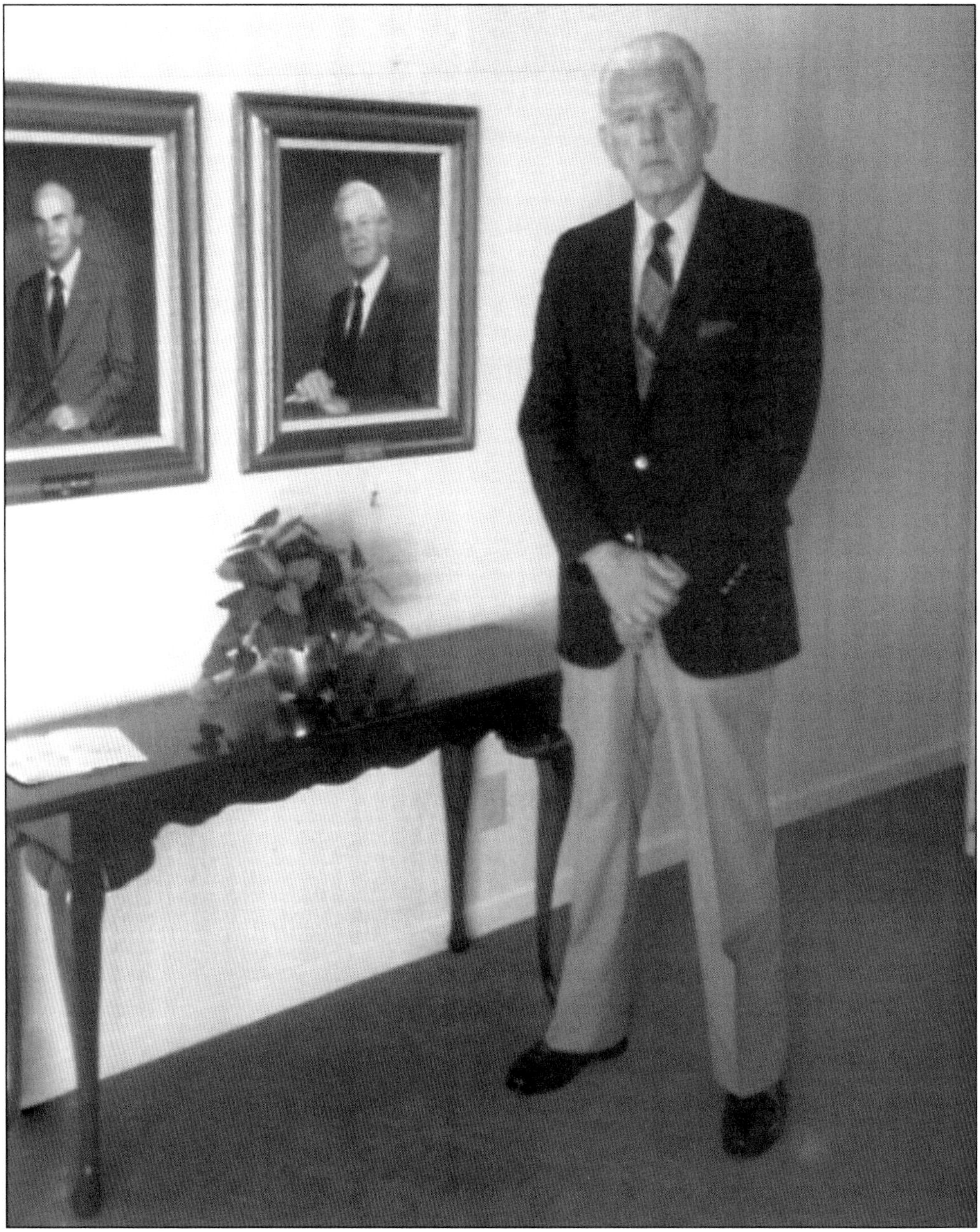

Robert Channing Rouse, 1988. Bob Rouse was known for his incredible ability to recall facts and stories from the past. He was the inspiration for the birth of the La Grange Historical Society. Rouse served the town of La Grange as a councilman, and he was a past winner of the La Grange Citizen of the Year award. (Courtesy of the Bob Rouse family.)

On the Cover: La Grange Fire Department, 1910. These men were very proud of their local fire department. Many of those pictured here were business owners. They took pride in the large volunteer base. The firefighters could get to a blaze quickly because the well was in the center of the town. These men were challenged in 1911, when La Grange's greatest fire swept quickly through town. (Courtesy of the Bob Rouse family.)

IMAGES
of America

LA GRANGE

Chris C. McCallister

ARCADIA
PUBLISHING

ISBN 978-1-4671-2030-2

Published by Arcadia Publishing
Charleston, South Carolina

Printed in the United States of America

Library of Congress Control Number: 2013934060

For all general information, please contact Arcadia Publishing:
Telephone 843-853-2070
Fax 843-853-0044
E-mail sales@arcadiapublishing.com
For customer service and orders:
Toll-Free 1-888-313-2665

Visit us on the Internet at www.arcadiapublishing.com

To Bob Rouse and Cecil Burke Jr. Both men inspired the town they loved. Their passion and dedication to La Grange history lives on.

Contents

Acknowledgments

Lynn Taylor is a local businessman whose help with this book was invaluable. Your passion for the town speaks volumes, shown by your actions openly and behind the scenes. You are the granite that this author relied on.

The La Grange Historical Society contains a wealth of information about La Grange. To Gary Fields, the current president of the society, thank you for your knowledge of and contribution to La Grange's history. Other members of the historical society that contributed to this book were Glen Fields, J.P. Walters III, Monica LeMastus, Dorethea Branch, K.D. Kennedy, and many more. Your research is a testament to your dedication to the town of La Grange. Also, thank you to the La Grange Frink Alumni Association and Speck and Sister Fields for inspiring me.

To Bob Rouse, there is not a day that went by that I did not hear your voice in my ear encouraging me to write. You are the inspiration and the true historian of La Grange. Your love for the people and for preserving the history of the town will always have your fingerprints on it. I miss the conversations we had in our yards. Thank you for your friendship and for being the best neighbor a man could have asked for.

Cecil (Cecil Burke Jr.) was a ball of energy; thank you for all of your insight and encouragement to write this book. La Grange has lost one of its liveliest and most wonderful characters. You inspired many with your kindness, and your testimony lives on in your sons Ray and Mike as well as in your grandchildren and your wife, Miss Grace.

Finally, thank you to the Jake and Christine Herring Jr. family. Sonny and Frank, your father was dear to me. Sonny, thank you for preserving the James Rouse photographs and contributing them to this work. To the fantastic people of La Grange, thank you for all that you gave to make this book a labor of love.

INTRODUCTION

La Grange began just a few miles from its current city limits as a small farming area known as Bear Creek. The settlement later grew into what would be known as Moseley Hall, which was begun in the early to mid-1700s by the Joshua Herring and Matthew Moseley families. Both of the families were farmers. The Moseley plantation, referred to as Moseley Hall, served as the main stagecoach station for Bear Creek, Jason, Moseley Hall, and Falling Creek townships. Soon, John Wooten, a hatter by trade, and his family came to the area from Pitt County, North Carolina, and Virginia. John Wooten and his son Council grew their land into a well-run and prosperous plantation. These three families became very successful at tobacco and cotton farming. By 1869, these families and others grew the surrounding settlements into La Grange.

Eventually, other families began to move in and settle the area, including the Rouse, Dawson, Fields, Mewborn, Sutton, Best, and Whitfield clans. In June 1858, the Atlantic & North Carolina Railroad opened 95 miles of track from Goldsboro to New Bern on to Morehead City. The railroad began construction in Moseley Hall (La Grange) in 1855. That year, there were three homes in Moseley Hall, owned by William Dunn Moseley, Drew Murphy, and George Franklin Whitfield. The railroad was completed in 1858. With the opening of the railroad, more and more people moved into the town. Later, La Grange became one of North Carolina's major warehousing depots for tobacco.

During the Civil War, First Missionary Baptist Church was used as a hospital. On April 10, 1869, Moseley Hall changed its name to La Grange. Dr. Hadley and Colonel Whitfield convinced the town to adopt the new name, chosen to honor the French general the Marquis de Lafayette. During Reconstruction (1865–1877), La Grange residents rebuilt the town. Union soldiers had eaten most of the town's food and burned down homes, such as Council Wooten's home, which was shot up. The residents turned to the task of reestablishing farms, and the town bounced back quickly. Also during Reconstruction, the town established its first police department, which was made up solely of African Americans. About five years later, Winfield Murchison became the sheriff. The first mayor of La Grange was a Mr. McIntyre.

In 1869, the La Grange Academy was established by local physician Preston Wilson Wooley. The academy was purchased in early 1881 by Joseph E. Kinsey and renamed Kinsey Seminary. The seminary today is Barton College. In 1880, the Davis Military Academy was founded. At one point, it had nearly 300 students. The school moved to Winston Salem in 1890.

By the turn of the century, La Grange had established itself. It now had a post office, whose first postmaster was Bill Best. The area's farming had once again rebounded and flourished. La Grange became the fourth-largest tobacco warehousing town in North Carolina. For convenience, the tobacco warehouses were located by the railroad. Supply trains could pull up and load their product with ease. The town established its first official volunteer fire department around 1905. During World Wars I and II, La Grange's Hardy-Newsome foundry, established in 1905, made camouflage and other items for the war effort. The foundry had great success with its soybean harvester. It would turn out 75–100 bushels a day, and this output was sold worldwide. The machine's popularity soared by 1918. The original bean harvester sold for $150.

Also in the early 1900s, La Grange became a part of the train route known as the "Shoofly." The Shoofly ran between Goldsboro and Morehead City, North Carolina. The train's porter was Eugene "Jim" Shaw, a La Grange citizen. He became the first African American porter on the Shoofly. It was Shaw who gave the town its nickname, "the Garden Spot."

Through the major events and eras of US history, La Grange adapted. The Great Depression was met with farmers feeding people; although money was short, food was not. La Grange citizens signed up to defend their country in World Wars I and II, Korea, Vietnam, Desert Storm, and the War on Terrorism. La Grange had some great people, and a few caught and catalogued those historical events, like Nannie Braxton Herring's history written document of 1917 and James L. Rouse's impressive photography collection.

As you read the words and view the images in this book, on behalf of the town of La Grange, let us welcome you to our town. Come visit us. You are always welcome, and it would be nice to meet a new friend. Come on by and have a sweet tea at Murray's, or pick up some local, farmer-grown sweet corn from the Garden Spot Hardware. Jim Shaw said it best: "Welcome to La Grange, the Garden Spot!"

One

La Grange, the Early Years

La Grange did not receive its name until 1869. Originally, the town's name came from the Matthew Moseley family. The Moseleys have been in North Carolina since the early 1700s. Edward Moseley, the surveyor general of the North Carolina province, was among the first to map North Carolina. The Moseleys of Moseley Hall (La Grange) were descendants of his. When the Moseleys moved to the area, they met up with the Joshua Herring family in the 1730s and 1740s. Eventually, the two families intermarried.

By the end of the 1700s, John Wooten had moved into the area and settled into farming. Wooten had influence in the newly formed Dobbs County, which incorporates Wayne and Lenoir Counties. He served in the House of Commons and thus began a line of public service for many of the Wooten family. By 1832, Wooten's son Council had established himself as a successful planter. Council entered into public service in the general assembly and was among the legislators that worked on the state's revised constitution of 1835.

Another Moseley Hall resident, William Dunn Moseley, Matthew's son, served the public in the state senate and was the Speaker. W.D. Moseley was well thought of throughout the state and ran for governor in 1834. He lost by a small margin to David Swain. In the years to come, more families moved into La Grange, and the town began to grow, especially after the Civil War. The town council changed the name Moseley Hall to La Grange on April 10, 1869. The name change came about under the influence of Dr. Jacob M. Hadley and George F. Whitfield. The town progressed after Reconstruction, installing its first police department and post office, and it began to see tobacco farming become a cash crop. After a 1911 fire, La Grange began to rebuild and to grow mightily.

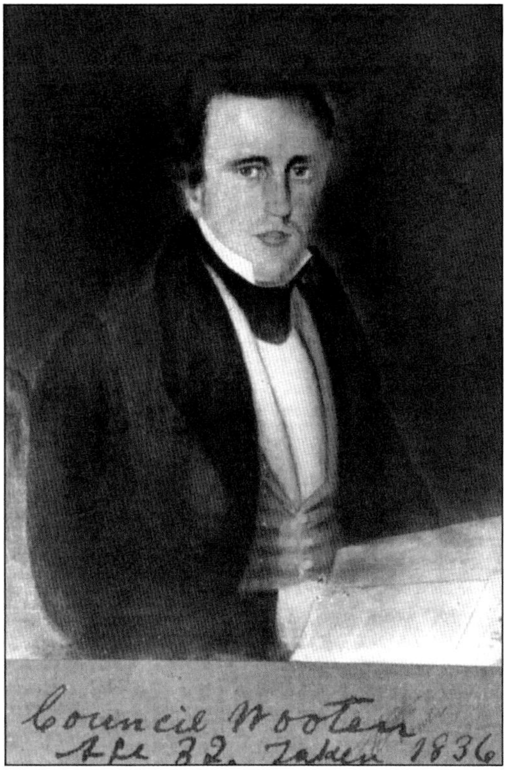

Council Wooten Sr., 1832. Council Wooten was a well-known politician in North Carolina. He was serving in the state's house when North Carolina revised its 1835 constitution. Wooten was also a successful farmer and a great leader in La Grange. (Courtesy of the North Carolina Museum of History.)

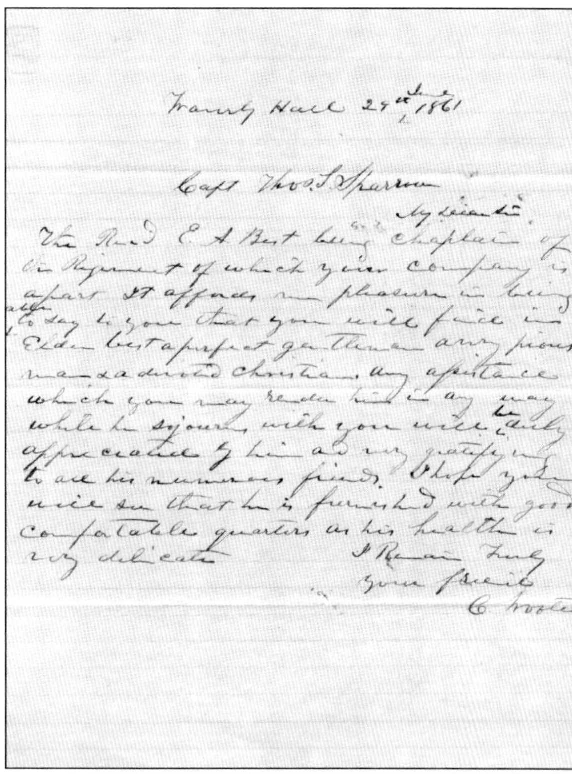

Moseley Hall 29th June 1861

Capt Thos. Sparrow
My dear Sir:
The Revd E A Best being chaplain of the Regiment of which your company is a part It affords me pleasure in being able to say to you that you will find in Elder Best a perfect gentleman and a pious man & a devoted Christian. Any assistance which you may render him in any way while he sojourns with you will be duly appreciated by him and very gratifying to all his numerous friends. I hope you will see that he is furnished with good comfortable quarters as his health is very delicate.
I Remain Truly
your friend
C Wooten

Council Wooten Letter, 1861. This letter is addressed to Capt. Thomas Sparrow, a lawyer before the war in Washington, North Carolina. This letter was an endorsement from Wooten of E.A. Best, the company's chaplain. As well, Wooten was asking that Best's living accommodations be as good as possible because of Best's "delicate health." (Courtesy of East Carolina University, Joyner Library Digital Collections.)

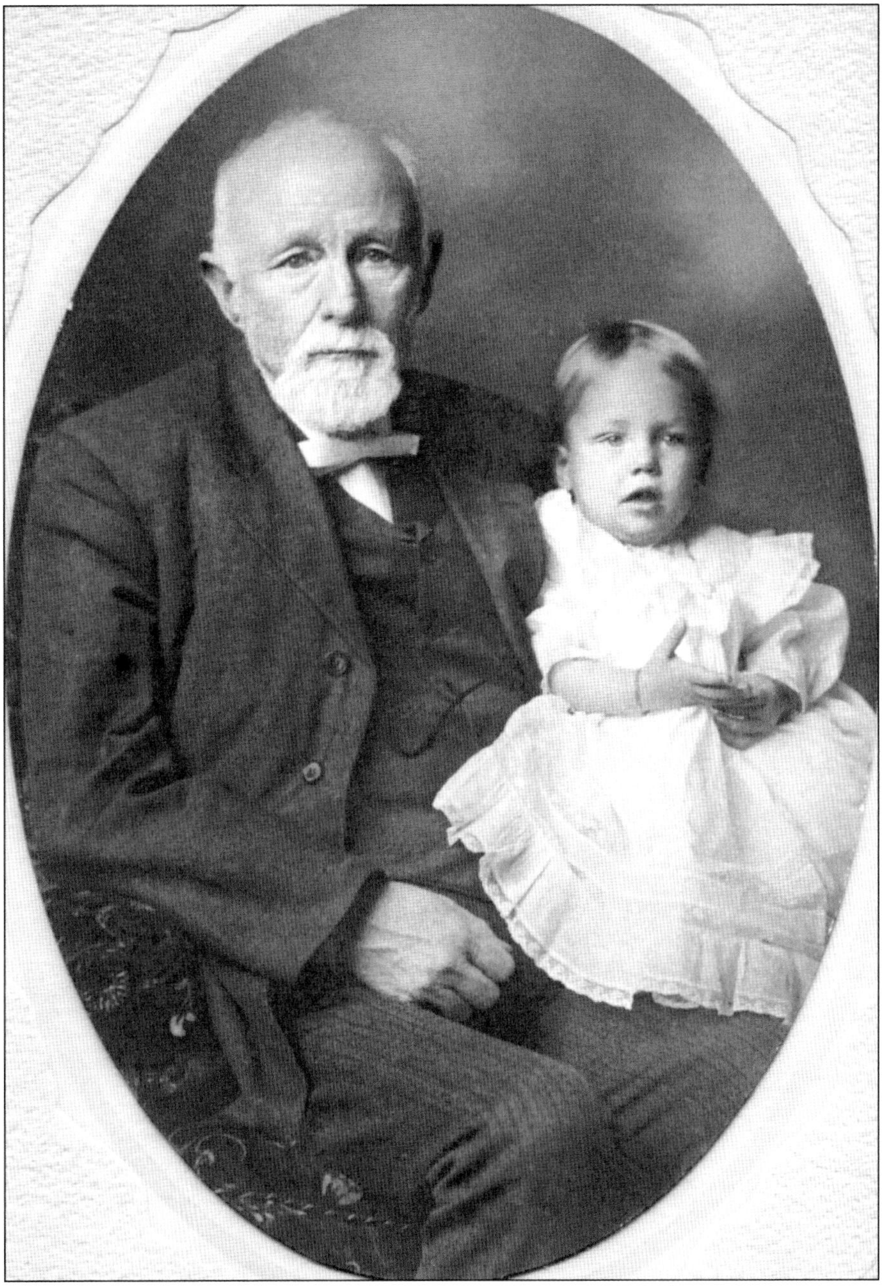

Council Simmons Wooten, 1926. Council Simmons, commonly known as "C.S.," was the son of Council Wooten Sr. He studied law at Wake Forest College when it was located in Wake Forest, North Carolina, and practiced law in neighboring Goldsboro. C.S. was a prolific writer, penning most of his 178 articles for the *Charlotte Observer*. During the Civil War, he served in the Confederate administration. He obtained amnesty in 1866 from Pres. Andrew Johnson. After the Civil War, he brought the family's farming business back to life from its desolation. In 1906, he wrote a complete biography of his father and his grandfather, John Wooten, and published it statewide. The column was reprinted in 1906 in the *La Grange Sentinel*. (Courtesy of the North Carolina Museum of History.)

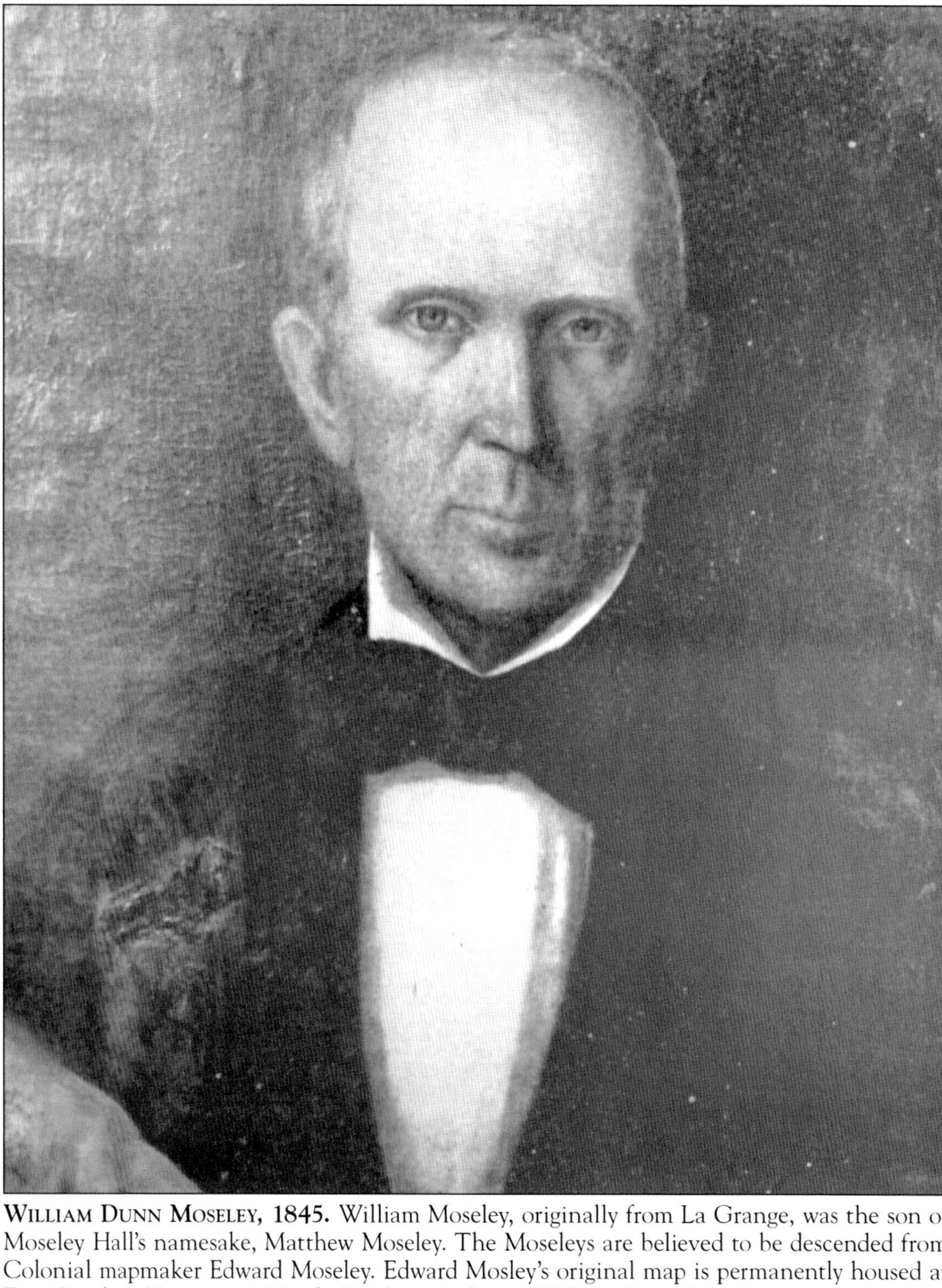

William Dunn Moseley, 1845. William Moseley, originally from La Grange, was the son of Moseley Hall's namesake, Matthew Moseley. The Moseleys are believed to be descended from Colonial mapmaker Edward Moseley. Edward Mosley's original map is permanently housed at East Carolina University's North Carolina Archives. William Dunn Moseley, an attorney, also represented Lenoir County in the state senate from 1829 to 1837. He ran for governor in North Carolina in 1834, losing to David Swain. Moseley garnered 45.41 percent, and Swain 49.49 percent of the vote. He moved to the Florida Territory about 1840 and became the state's first governor in 1845. In the election, Moseley defeated the well-known Richard Keith Call. Moseley was an agrarian governor, encouraging farmers to plant citrus and avocados. (Courtesy of the State Archives of Florida, Florida Photographic Collection.)

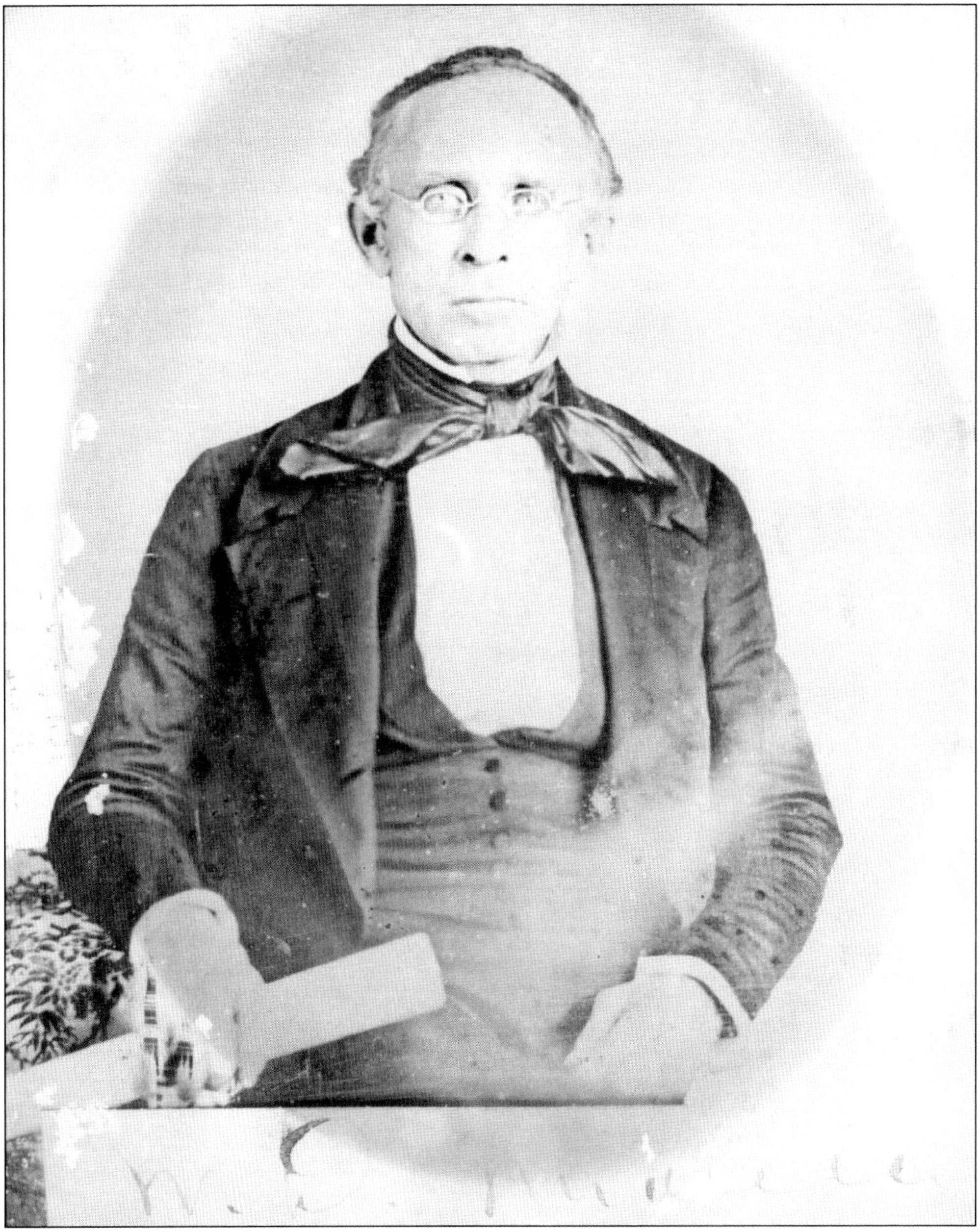

William Dunn Moseley, 1855–1860. This rare photograph of William "W.D." Moseley was taken during his retired years. Prior to becoming Florida's governor, Moseley served in the Florida territorial House of Representatives. As a politician, he was an advocate of states' rights. It was Moseley who put the state government of Florida in place. Moseley, due in part to his extensive agricultural background, encouraged Florida farmers to embrace the growing of citrus, cotton, and other cash crops. Among his accomplishments were overseeing Florida's role in the Mexican War and conflicts between settlers and the Seminole Indian Nation. Moseley was an advocate for public education. After serving as governor (1845–1849), he retired to his original plantation in Jefferson County. Later in life, he moved to Palatka, Putnam County, Florida. (Courtesy of the State Archives of Florida, Florida Photographic Collection.)

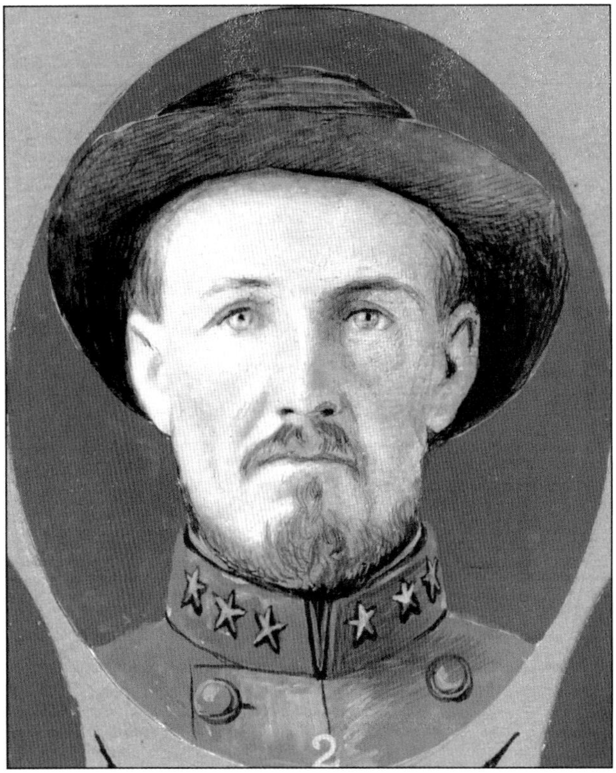

Col. George Franklin Whitfield, 1865. George Whitfield was one of the first to build a home in La Grange, between 1855 and 1858. During the Civil War, Whitfield served with and helped to establish the North Carolina 27th Regiment, Company C. Whitfield was wounded many times in the war. (Courtesy of the North Carolina Museum of History.)

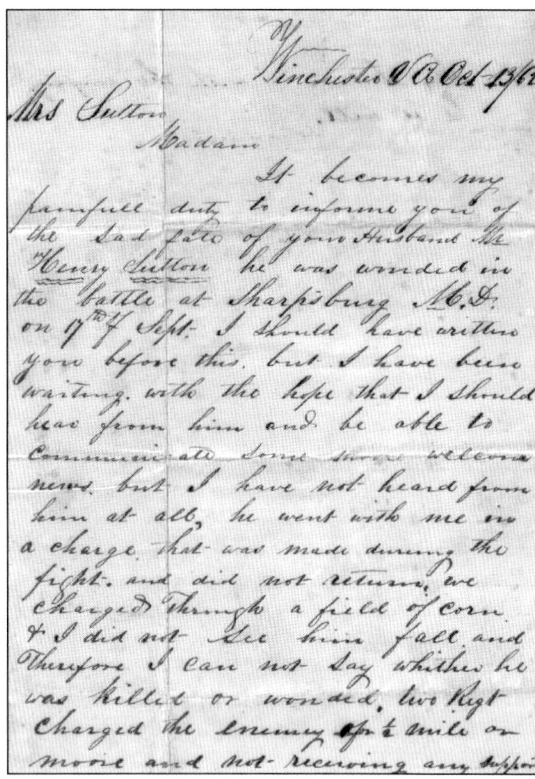

Winchester VA Oct 13/62

Mrs Sutton

Madam

It becomes my painfull duty to inform you of the sad fate of your Husband Mr Henry Sutton he was wonded in the battle at Sharpsburg MD on 17th of Sept. I should have written you before this. but I have been waiting. with the hope that I should hear from him and be able to Communicate some more welcome news. but I have not heard from him at all, he went with me in a charge that was made during the fight. and did not return, we charged through a field of corn & I did not see him fall and therefore I can not say whither he was killed or wonded, our Regt charged the enemy for ½ mile or more and not receiving any support

Letter from George Whitfield, 1862. This very rare letter was written on October 13, 1862, during the Civil War, after the Battle of Sharpsburg. Whitfield wrote the letter to his wife, Polly. He requested that she personally speak with Henry Sutton's wife. The letter explains that Henry died bravely during the battle. (Courtesy of Glen Fields.)

GEORGIANA COKER FIELDS, C. 1890. Fields was the daughter of Francis Coker, a private in the Lenoir Braves, Company A, 40th North Carolina State Troops. Georgiana Fields lived on the outskirts of La Grange, near Jason. She, like many farmers' wives, helped with the budget, kept the store books, and tended to the family's local garden. (Courtesy of Gary Fields.)

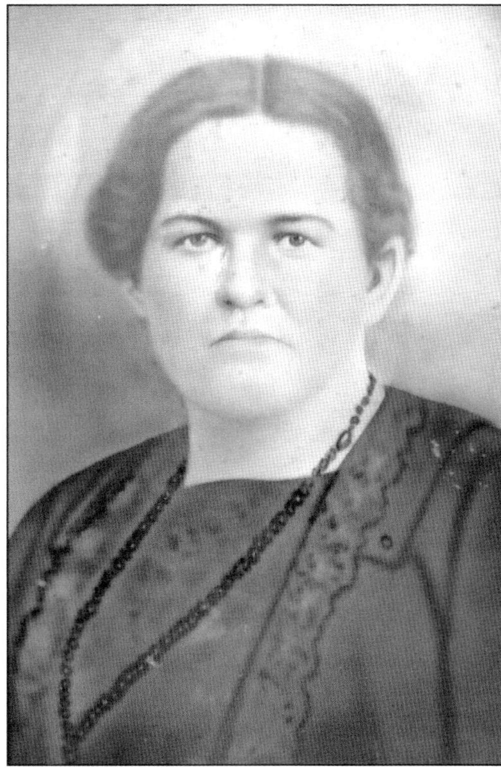

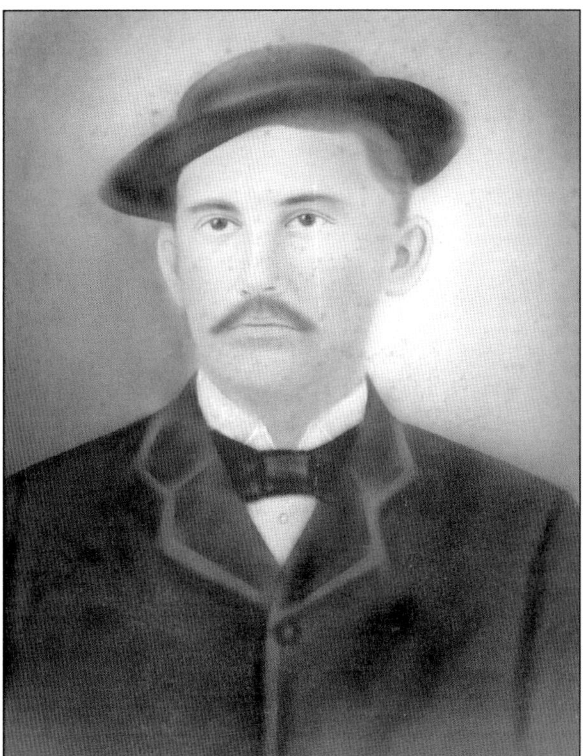

ABNER FIELDS, C. 1890. Fields, a farmer, also ran Abner's General Store from 1890 to 1932. He would buy all types of grain, cotton, corn, and tobacco. Much of what he bought was from local farmers. He would purchase the last gleanings of harvest and resell them. He made wine and apple and peach brandy. (Courtesy of Gary Fields.)

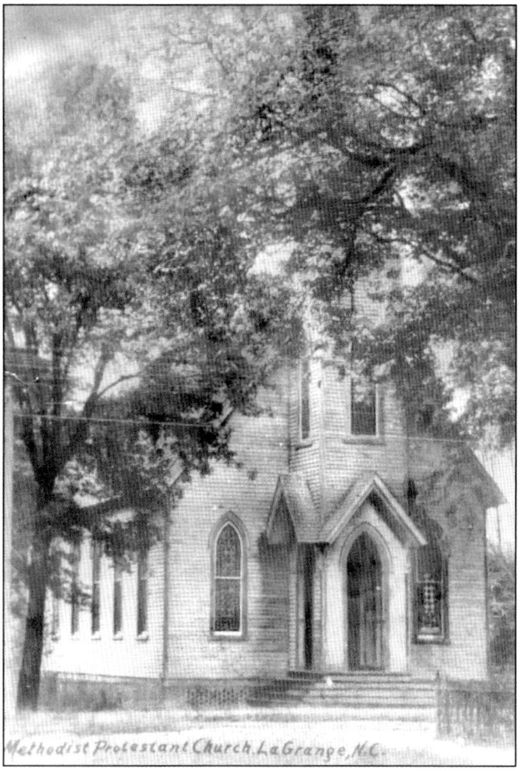

METHODIST PROTESTANT CHURCH, C. 1900. Established in 1881, this church is in good repair today. It is located on the corner of James and Caswell Streets. Civil War surgeon Jacob Hadley was a longtime member of the church. Hadley donated glass for the church's windows. The church underwent a split and eventually became the Southern Methodist Church. (Courtesy of Grace Burke.)

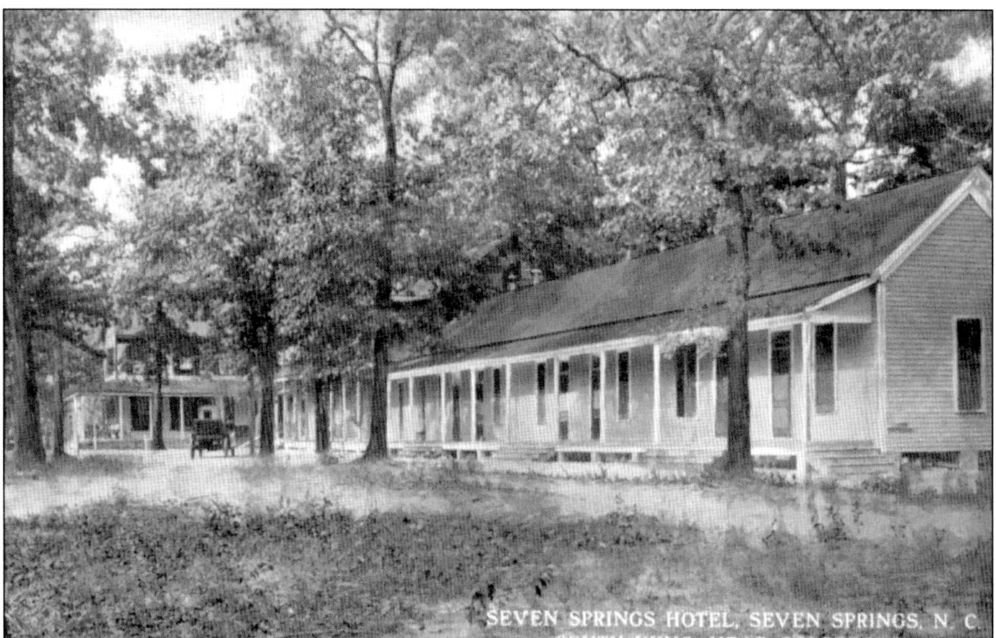

SEVEN SPRINGS HOTEL, 1910–1915. The Seven Springs Hotel was a luxury vacation spot for more than 50 years. Seven Springs, North Carolina, was known for its springwater. People would come to the area to be healed of various maladies. The hotel sold water by the gallon until the source dried up. (Courtesy of East Carolina University, Joyner Library Digital Collections.)

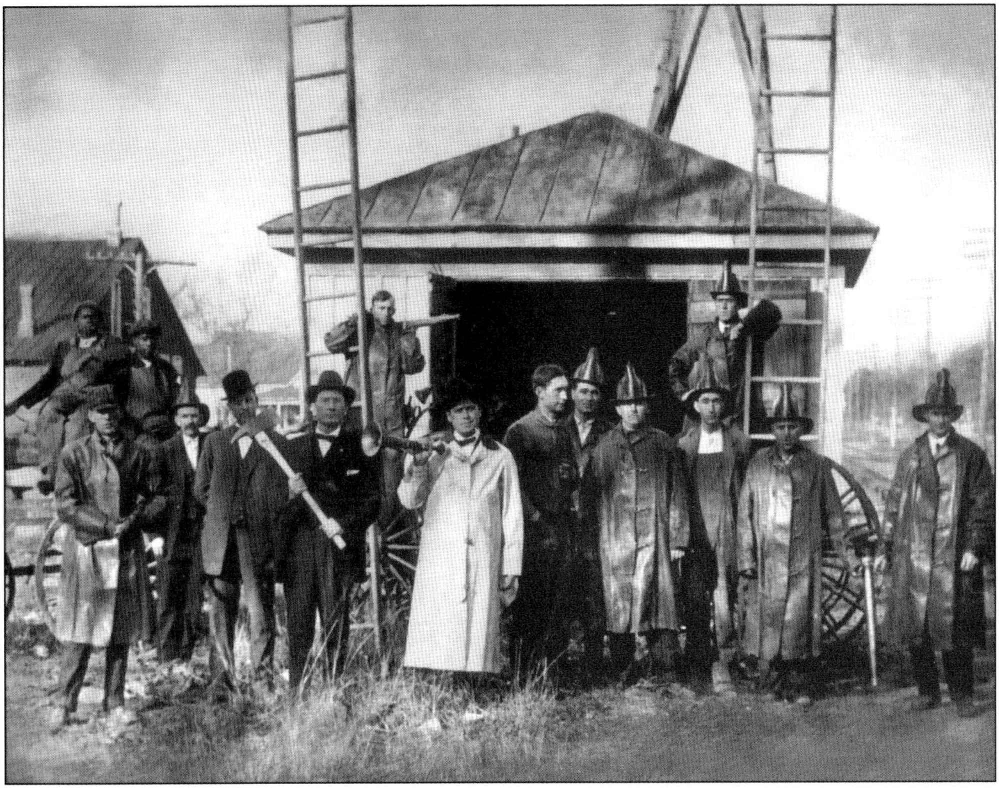

La Grange Fire Department, 1910. Pictured from left to right are (first row) three unidentified, John H. Rouse (holding an axe), fire chief Floyd Barwick (in a long white coat), three unidentified, fireman Smith, fireman Fields, and Joseph Walter "J.W." Wilson; (second row) John Henry Collie, Steve Collie, Cecil Burke Sr. (holding water hose), and unidentified. (Courtesy of the Bob Rouse family.)

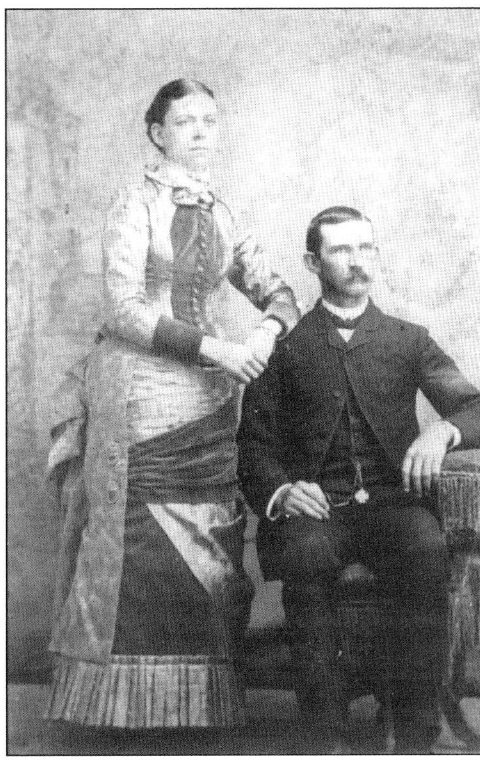

Joshua Parrott and Ida Varina Wooten Mewborn, 1885. This is the couple's wedding portrait. Joshua attended the Davis Military School, and Ida was enrolled in the Kinsey Seminary. Joshua's grandfather was Thomas Wooten, brother of Council Wooten Sr. Joshua, a farmer and a lawyer, practiced law in Kinston for the district attorney's office. He was also a justice of the peace. (Courtesy of Gary Fields.)

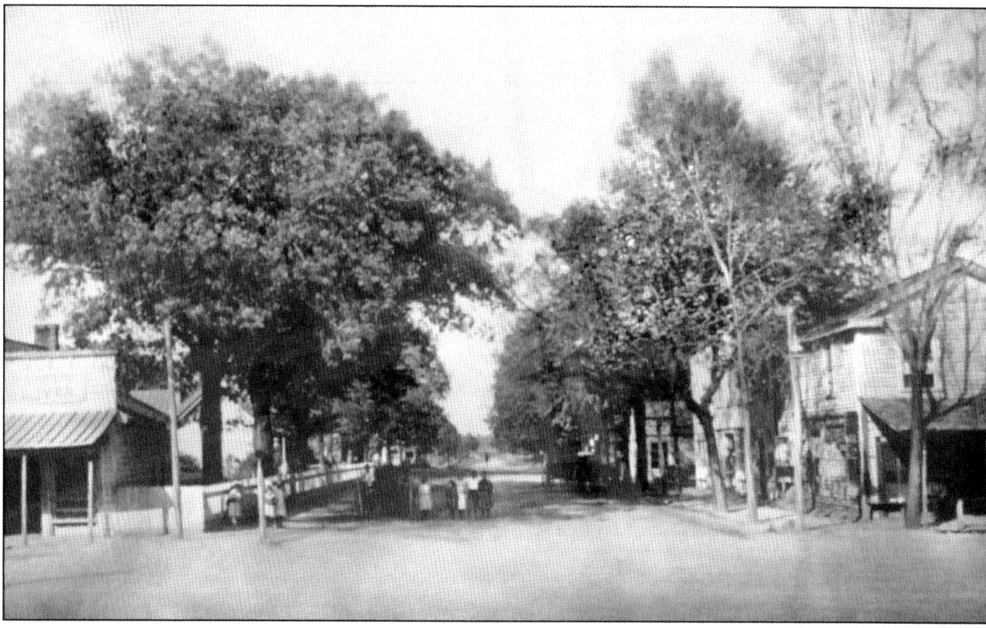

CASWELL STREET, LATE 1880S. This photograph, taken from the corner of Washington and Caswell Streets, shows the town's vegetation prior to the fire of 1911. In the distance, a lone horseman is riding into town. From the rider's direction, it is assumed that he is coming from the Moseley plantation. (Courtesy of Rouse Funeral Home.)

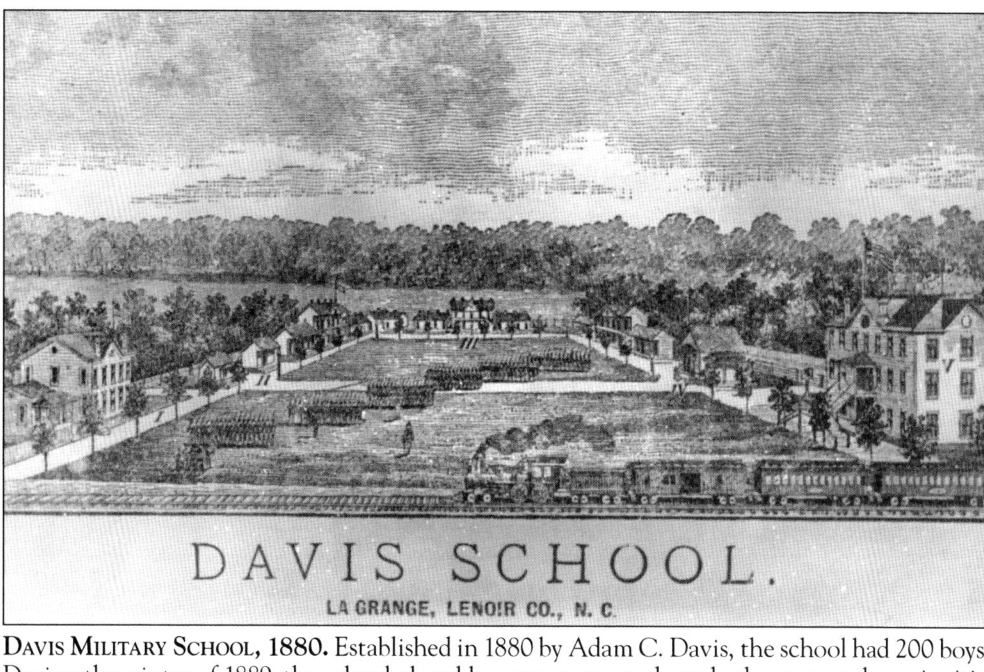

DAVIS MILITARY SCHOOL, 1880. Established in 1880 by Adam C. Davis, the school had 200 boys. During the winter of 1889, the school closed because some students had contracted meningitis. The school moved to Winston Salem, North Carolina, in 1890. It kept its original name and is still in operation today. (Courtesy of Grace Burke.)

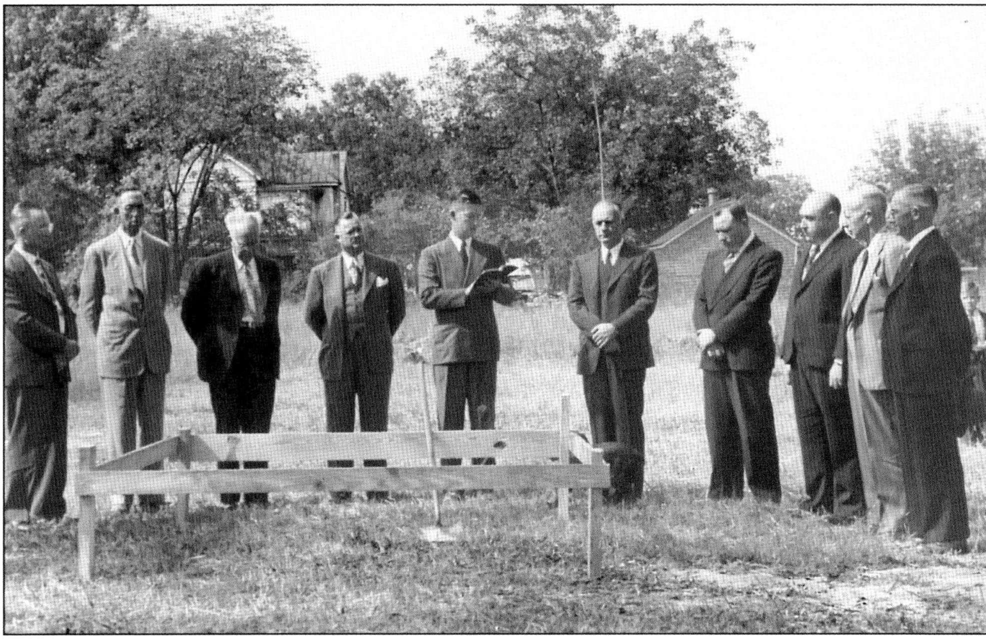

A GROUND BREAKING, C. 1930. According to the La Grange Historical Society, this ground breaking is believed to be of a local church. The historical society believes that this event took place in the Palmer Town area of La Grange. Today, this area has two well-established churches. (Courtesy of Sonny Herring.)

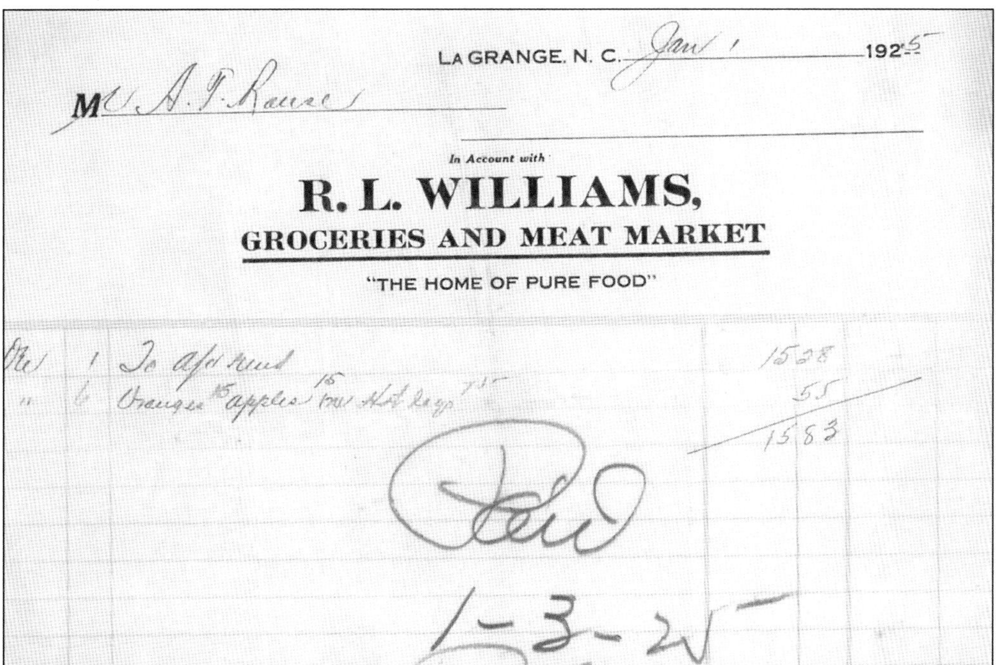

LA GRANGE, N. C. ______ 192__

M______

In Account with

R. L. WILLIAMS,

GROCERIES AND MEAT MARKET

"THE HOME OF PURE FOOD"

R.L. WILLIAMS GROCERY, 1925. This receipt is from a time in La Grange when groceries could be charged on account. Note the prices: six oranges, apples, and hot dogs cost a total of 55¢. Most of the food sold at the grocery was from farmers in the La Grange area. (Courtesy of Grace Burke.)

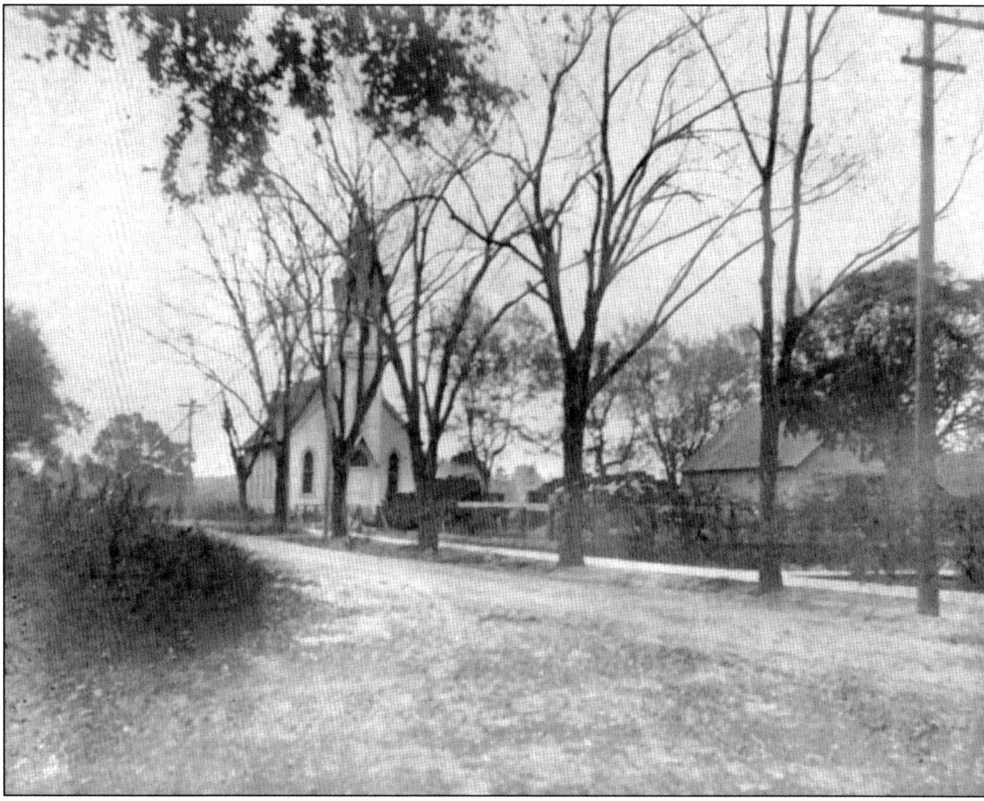

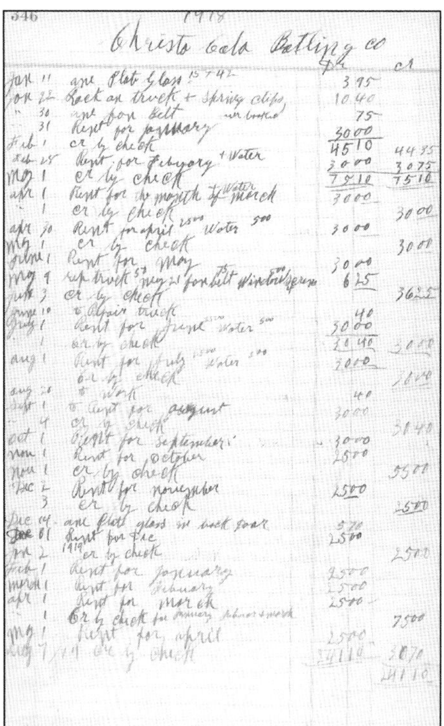

PRESBYTERIAN CHURCH, 1910. Founded in 1881, this church has received great care for many years. During Hurricane Fran, the steeple was severely damaged, and it was replaced in 1996. The church is not active today, but it is used for various local activities and is the home of the La Grange Rotary Club. (Courtesy of Grace Burke.)

LEDGER BOOK, 1918. This ledger book shows that Christo Cola was sold in La Grange. Christo Cola, a soda company based out of Richmond, Virginia, was in business for only a few years, but it was very popular in La Grange. Pepsi and Coca-Cola were also sold in town. (Courtesy of the Bob Rouse family.)

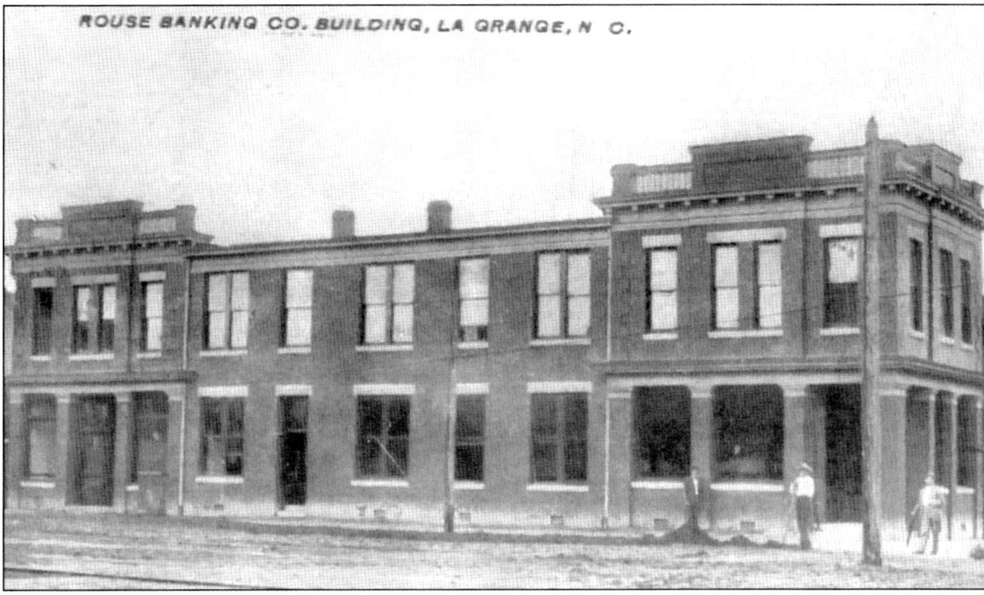

Rouse Banking Company, 1908–1910. At one time, the main streets of the town were filled with oyster shells and lined with beautiful oak trees. Due to fires, many of the buildings and trees were destroyed. The front right section of this brick building is the Rouse Bank. The bank is still functioning today as the Little Bank. (Courtesy of the Bob Rouse family.)

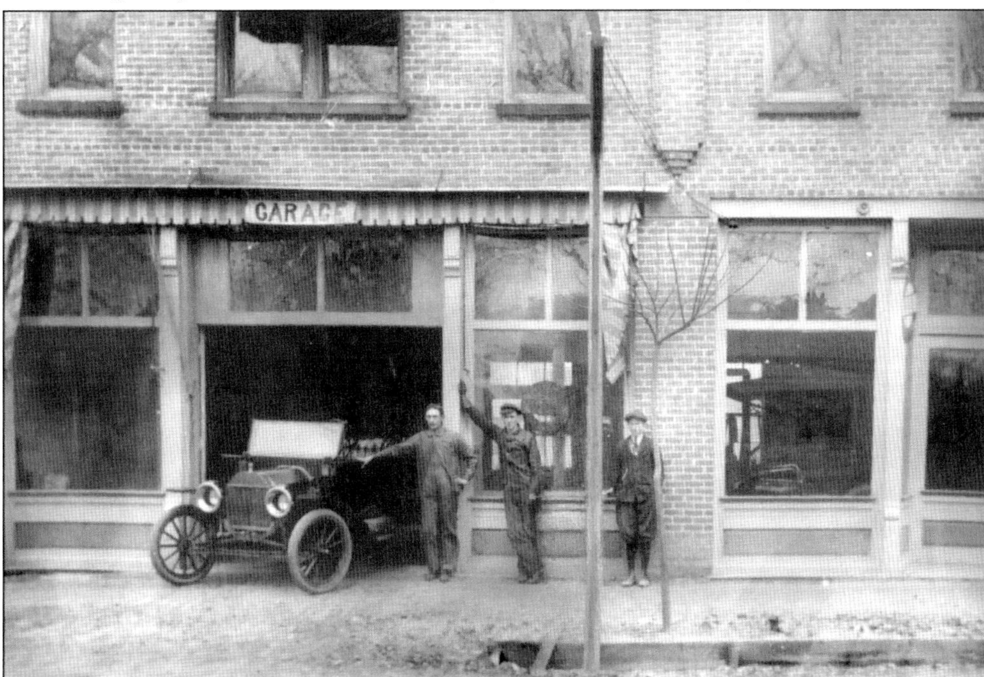

Rouse Motor Car Company and Metz Car Dealership, 1911–1914. Hal Rouse, John H. Rouse's eldest son, is on the left, leaning on the car, a Metz 22 automobile. The car's original cost was $495. When purchased, it arrived in 14 major parts that then required assembling. Among the first to purchase the car was local physician J.W.P. Smithwick. (Courtesy of the Bob Rouse family.)

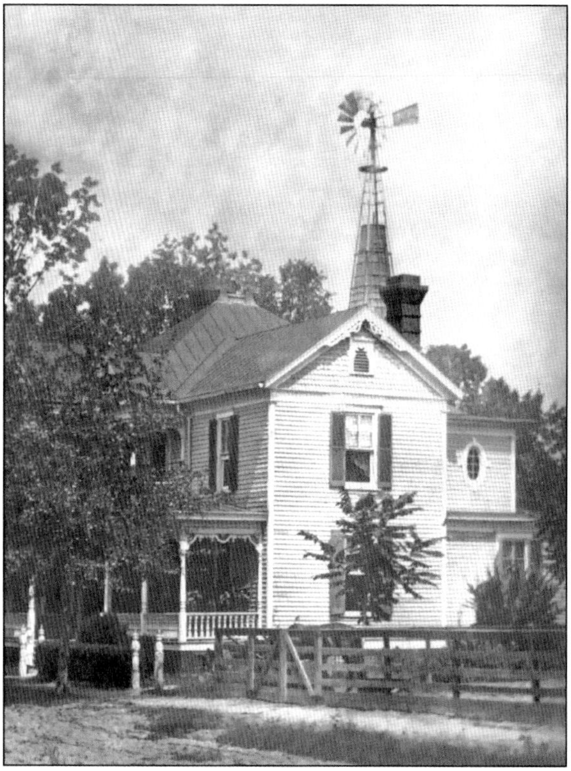

John H. Rouse House, 1890. This house was built in 1890. Behind the home, a Civil War Union cavalry officer's sword was found. The windmill in the back supplied water to Rouse's buggy factory on Caswell Street. John H. Rouse connected Dr. Hadley into the water line and, eventually, did so for the town of La Grange. (Courtesy of the Bob Rouse family.)

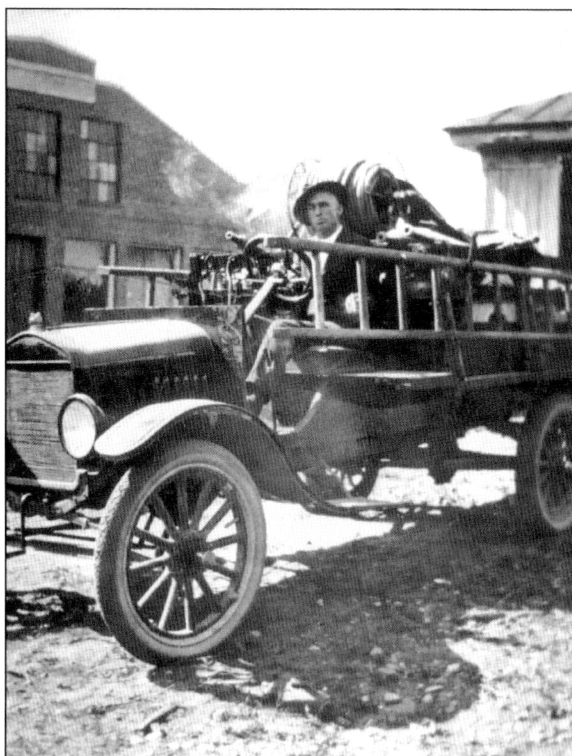

La Grange's First Fire Engine, c. 1910. Cecil Burke Sr. was the town's first fire-engine driver. In the background is the Harper Hotel, the only hotel in La Grange in 1906. Established in 1903, it was well known for having telephone service to Kinston and Goldsboro. (Courtesy of Grace Burke.)

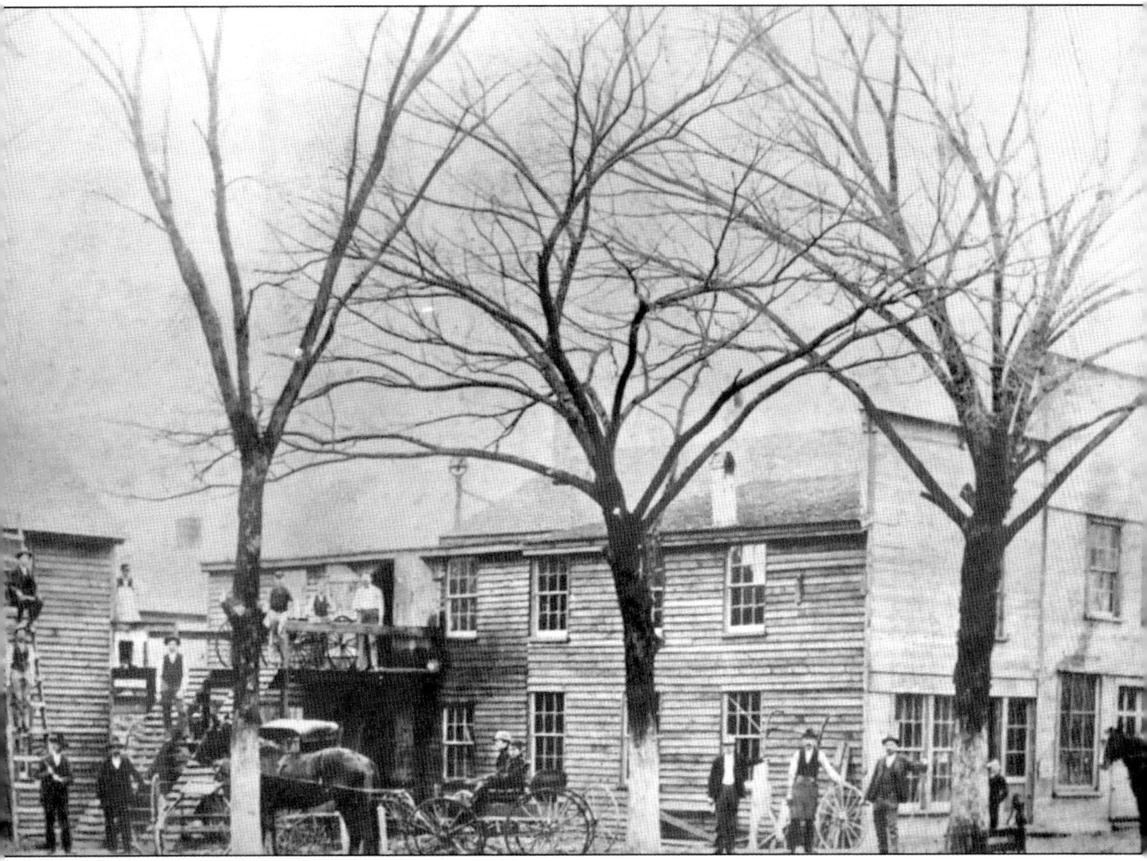

Rouse Funeral Home, 1882. Located at 108 North Caswell Street, Rouse Funeral Home is believed to be the oldest privately owned funeral home in North Carolina. It was operated by only the second generation of the founding family. It is the oldest continuous business in La Grange. In the 1870s, when the United States was approaching its centennial, John H. Rouse Sr. came to La Grange. Around 1882, he opened a buggy factory, known as the Rouse Buggy Factor, where he manufactured the lightweight sports model "Rouse Buggies." On his stationery appeared the famous slogan, "The World Do Move, So Do Rouse Buggies." The Rouse Buggy Factory grew into a big business in its day, at one time employing about 80 men. The buggies were sold locally and also shipped, unassembled, by rail throughout North Carolina, South Carolina, and Georgia. (Courtesy of the Bob Rouse family.)

Jenny Lind -- What's In The Name?

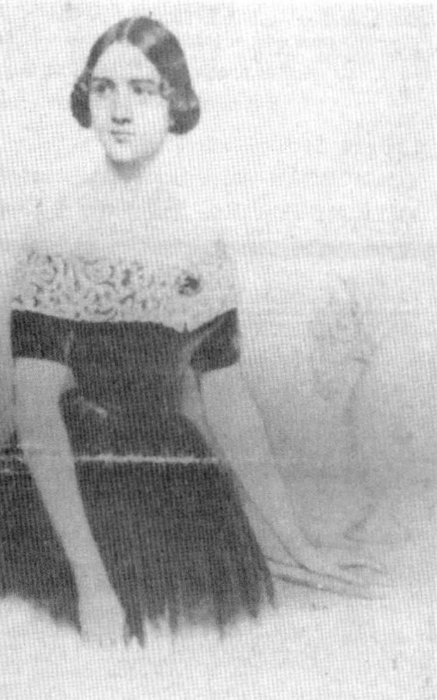

PORTRAIT OF JENNY LIND

By LISA K. BRITT

(Writer's Note: I wish to thank all of the people who assisted me in my research for writing this arricle. All of the calls and information are greatly appreciated.)

There are several theories as to the way the rural community Jenny Lind was named. While the theories are relatively different, they are similar in that they all evolve around the Swedish nightingale Jenny Lind.

Jenny Lind, born Johanna Maria Lind on October 6, 1820, in Stockholm, Sweden, began captivating audiences all over Sweden, Germany, France (mainly Paris,) England, and the United States with her coloratura soprano voice in 1838 with her operatic debut in Stockholm. With unique vocal control and technique, Miss Lind was a virtuoso of the opera and concert stage. She was also known for her charitable and generous nature as she would often give proceeds from concerts to struggling institutions and loyal, destitute fans.

Miss Lind was engaged in an American tour from 1850 - 1852 with P.T. Barnum. During this time, she performed in New York, Boston, Philadelphia, Maryland, and as far south as Charleston, S.C. She died on November 2, 1887, in Malvern Hills, England.

Local legend has it that Jenny Lind actually came to the rural community and sang under a tree that was located near the community store. Mrs. Lorraine Bell of LaGrange explains, "It was told years ago that she came down here and sang. The people liked it so much that the place was named after her."

This legend is quite popular among the people of the Jenny Lind community and LaGrange. Another response received also claims that Jenny Lind came through the community; however, there is a slight variation in the story. Mrs. Eunice Rouse of Route 4, LaGrange, notes, "She (Jenny Lind) was a singer who went through there during an election. My dad was down there. They got drunk and started fighting. She was shot, and it was called Jenny Lind after that."

Mrs. Mary Mitchell, a former resident of the Jenny Lind area who now lives at 205 South Charles Street, LaGrange, has another story. Mrs. Mitchell tells a tale that her father, Rotheus Caswell Croom, passed down to her family.

Mrs. Mitchell's grandfather, John Leighton Croom, ran the local store in the community and got his goods up the river. Mrs. Mitchell comments, "At this time, he went to New York City to buy goods, and he heard Jenny Lind sing. He said it was the most wonderful thing he had ever heard in his life. When he came back home, he named his store Jenny Lind. That's the way it got its name." After the store was named Jenny Lind, the community also picked up the name.

"When he came back, he brought his baby a Jenny Lind doll. When he walked in at the door, his baby was dead. They put the Jenny Lind doll in the coffin with her," she continues. The grave is located approximately a mile past Marvin Hardison's Store. Several years after the burial, some people tried to open the grave back up and found the China part of the doll. Mrs. Mitchell claims that there is now too much growth over the grave to get into it again.

Knowing the legendary tale that Jenny Lind actually came to the community, Mrs. Mitchell notes that the tale cannot be true. At the death of her nephew in Washington, D.C., a Mr. Peterson, a friend of her nephew, came to the Jenny Lind area for services and became interested in the community and how it was named.

Mrs. Mitchell explains, "When he went back (to Washington, D.C.), he said he checked the records. The records said that she never came to North Carolina, but she did go to Charleston, South Carolina. So, that killed what folks thought, you know, that she sang under the tree."

However, researched evidence reveals that Jenny Lind did sail from Wilmington, N.C., on her way to Charleston; but there is no information as to whether she came to this area. Research also reveals the time of Miss Lind's death; consequently, she was not shot here. Therefore, all of the stories leave room for error.

No one really seems to know exactly how the Jenny Lind community was named. One thing, however, is certain. Whether Jenny Lind came to this area or not, the community is named in honor of the Swedish prima donna of song. What a privilege for any community!

JENNY LIND, c. 1969. This article from the *Weekly Gazette*, about Jenny Lind, touches on one of the most intriguing stories in La Grange. It is believed that this Swedish actress visited just outside of La Grange and gave a performance under a tree. Local residents were so captivated that they named this area after her, Jenny Lind. She was a very popular singer with P.T. Barnum. Another version of the story is that storeowner Joshua Leighton Croom went to New York and heard her sing. He was so taken by the performance that he named his store after her, and the community also adopted the name. Barnum and Lind toured the Southern states in 1851–1852, performing at many halls in the South. (Courtesy of Grace Burke.)

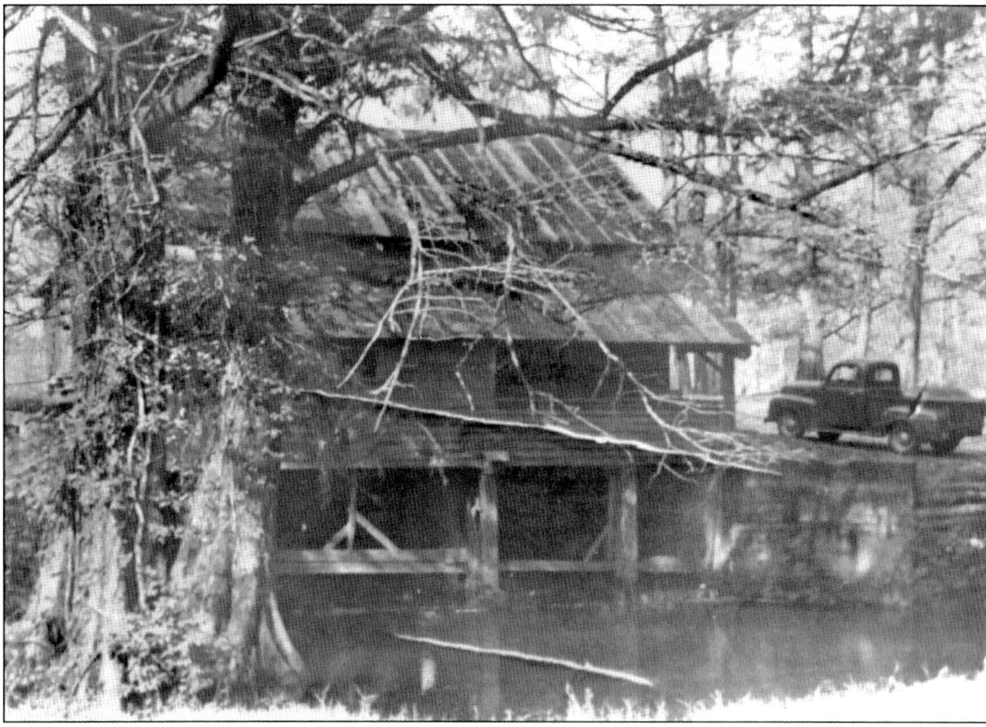

Walters Mill, Mid-1950s. This mill was named after John N. Walters. According to local historian Gary Fields, it was originally owned by the Dawson family during the Civil War. The mill was used for various grain milling, and it later became a place for social gatherings. (Courtesy of Sonny Herring.)

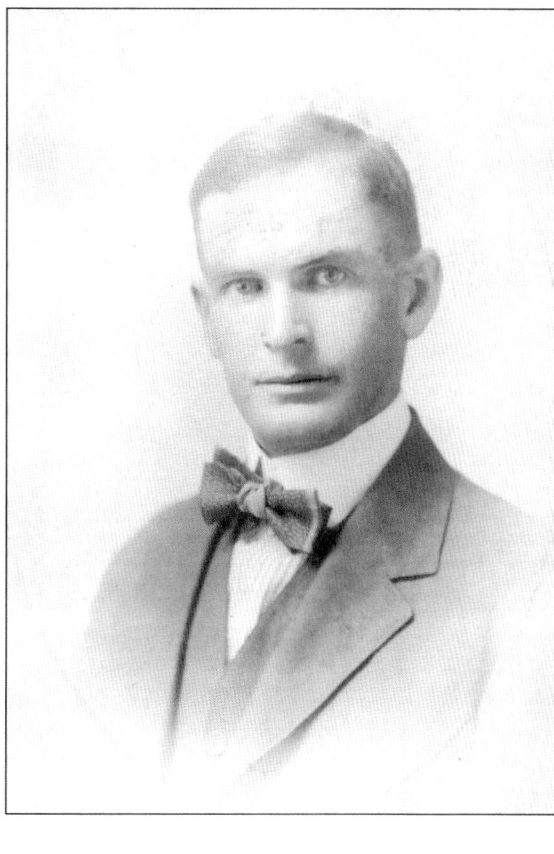

Egbert Herring Sr., c. 1900. Herring farmed land by State Road 1001. He inherited two tracts of the original farm from his father, Allen James Herring. His grandfather, Benjamin Franklin Herring, was a Civil War sergeant. Egbert solidified the Herring farmland. The Herrings still farm this area. (Courtesy of Sonny Herring.)

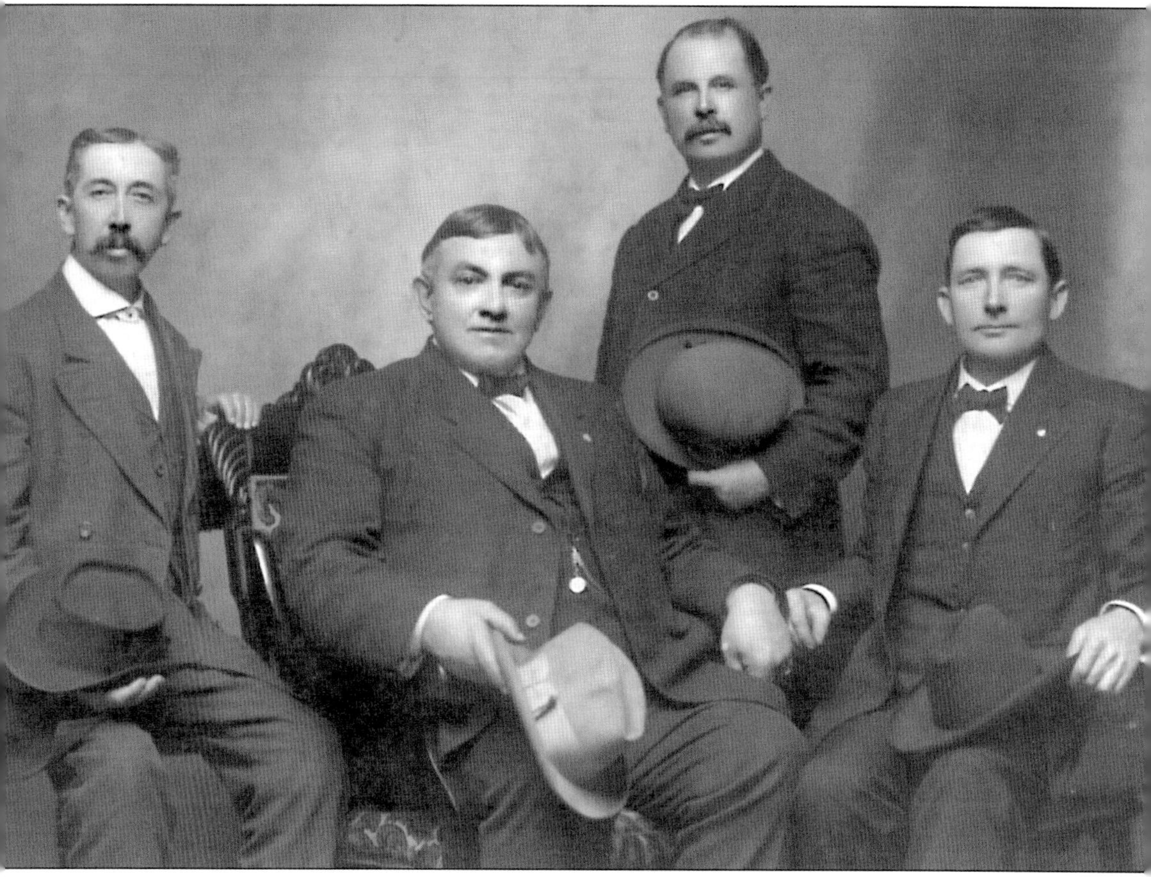

DISTINGUISHED GENTLEMEN, 1910. Shown here are some of La Grange's leading businessmen. They are, from left to right, William Malachi Fields, Floyd Barwick (believed to be the town's fire chief), Dr. J. Marcus Hodges, and John H. Rouse. (Courtesy of Speck and Sister Fields.)

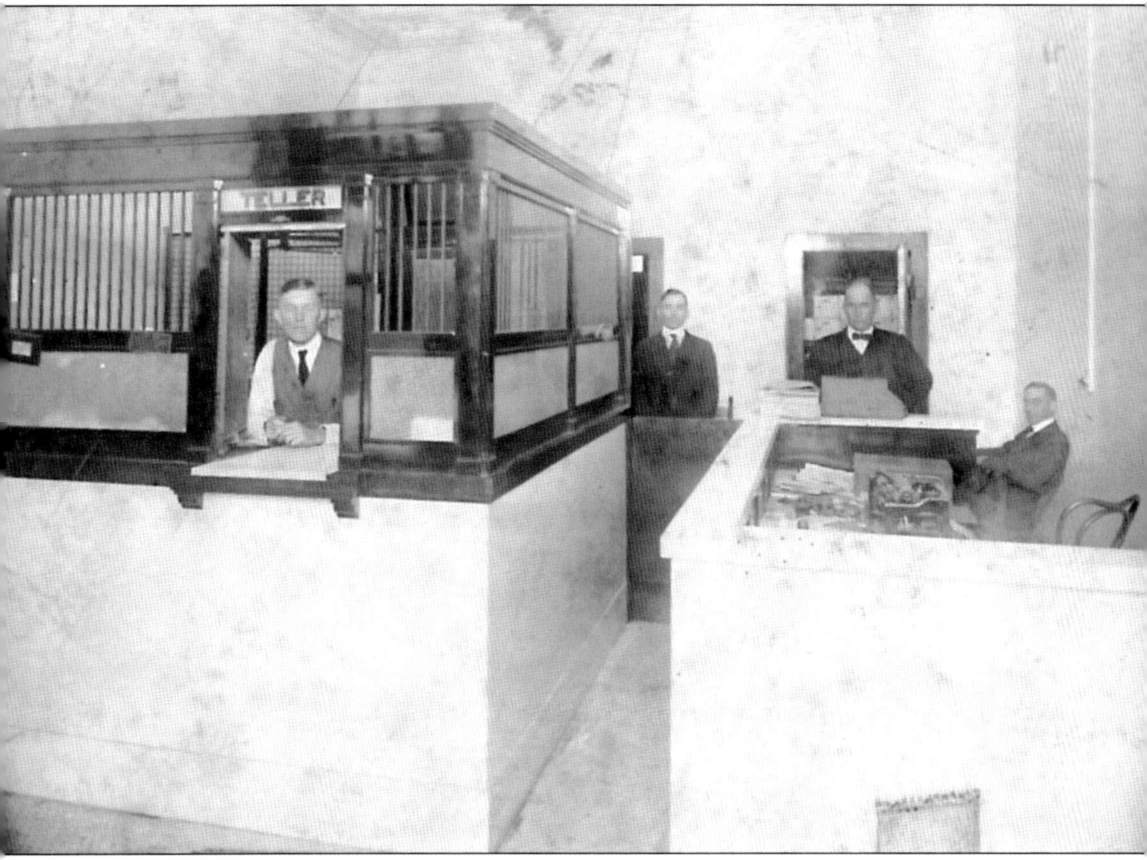

Rouse Banking Company, 1910. This was one of the first successful banks in La Grange. The teller in the window is Henry T. Abbott Sr. In the back are, from left to right, Sam Abbott, Eddie R. Burke, and, possibly, A.T. Rouse. Today, this institution is the Little Bank. (Courtesy of Jean Abbott.)

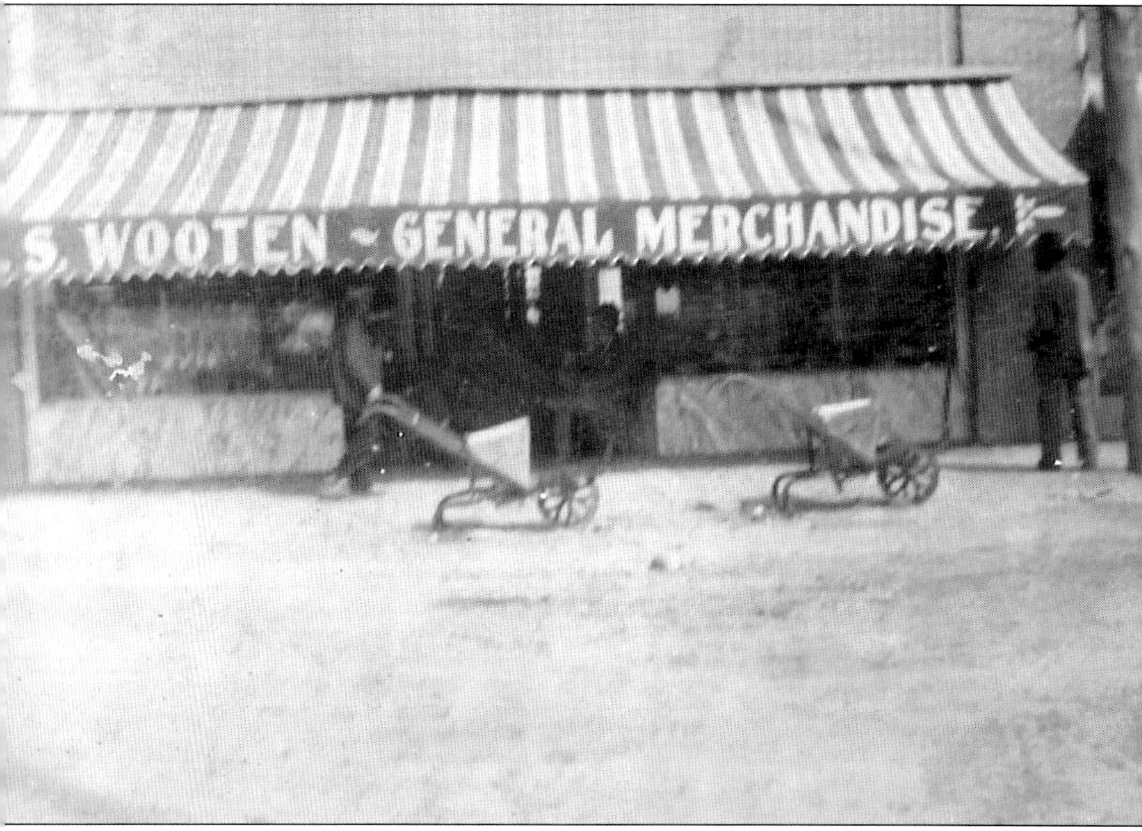

WOOTEN STORE, C. 1912. General merchandising stores were popular for almost 65 years. Farmers in outlying areas came to town for supplies. The Wooten store was the main retailer in town. Shown here are two grain spreaders, a new technology of the time. General stores offered a solid inventory of feed, food, clothing, tools, and fertilizer. They also supplied townspeople with food staples such as milk, cheese, and bread as well as household items. Also popular at the general merchandise store was candy, including stick candy, also referred to as "penny candy." (Courtesy of the Bob Rouse family.)

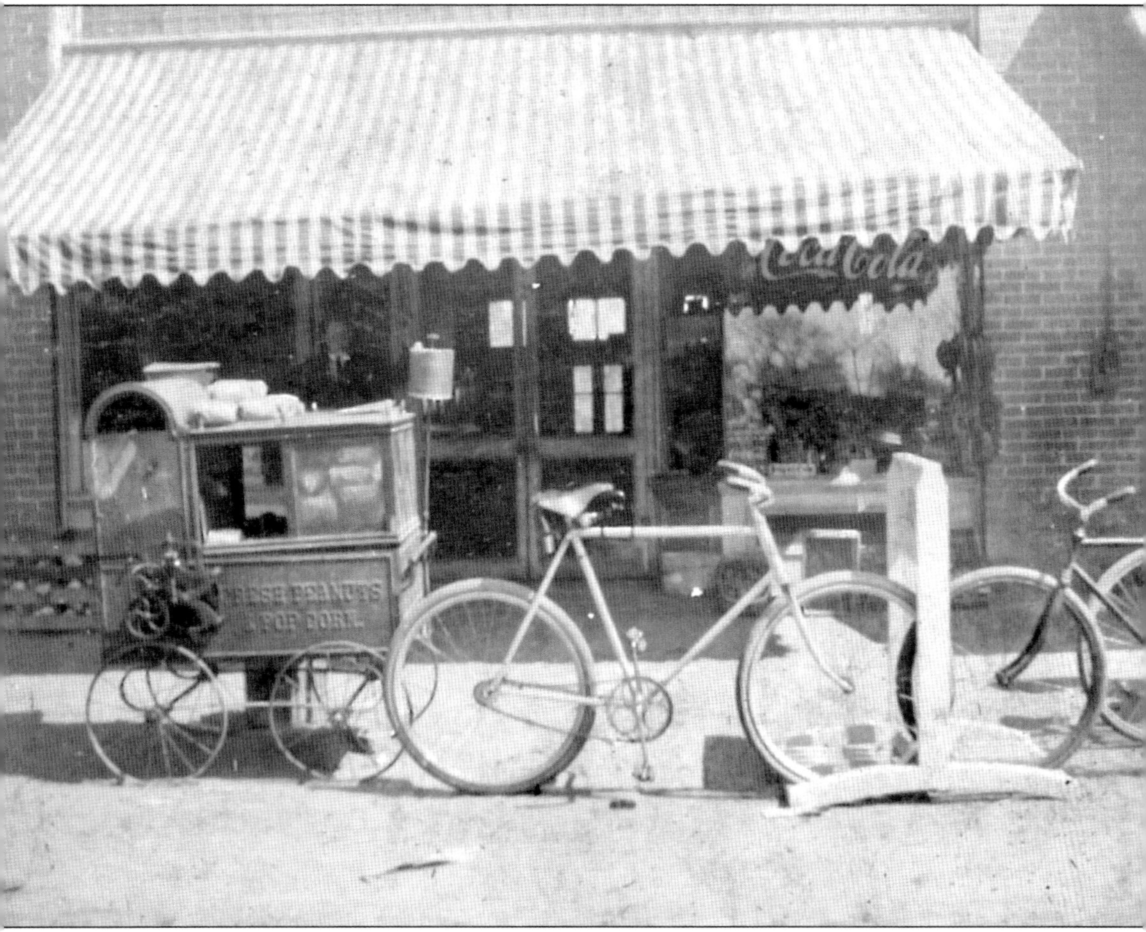

POPCORN MACHINE, C. 1912. Selling popcorn on the street was popular until the 1930s. Many businesses sold popcorn at public movies, shown on the side of buildings on Railroad Street. A resident who recalled the machines stated, "The streets of La Grange would be filled with the aroma of popcorn and peanuts being popped and roasted. It was a heavenly odor that countered the odor of horses and other animals." These popcorn machines were powered by steam and later by small mechanical engines. (Courtesy of the Bob Rouse family.)

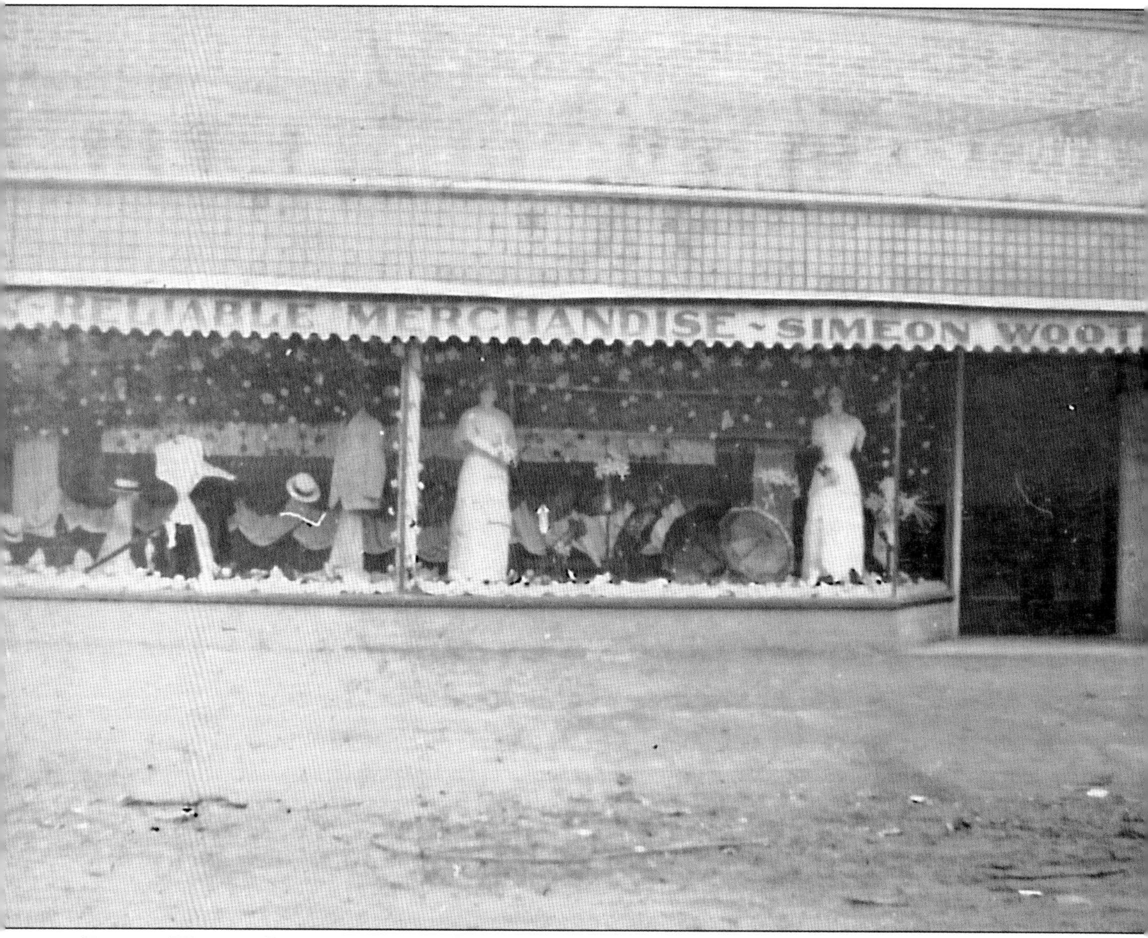

SIMEON WOOTEN STORE, C. 1912. This store was located at 121 South Caswell Street. Note the parasols, a modern-day fashion statement for the ladies. This photograph was taken when the Wootens Store was a brand-new building. When Wooten had the store built, he engraved his name in the mortar in large lettering, simply reading "Simeon Wooten." Regarding the dresses in the storefront, it was common for women to wear homemade dresses and never wear pants. The homemade clothing was considered "work clothes." Many women had only one or two store-bought dresses. The men's hats on display are straw boater hats. They were very popular from 1880 to 1920. (Courtesy of the Bob Rouse family.)

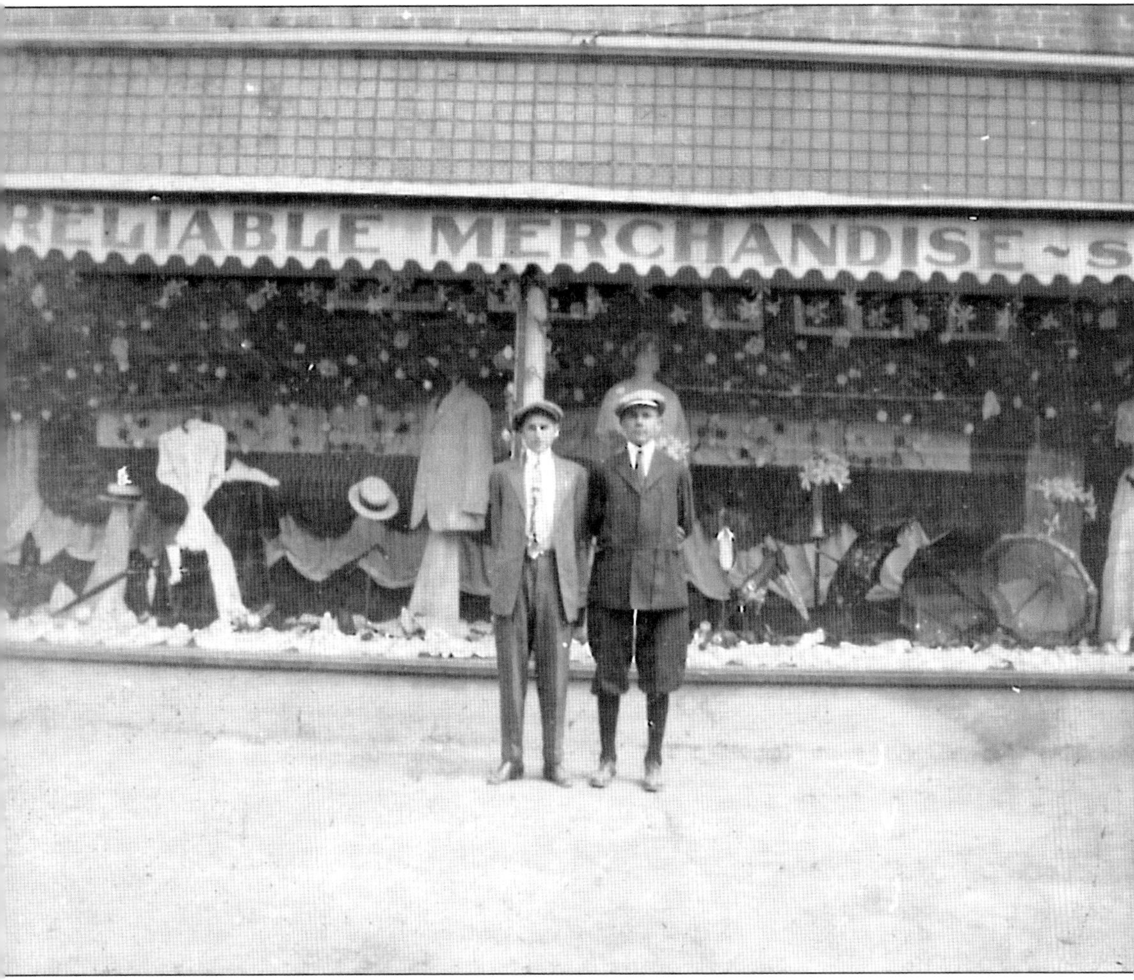

SIMEON WOOTEN, 1908–1910. The man on the right may be Simeon Wooten. This photograph offers a closer view of the fashion of the day. The parasols on display were from an era of fashion before World War I. The parasol was considered to be an essential part of a lady's outfit. Parasols were considered accessories, along with gloves, hats, shoes, stockings, and purses. Although the parasol was popular, it gave way to the umbrella and lost its luster by the 1920s. The man on the right is wearing what appears to be a Norfolk jacket. Men were never seen in public without a hat, and these two men are wearing the fashionable flat cap, which had a button on the bill that held the cap in place. (Courtesy of the Bob Rouse family.)

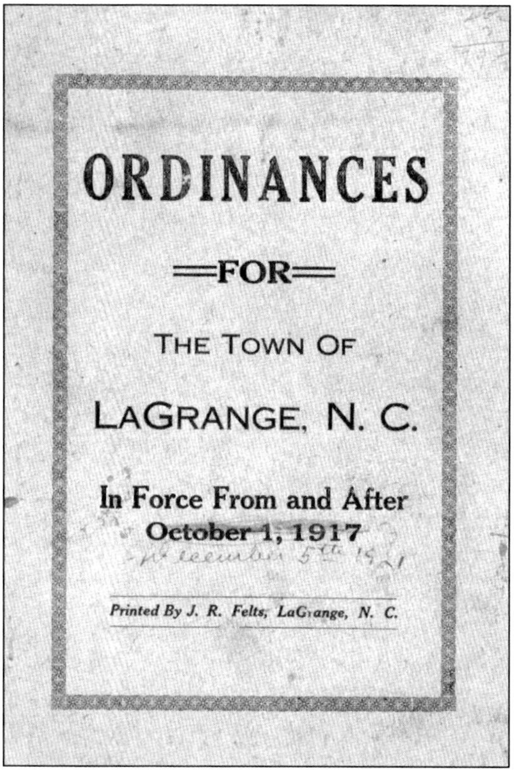

ORDINANCES

FOR

THE TOWN OF

LAGRANGE, N. C.

In Force From and After

October 1, 1917

Printed By J. R. Felts, LaGrange, N. C.

TOWN ORDINANCES, 1917. The ordinances in this booklet are, by today's standards, antiquated to say the least. Fines ranged from $1 to $50. A close look reveals an emendation written across the front: "December 5th 1921." The town, rather than reproducing the booklet each year, had small pieces of updated information taped or placed inside the booklet. (Courtesy of Speck and Sister Fields.)

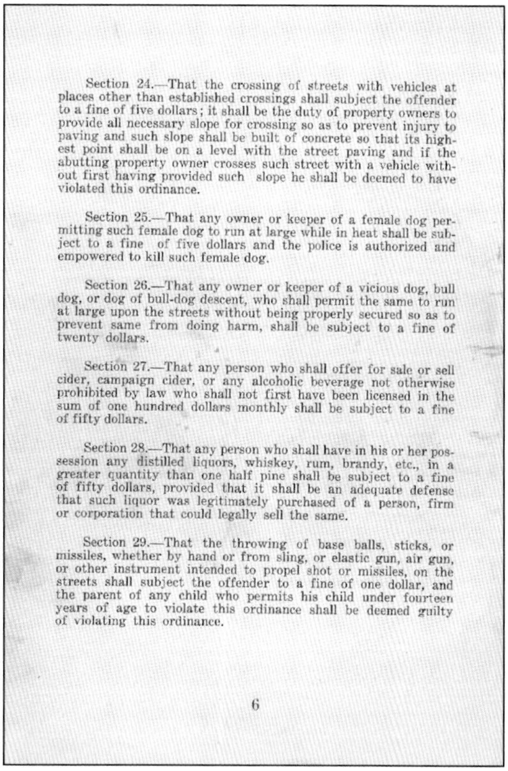

Section 24.—That the crossing of streets with vehicles at places other than established crossings shall subject the offender to a fine of five dollars; it shall be the duty of property owners to provide all necessary slope for crossing so as to prevent injury to paving and such slope shall be built of concrete so that its highest point shall be on a level with the street paving and if the abutting property owner crosses such street with a vehicle without first having provided such slope he shall be deemed to have violated this ordinance.

Section 25.—That any owner or keeper of a female dog permitting such female dog to run at large while in heat shall be subject to a fine of five dollars and the police is authorized and empowered to kill such female dog.

Section 26.—That any owner or keeper of a vicious dog, bull dog, or dog of bull-dog descent, who shall permit the same to run at large upon the streets without being properly secured so as to prevent same from doing harm, shall be subject to a fine of twenty dollars.

Section 27.—That any person who shall offer for sale or sell cider, campaign cider, or any alcoholic beverage not otherwise prohibited by law who shall not first have been licensed in the sum of one hundred dollars monthly shall be subject to a fine of fifty dollars.

Section 28.—That any person who shall have in his or her possession any distilled liquors, whiskey, rum, brandy, etc., in a greater quantity than one half pine shall be subject to a fine of fifty dollars, provided that it shall be an adequate defense that such liquor was legitimately purchased of a person, firm or corporation that could legally sell the same.

Section 29.—That the throwing of base balls, sticks, or missiles, whether by hand or from sling, or elastic gun, air gun, or other instrument intended to propel shot or missiles, on the streets shall subject the offender to a fine of one dollar, and the parent of any child who permits his child under fourteen years of age to violate this ordinance shall be deemed guilty of violating this ordinance.

6

ORDINANCES SECTIONS, 1917. Here are a few sections from the 1917 town ordinance booklet. Section 25 describes a fine for owners of female dogs who allow them to run about town freely. The police had the authority to "kill such female dog." Section 44 involved a fine of $5 for selling merchandise on Sunday. (Courtesy of Speck and Sister Fields.)

Two

School Days

The first school in La Grange began in the early 1830s on the Wooten plantation. Many of the neighboring children attended this private school, which used as one of its texts the King James Bible. Preston Wooley established a school in 1869. This was the first public school in the township. Wooley's school brought an end to the Wooten private school.

In the late 19th century, many schools were established in La Grange. Those of importance were the Kinsey Seminary and the Davis Military School. Joseph E. Kinsey and his brother R.B. Kinsey came to La Grange to teach at the La Grange Academy. In 1881, Wooley's La Grange Academy became the Kinsey Seminary. The institution had 60 female students and 8 teachers. It was about this time that La Grange was getting its reputation as a school town. By 1891, the Kinsey Seminary was purchased by the Christian Church (Disciples of Christ) and moved to Wilson. The Davis Military School stretched two blocks down Railroad Street and was two blocks in width, reaching Jones Street. The uniforms were gray and gold, the color of the Confederacy. This was to honor the students' fathers and grandfathers. The school closed in 1890 and was purchased and moved to Winston Salem.

After the Kinsey Seminary moved to Wilson, a Mr. Witherspoon and, afterward, a Mr. Debnaux (former Greene County superintendent of public instruction) reopened the Kinsey building, and in 1907, a brick building was erected. In its inaugural year, this school had nine grades. In 1912, the 10th grade was added and, by 1915, the 11th. In addition to this all-white school, the La Grange Colored School (LGCS) was in operation by 1920. LGCS had seven grades and five teachers, with a nine-month school term. LGCS burned down in 1927. The new LGCS was a historic Rosenwald School, made completely of brick. In 1933, Emmett Bentley "E.B." Frink became the principal. He grew the school to include 34 teachers and 1,100 students.

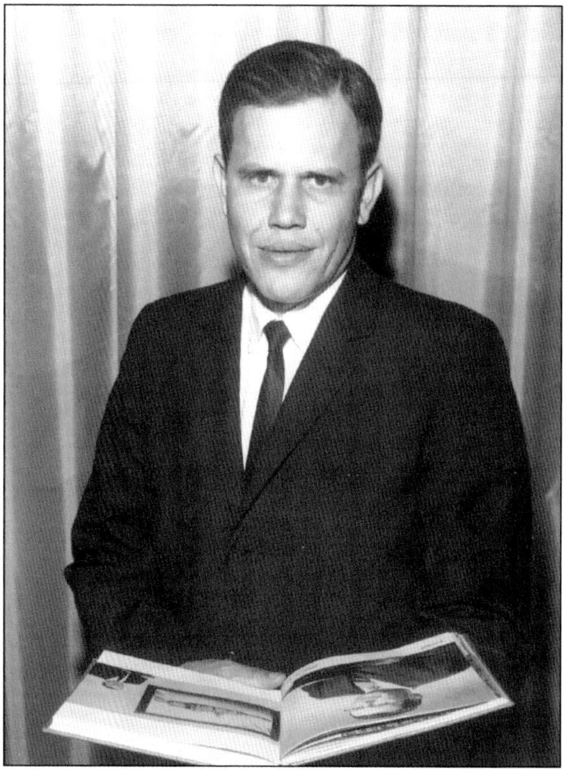

Raymond L. Davis, 1965. Davis was the first principal of North Lenoir High School. Previously known as La Grange High School, it was located on Railroad Street. After 1964, the building became the property of the elementary school. In 2006–2007, the original La Grange High School was taken down to build a modern elementary school. (Courtesy of Sonny Herring.)

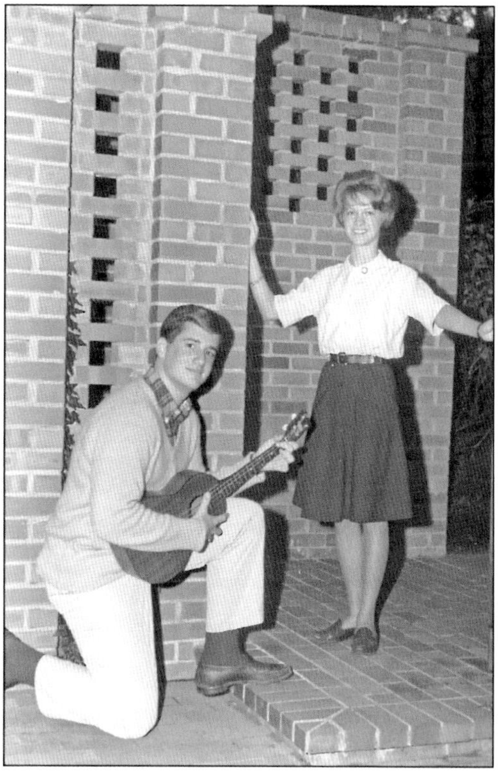

J.P. Walters and Mattie Kate Harrison Aycock, 1962. The caption for this photograph in the 1963 La Grange High School annual reads, "The Talented." J.P. Walters is a member of the La Grange Historical Society. The photograph was taken by James L. Rouse at Dr. J.C. Teele's house in Kinston. (Courtesy of Sonny Herring.)

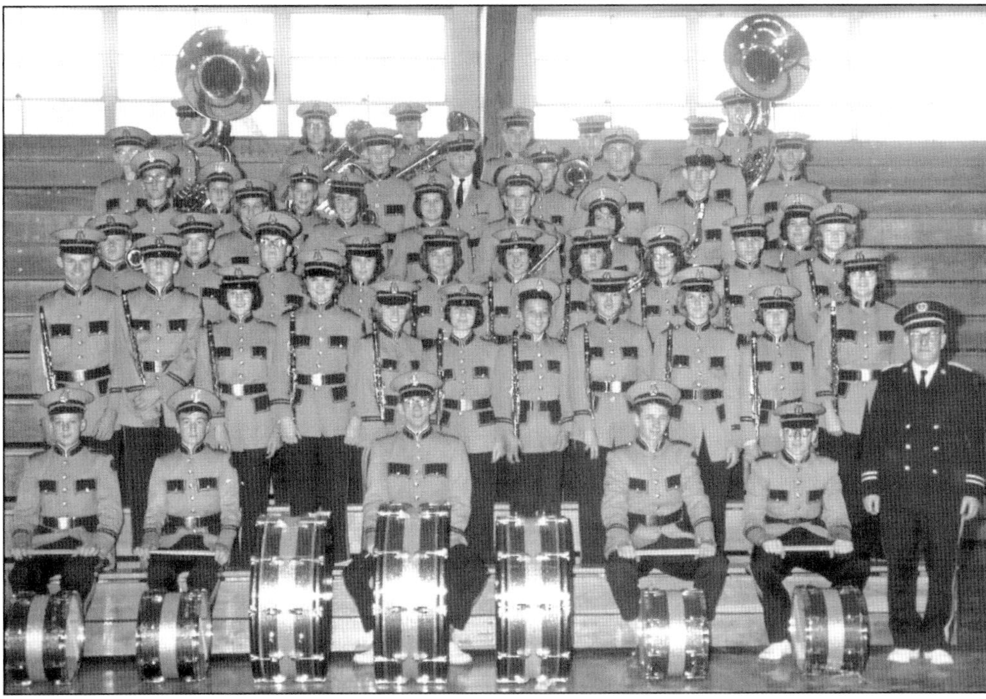

La Grange High School Band, 1962. The band is shown here with director Lionel Croteau. He was from the Kinston area and served in the military. He originally taught music at La Grange High School and moved with the school in 1965 to North Lenoir's current location. (Courtesy of Sonny Herring.)

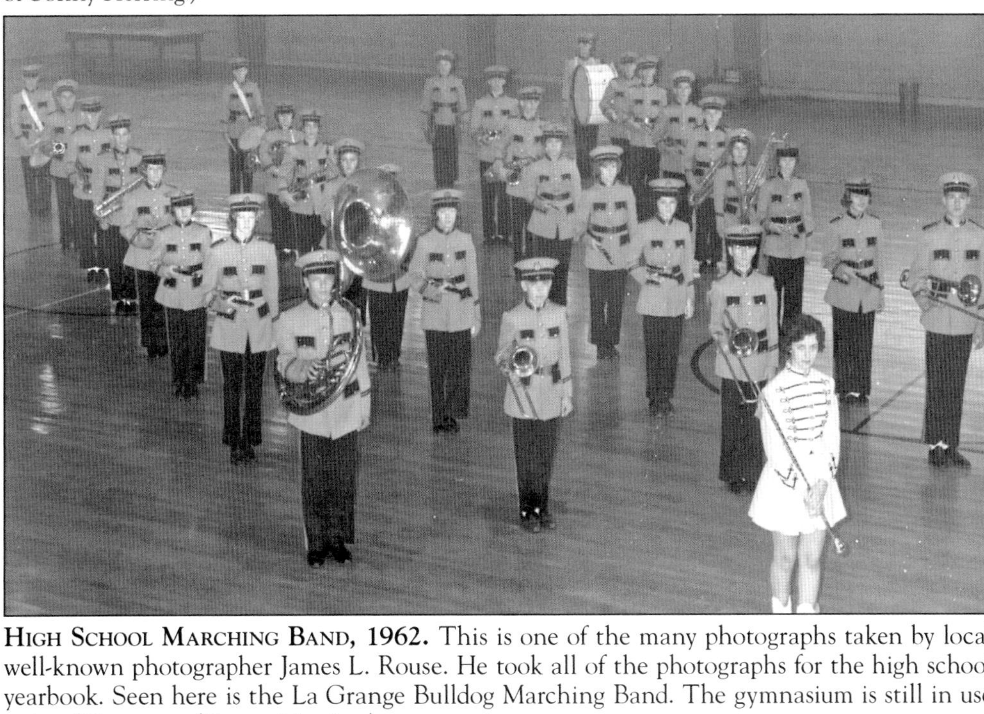

High School Marching Band, 1962. This is one of the many photographs taken by local well-known photographer James L. Rouse. He took all of the photographs for the high school yearbook. Seen here is the La Grange Bulldog Marching Band. The gymnasium is still in use today. (Courtesy of Sonny Herring.)

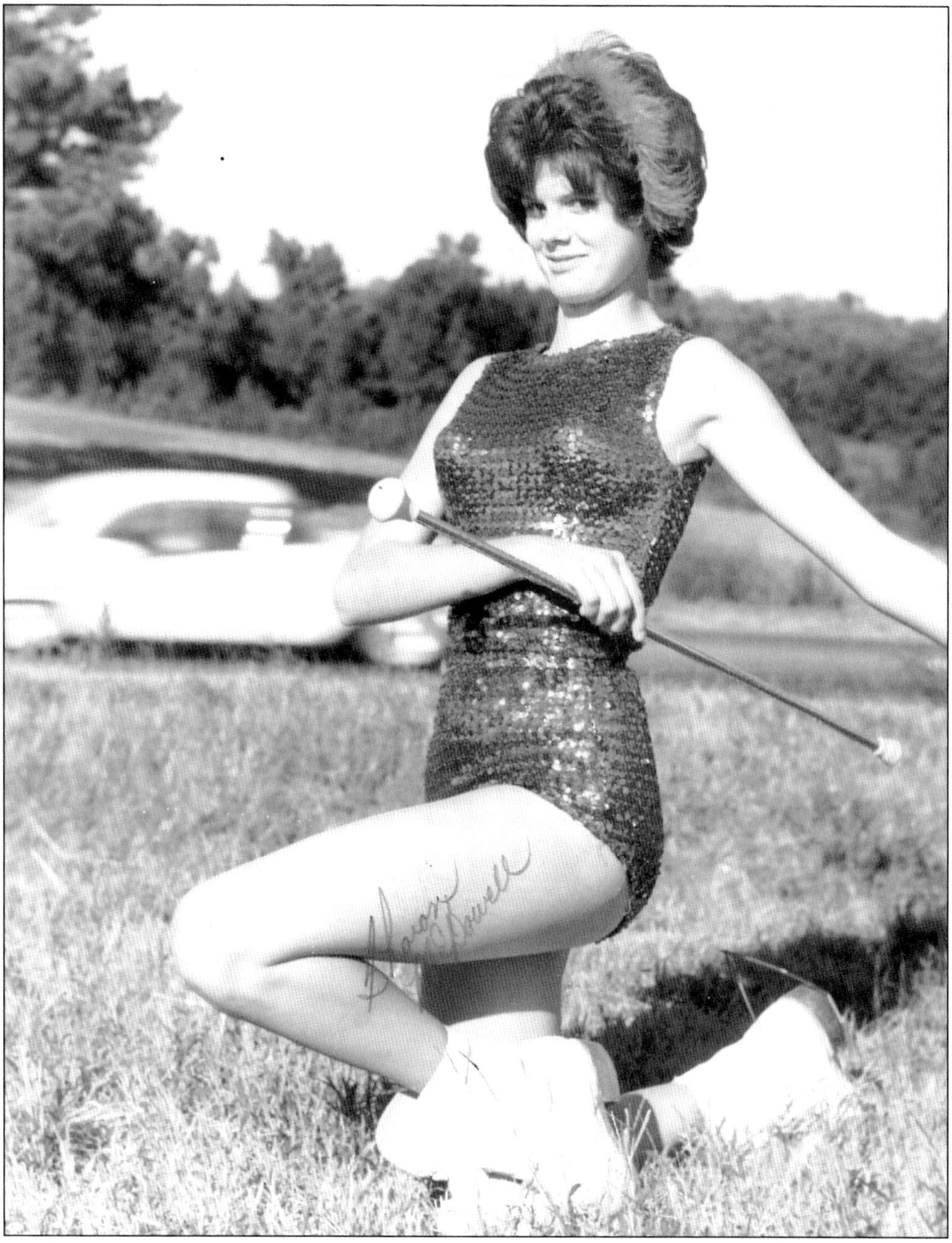

La Grange High School Majorette, 1964. Sharon McDowell poses in this photograph by James L. Rouse. McDowell autographed this photograph for an unidentified recipient. This was the last year of the marching band in La Grange. McDowell was a part of the majorette drum corps. The position of drum majorette was very popular between the 1950s and 1970s. They were not considered cheerleaders or flag bearers. In many cases, they led the marching band in accordance with the drum's cadence and the direction of the bandleader. Majorettes often performed solo acts with the band, including baton twirling and other feats and dances requiring coordination. Today, majorettes have lost their original luster. (Courtesy of Sonny Herring.)

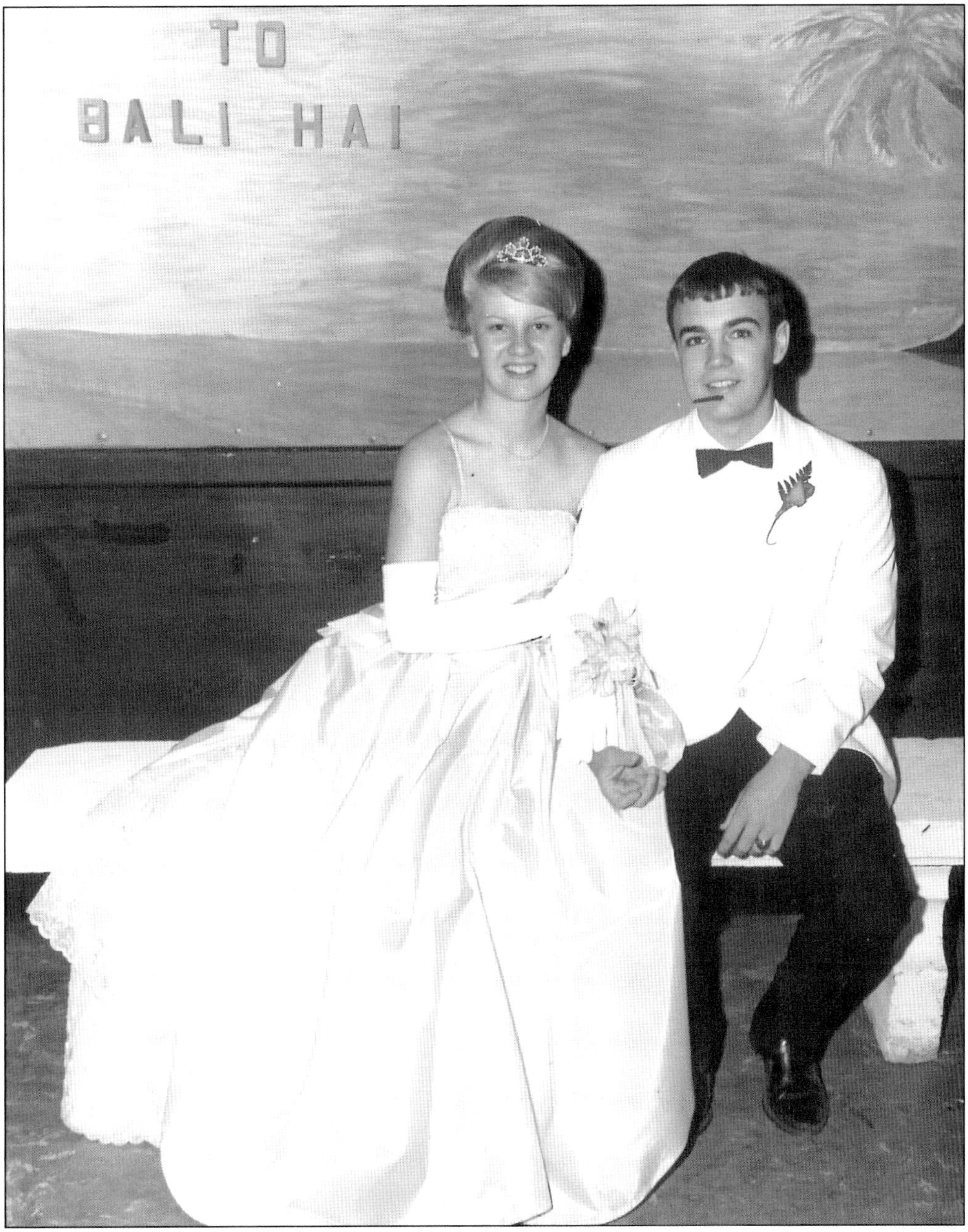

Bob Walker and Vicki Wallace, 1965. The theme for this junior/senior homecoming dance was a tropical one, as can be seen by the hand-drawn background and lettering. Bob Walker's mother taught English at North Lenoir High School. He and Vicki Wallace were sweethearts for a time. Walker played basketball and football for both La Grange and North Lenoir, including as quarterback for North Lenoir in 1965. That year, North Lenoir's football team came in second place in the conference, with a 7-3 record. Wallace was a cheerleader at La Grange and North Lenoir. She was the first chief cheerleader at North Lenoir, in 1964–1965. Unlike the cheerleaders of today, these cheerleaders did not perform dance and gymnastics but simply cheered and did so loudly. (Courtesy of Sonny Herring.)

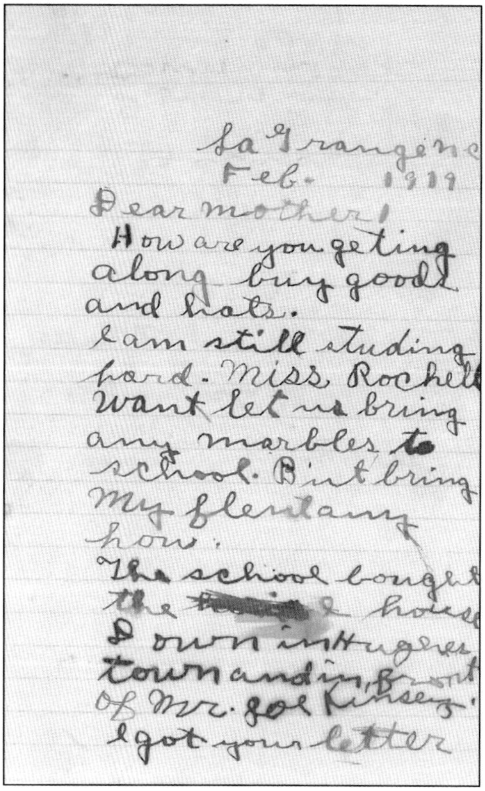

La Grange N.C.
Feb. 1919
Dear mother!
How are you geting along buy goods and hats.
I am still studing hard. Miss Rochelle want let us bring any marbles to school. But bring my [illegible] now.
The school bought the [illegible] house down in [illegible] town and in front of Mr. Joe Kinsey.
I got your letter

LETTER, 1919. J.W. Fields wrote this letter to his mother. In the letter, a Ms. Rochelle is mentioned. She was a well-known teacher in Lenoir County. Rochelle Middle School in Kinston was named in her honor. There is also a reference to Joe Kinsey. The Kinsey home was located downtown, on Washington Street. (Courtesy of Speck and Sister Fields.)

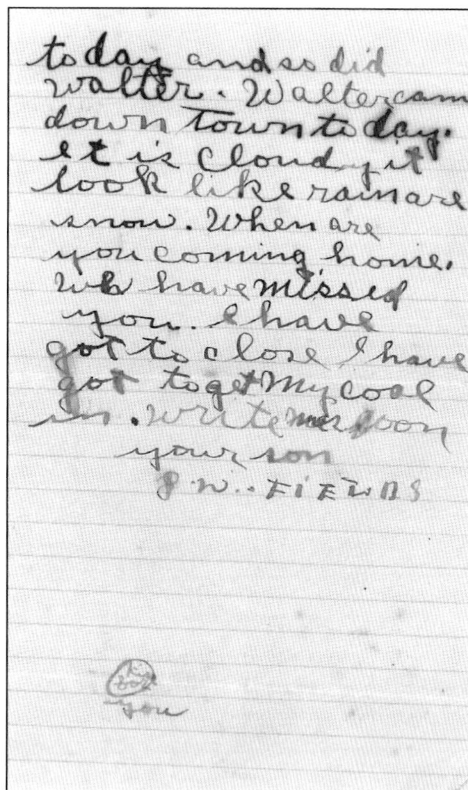

today and so did walter. Walter came down town today. it is Cloudy it look like rain are snow. When are you coming home. we have missed you. I have got to close I have got to get my coal in. write me soon
your son
J.W. FIELDS

J.W. FIELDS LETTER, 1919. It is interesting to note that Fields mentions that he must get his "coal in." This was common in La Grange in that era. Many churches, schools, and homes were heated by coal that came in on the old Shoofly train route. Bringing the coal into the house was usually a boy's chore. (Courtesy of Speck and Sister Fields.)

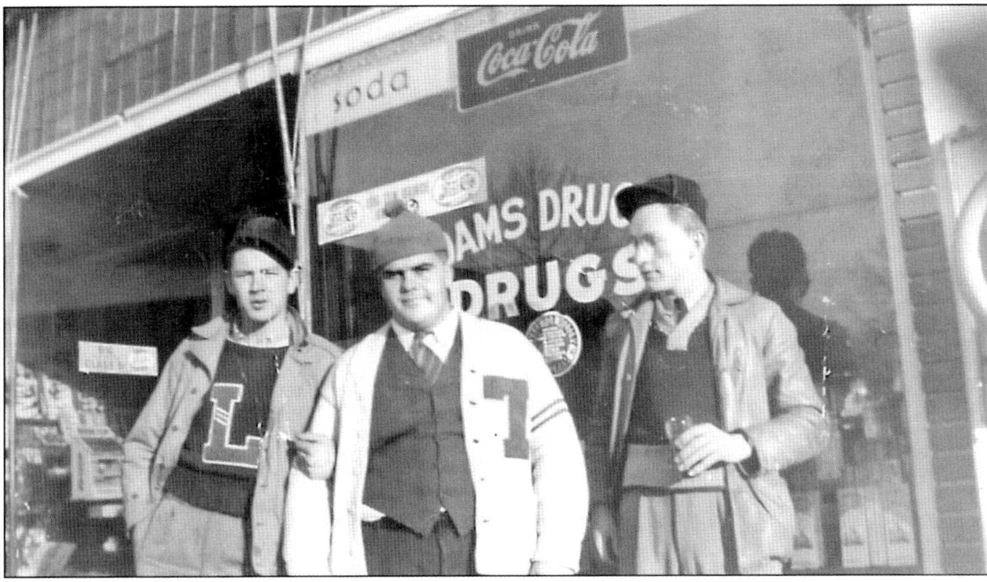

Hanging Out at the Soda Fountain, 1943. Bob Rouse (left), Rockefeller Venters (center), and Jack Crews stand outside of Adams Drugs Store. The store originally stood on the corner of Caswell and Railroad Streets. It made malts and sodas from scratch. Just months after this photograph was taken, these boys enlisted into the military. (Courtesy of the Bob Rouse family.)

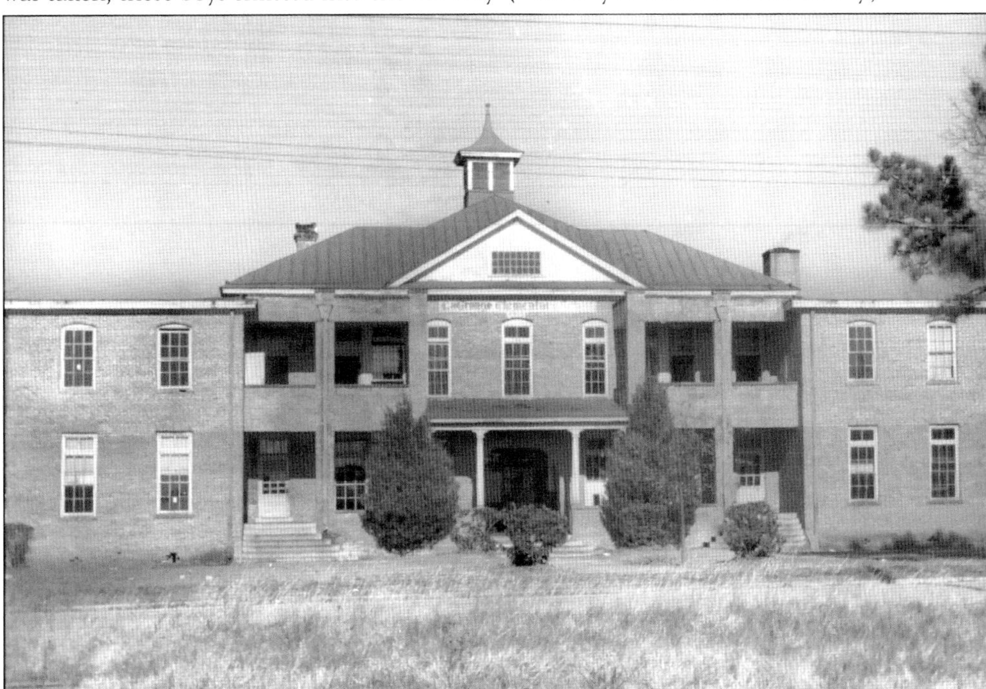

La Grange Elementary School, 1945. The school was established in 1906. According to local historian Nannie Braxton Herring, the school had only nine grades when it first opened. The 10th grade was added in 1912 and the 11th in 1915. In 1919, the school had 11 grades and 11 teachers. The building has since been torn down to erect a new, up-to-date school. (Courtesy of George Foss.)

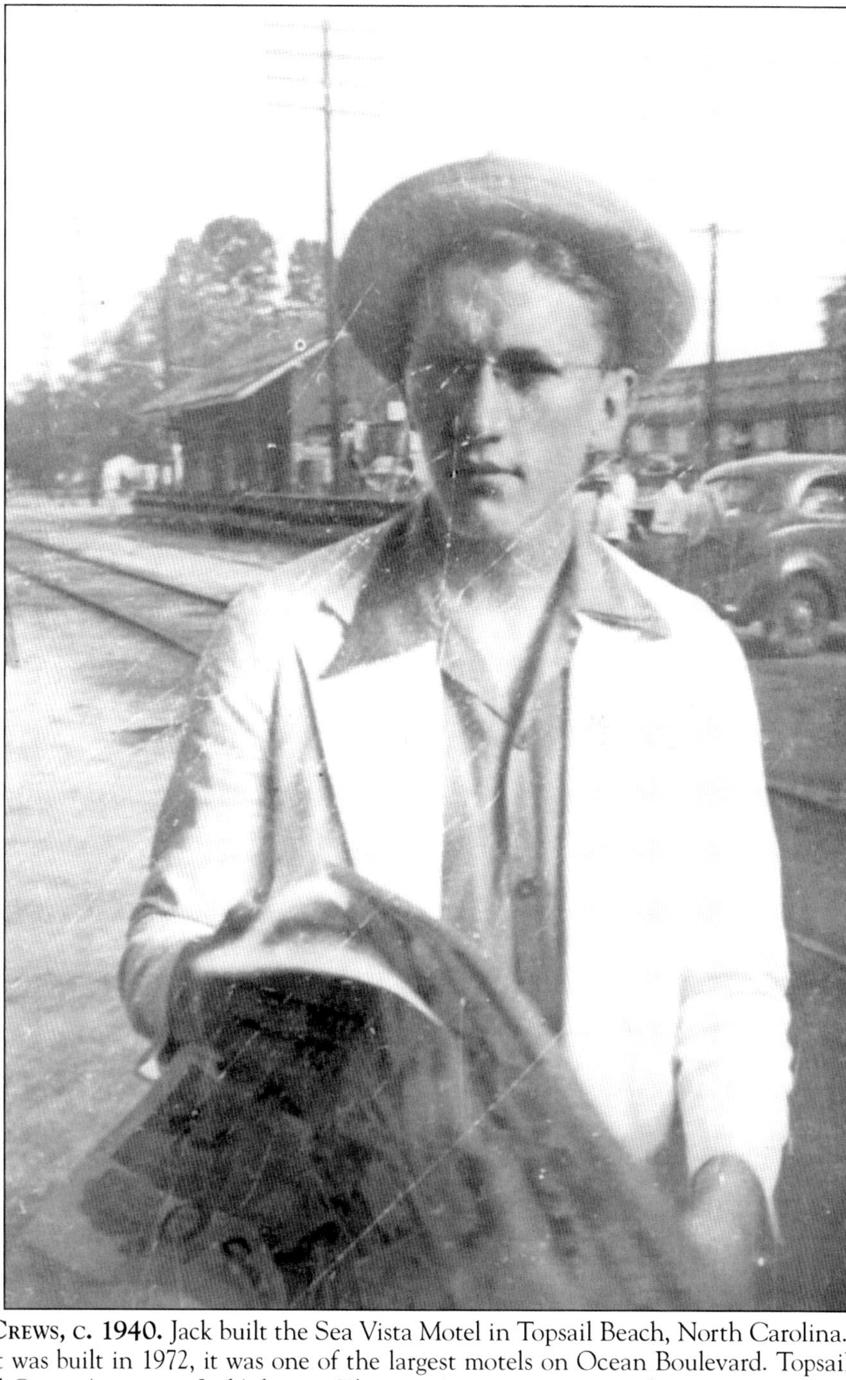

JACK CREWS, C. 1940. Jack built the Sea Vista Motel in Topsail Beach, North Carolina. At the time it was built in 1972, it was one of the largest motels on Ocean Boulevard. Topsail Beach named Crews Avenue in Jack's honor. The town's water-treatment plant is stationed on Crews Avenue. Many of the residents of La Grange in the 1940s, and even today, vacation or have a "place" at the beach. Topsail Beach is still a favorite vacation spot. It is a local pastime to head to the beach for brief three- or four-day vacations and for more lengthy stays during the summer. In this photograph, the old train depot is visible in the background. (Courtesy of the Jack Crews family.)

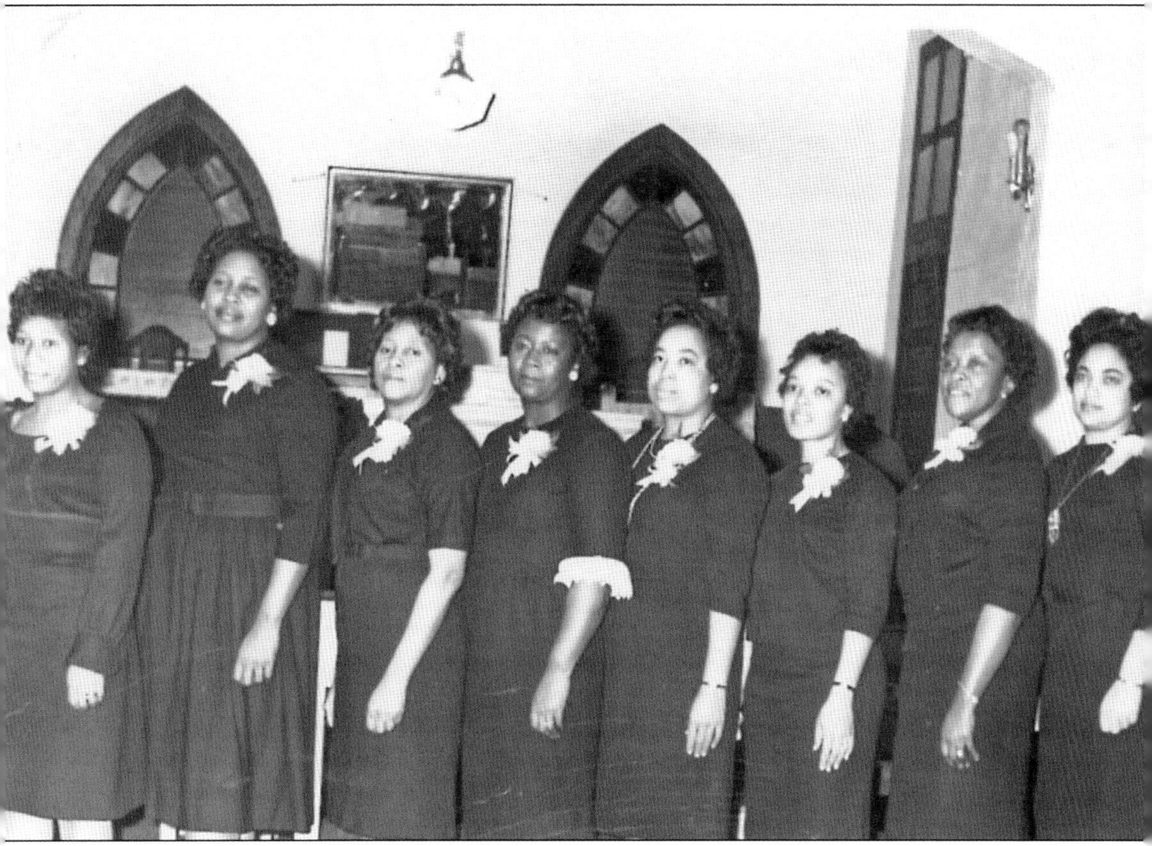

La Grange Colored High School Faculty, 1955–1960. This is a treasured photograph of some of the female faculty of La Grange Colored High School/Frink High School. These women served thousands of students during their tenure. The photograph was taken at Ebenezer Missionary Baptist Church in La Grange. Many town leaders were members of Ebenezer, such as Jim Shaw, who taught Sunday school; E.B. Frink; and Ira Branch. Ebenezer was formed in 1871, making it one of the oldest historically African American churches in La Grange. The original wood frame church burned down in 1918. It was rebuilt in 1920 by Rev. R.W. Pate, a brick-maker by trade who did most of the physical labor himself on the new church. (Courtesy of Dorethea Branch.)

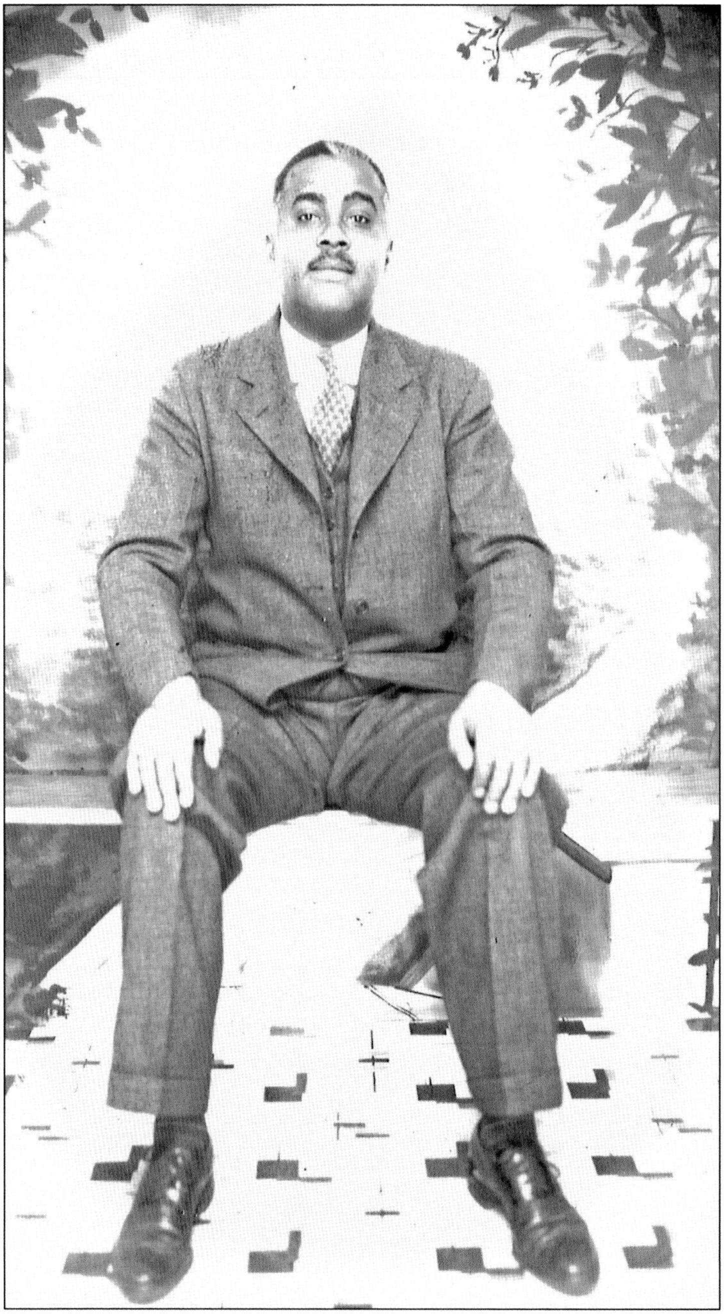

EMMETT BENTLEY FRINK, 1945–1951. Frink was one of the most beloved citizens of La Grange. He was involved with the Masonic lodge and Ebenezer Missionary Baptist Church. At Ebenezer, he served as a Sunday school teacher. Frink came to La Grange in 1932. He was the first African American to procure a bus for the school. When he came to La Grange Colored School, there were only seven teachers. Frink grew the school to be one of the largest African American schools in North Carolina. The son of a fisherman, Frink was also a scholar and administrator. To this day, those who knew him personally or were his students refer to him by the nickname "Fessor." The Frink Alumni and Friends Association is named in his honor. (Courtesy of Dorethea Branch.)

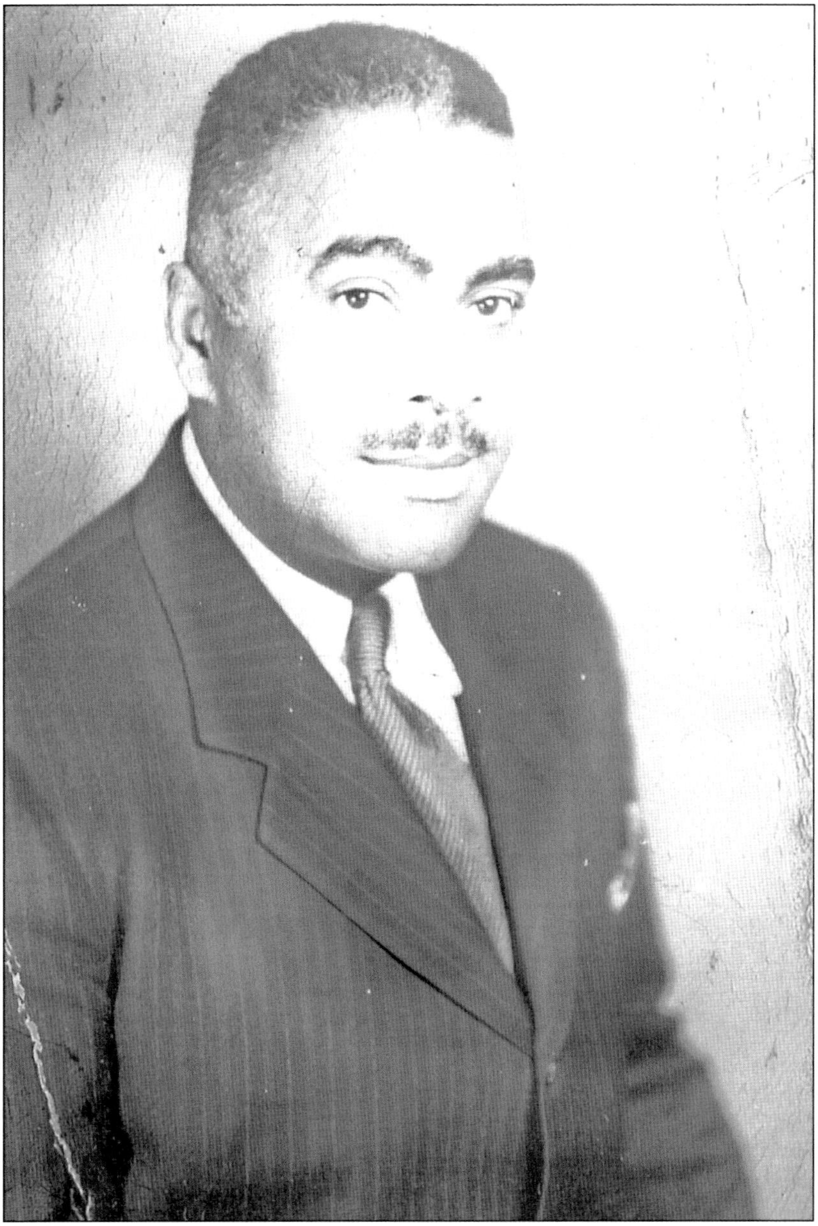

"Fessor" E.B. Frink, 1950. Frink died in 1951 of an apparent heart attack in his home. At the time of his death, he had 1,100 students. He personally drove the school's only bus into the country to pick up African American students. He taught three classes, including Problems in Democracy and civics. The Frink family, still active in the school today, sponsors two awards annually, The Emmett Bentley Frink Award, which acknowledges a student with a consistent 95 average from grades six through eight. The recipient must also have a proven track record of civic and academic leadership. The family also sponsors the Ophelia Winslet Frink Award, which recognizes one eighth-grade student for his or her academic skills and contribution to knowledge. Both awards come with monetary gifts. Emmett Frink's son Sam Frink speaks annually at the eighth-grade graduation. The day before graduation, students are required to hear a motivating speech from Sam Frink. (Courtesy of Dorethea Branch.)

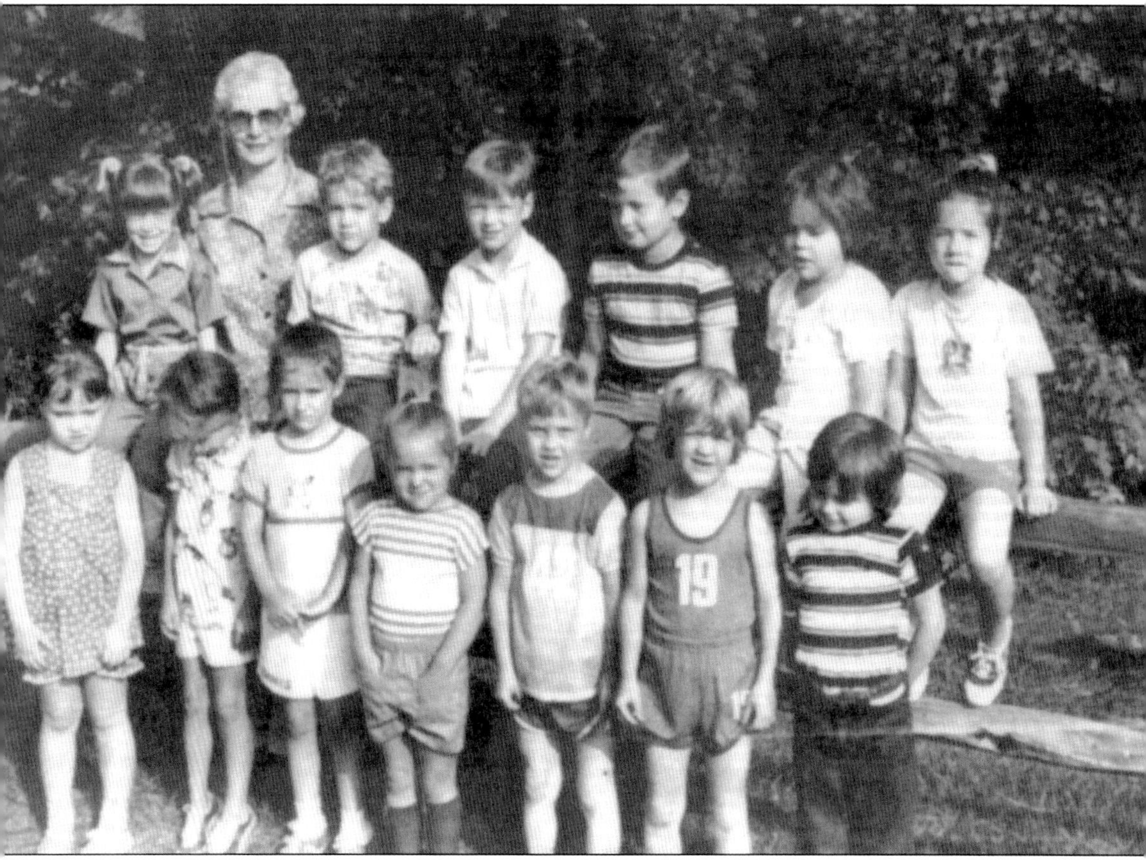

Grace Burke's Kindergarten Class, 1978. Grace Burke and her kindergarten class pose for a photograph on May 29, 1978, at the end of the school year. The occasion was a trip to the children's museum in Rocky Mount, North Carolina. The children also visited Figures, Inc., and stopped at a large playground for some playtime. Shown here are, in no particular order, Grace Burke, Amy Aldridge, Mark Alphin, Tammy Carter, Tommy Colie, Chris Creech, Jon Dawson, Heather Fields, Tracey Harrison, Diane Heath, Deanna Layden, Tommy Reid, Reid Rouse, Michelle Sutton, and Jennifer Rouse. The students had just completed their Parents Night Commencement program on May 26. All students were involved in putting on the program. Burke taught kindergarten in La Grange until 1980. She taught at the First Missionary Baptist Church and eventually in her home. The church's current pastor, Brad Mitchell, was one of her students. (Courtesy of Grace Burke.)

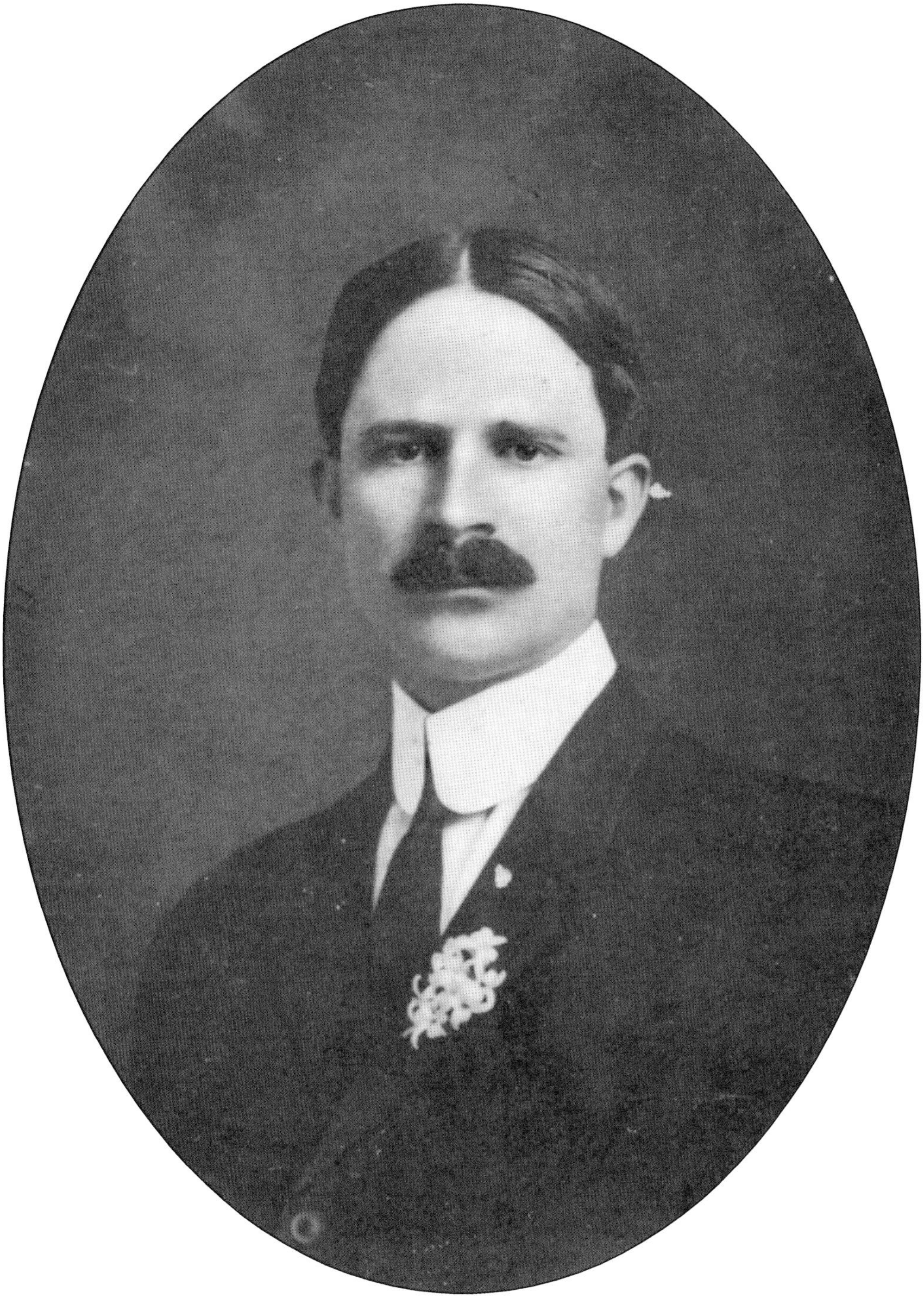

Supt. Braxton Craven, 1911–1912. Craven was the superintendent of Lenoir County Schools after 1906. The first school superintendent was James W. Harper, followed by J.Y. Joyner; Capt. W.S. Byrd, who died in office; Col. W.D. Pollock; and, in 1890, Rev. C.W. Howard. After the district went without a superintendent for a few short years, Howard returned. (Courtesy of the Heritage Place, Lenoir Community College.)

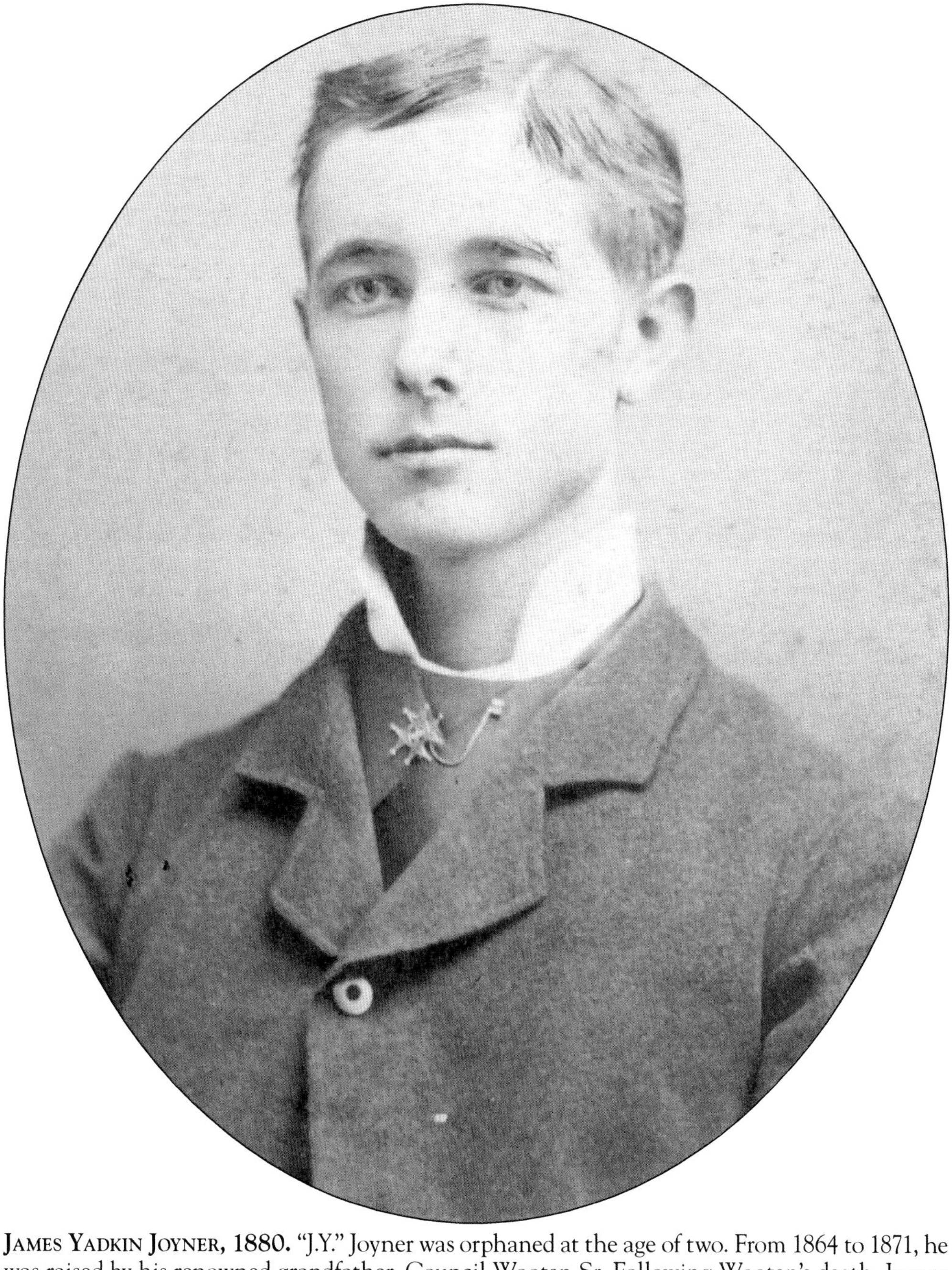

JAMES YADKIN JOYNER, 1880. "J.Y." Joyner was orphaned at the age of two. From 1864 to 1871, he was raised by his renowned grandfather, Council Wooten Sr. Following Wooten's death, Joyner lived with his other grandfather, Uncle Shade I. Joyner attended the University of North Carolina when he was 16 years old. Years later, he was given an honorary LLD from the University of North Carolina. Joyner was Lenoir County's superintendent of schools from 1882 to 1884. He was a devoted member of the First Missionary Baptist Church. When he retired in 1919, he returned to La Grange and became involved with the North Carolina Tobacco Growers Association. He became the association's president in 1922. He also was an agent for Prudential Life Insurance Company. (Courtesy of East Carolina University, Joyner Library Digital Collections.)

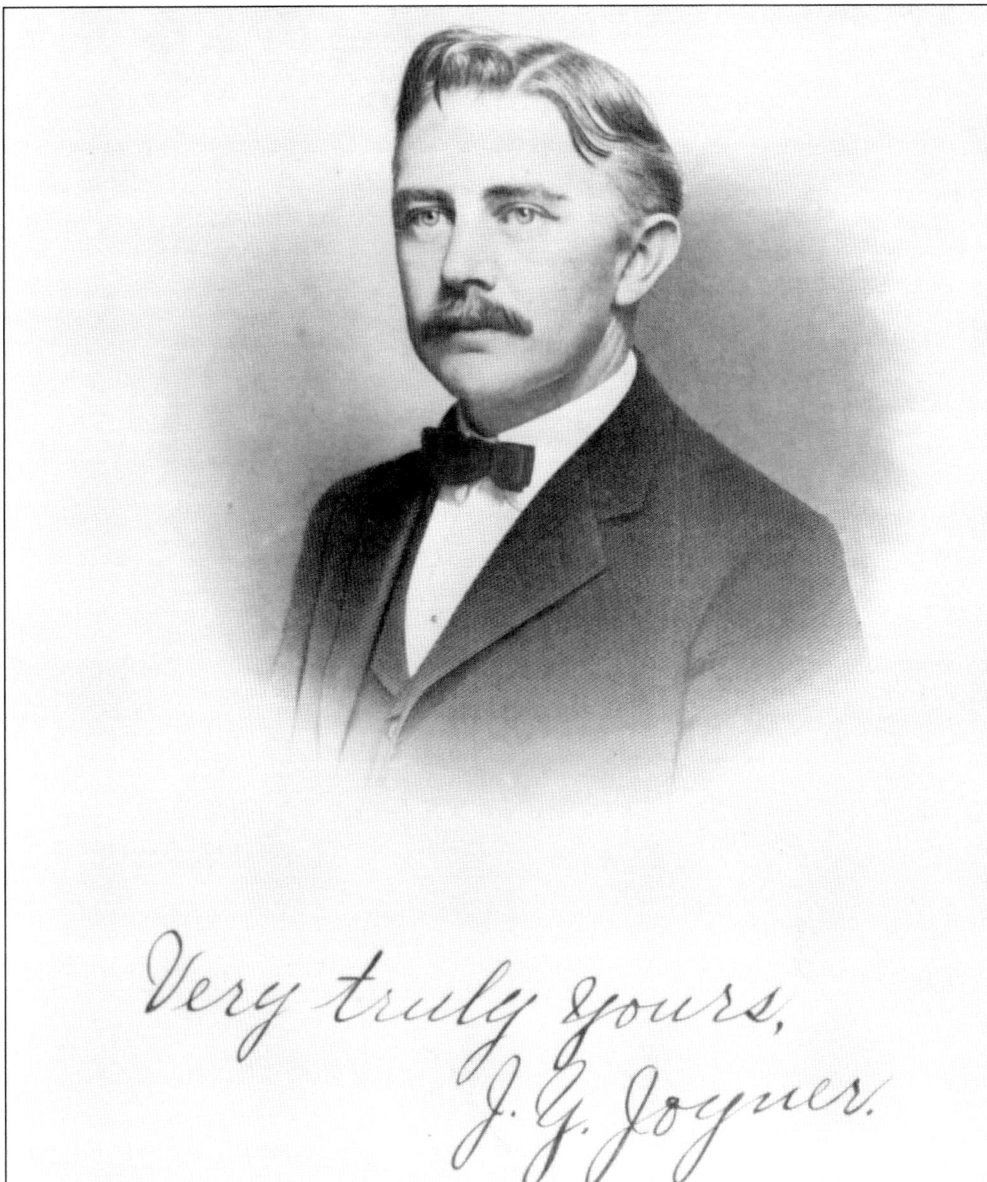

J.Y. Joyner, c. 1915. The East Carolina University Archives includes the following description of Joyner: "He helped operate La Grange Academy and La Grange Collegiate Institute (1881–1884), taught at the Winston Graded Schools (1884–1885), served as superintendent of the Goldsboro Graded Schools (1889–1893), and helped organize teachers' institutes throughout North Carolina. Joyner studied law at the Greensboro Law School operated by Robert Paine Dick (1885–1886) and practiced law in the firm of Faircloth, Allen and Joyner in Goldsboro (1886–1889)." Accepting the call of his classmate at Chapel Hill, Charles Duncan McIver, Joyner chaired the Department of English at the Normal and Industrial College for Women in Greensboro (1893–1902). In 1902, Gov. Charles Brantley Aycock appointed Joyner superintendent of public instruction. Joyner held the position until January 1, 1919, during which time he instituted sweeping reforms in the state's system of public education. He presided over the National Education Association in 1910. (Courtesy of East Carolina University, Joyner Library Digital Collections.)

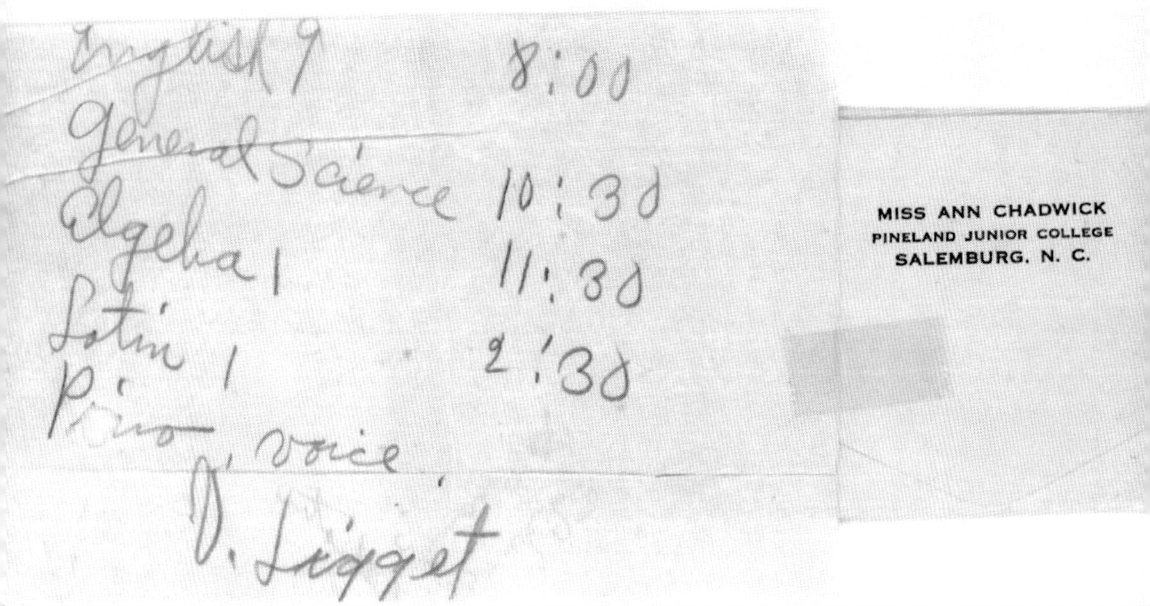

CLASS SCHEDULE, 1947. Ann Cashwell went to Pineland Junior College, a private high school for girls, in her junior year. Shown here is her academic schedule for the semester. She use to say, with a wonderful sense of humor, "I was sent to Pineland to get straighten out but it didn't work." Founded in 1875, the school's original name was Salemburg Academy. Pineland was located in Salemsburg, North Carolina, outside of Fayetteville. The school closed in 1973. Cashwell came back to La Grange the following year and graduated from La Grange High School. She is another local historian that has had a consistently great record of separating lore from fact. Many of the town's historians appreciated her contributions to preserving local history. (Courtesy of Ann Cashwell and Penny Chadwick Dawson.)

Three

Family, Friends, and the Garden Spot Community

Many citizens of La Grange still hold great memories of the community. The Rouse family has created memories for many folks. Bob Rouse was one of those Rouses who have maintained the admiration of the town for many years. He and his brother Phil were greatly admired for their contributions to history and for their preservation of local history. Both men were sons of entrepreneur John H. Rouse Sr. Bob and Jake Herring Jr. lectured each year at E.B. Frink Middle School on the history of La Grange. Bob left the town a DVD lecture, which was, and is, a treasure.

The Fields, Herrings, Suttons, Dawsons, Britts, Mewborns, Wootens, Shaws, Branches, Fosses, and so many others helped to grow the town into the wonderful community it is today. Demographically, the town is evenly divided by race, and yet, La Grange is a beacon of light to the country of how the races can get along, living side-by-side with one another. The key to this accomplishment is simple: they were, and are, friends.

In an interview several years ago, Jake Herring Jr. put it best: "We took care of one another out here. Nobody went hungry and everyone here, black and white, watched out after each other." This was in response to the effects of the Great Depression. Also, when change came, change was accepted. Many citizens of La Grange supported the civil rights movement, for example. Such changes made La Grange an even better place to live.

Today, the residents are still friends. They will greet others with a smile and ask about their family. In this little Southern town, doors are still opened for ladies, and folks say "yes, sir" and "yes, ma'am." Visitors, and those who have recently moved to town, can count on having a friend here. This chapter tells the stories of some great families and friends that have made La Grange what it is today.

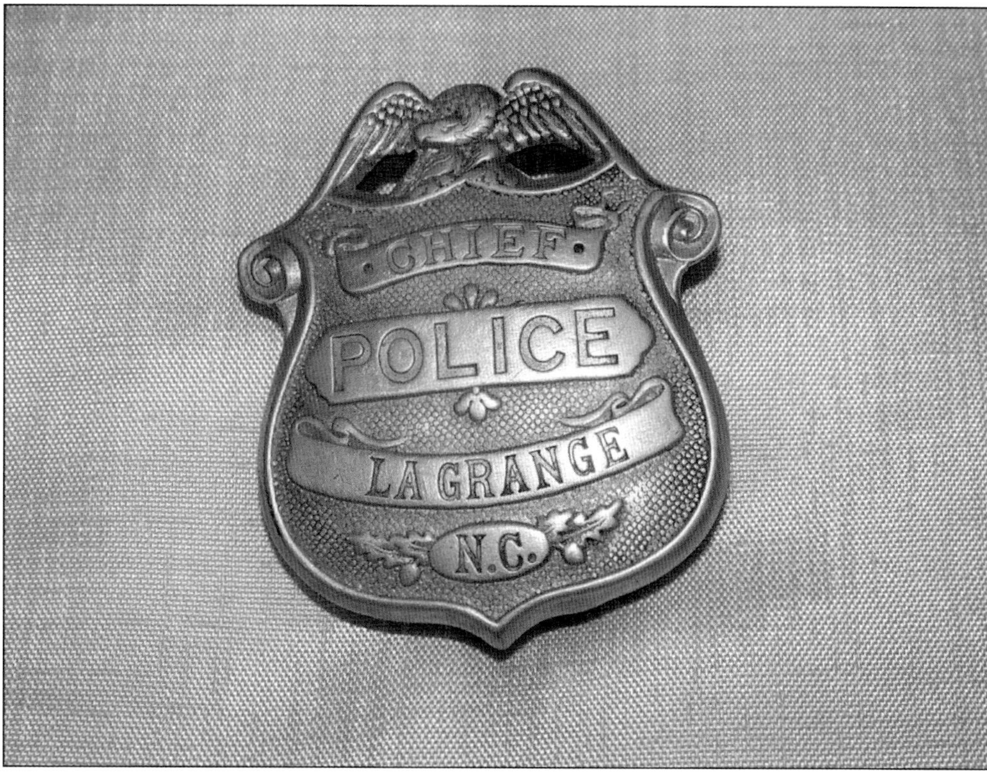

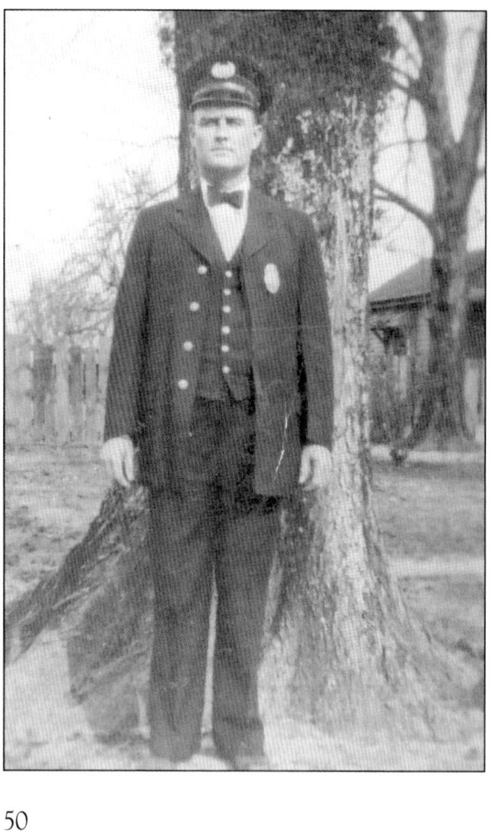

Matthew Tripp Police Badge, 1920–1925. This is a rare find, and it is more than likely the oldest La Grange police badge in existence today. The La Grange Police Department was created shortly after the Civil War. Prior to the war, La Grange was run by community leaders, who managed the town's laws. Legal matters were usually sent to Kinston. (Courtesy of Frances DeTuro Rosiello.)

Matthew Tripp, Early 1920s. Tripp was one of the first five chiefs of police in La Grange. He is seen here outside of his home. Tripp served as the chief from 1913 until the 1920s. Eventually, he moved to Goldsboro, where he retired. (Courtesy of Frances DeTuro Rosiello.)

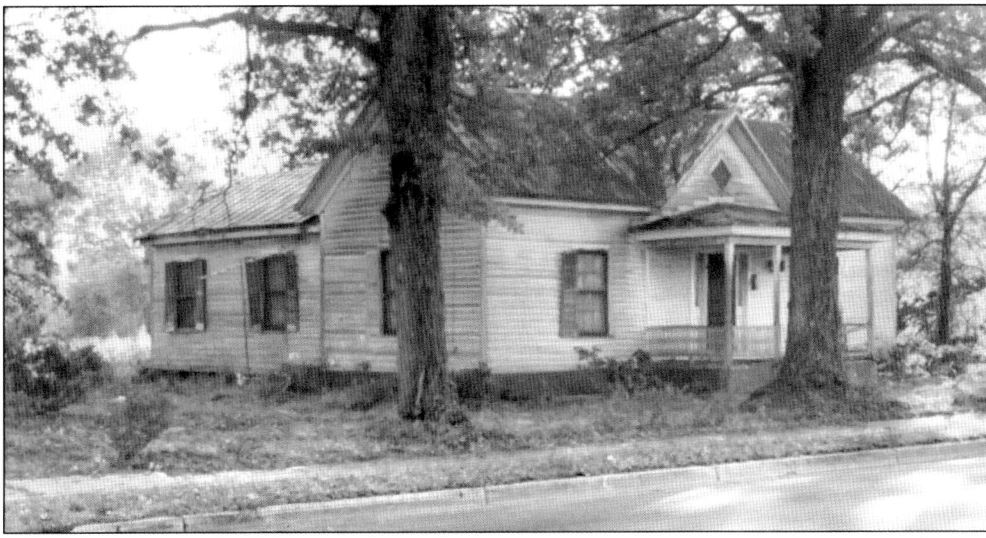

Bessie Tripp House, c. 1984. The house used to stand at 407 North Railroad Street. At the time of this photograph, it was in a state of disrepair, and it was torn down in the early 1990s. Bessie Tripp purchased the home about 1945. She married former La Grange police chief Matthew Tripp in 1913, and the Tripps had four children. (Courtesy of Frances DeTuro Rosiello.)

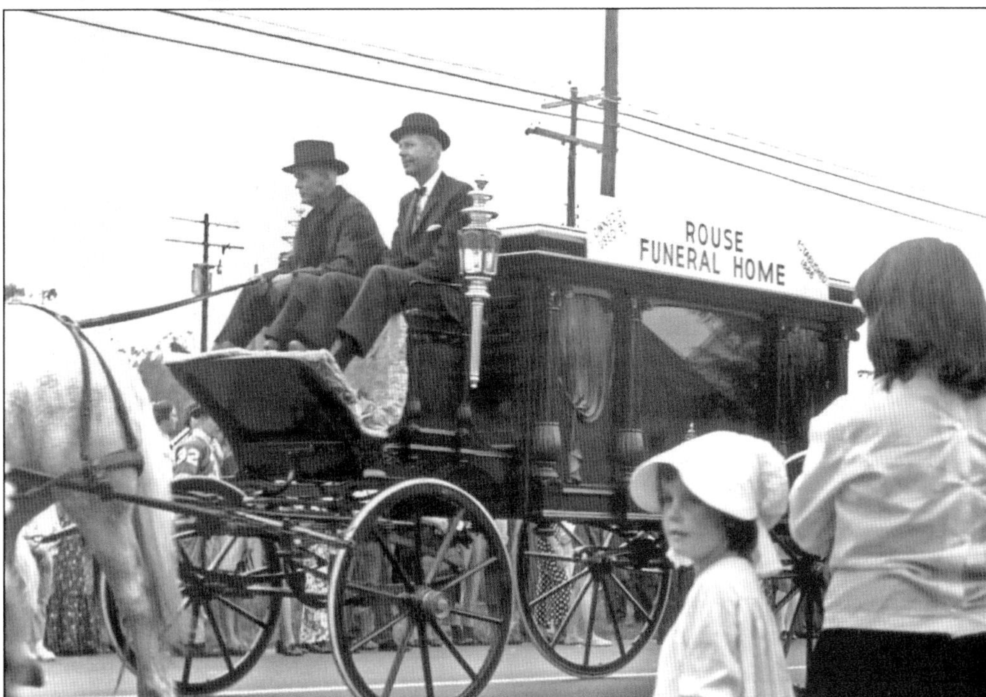

Rouse Funeral Home Hearse, 1969. Phil Rouse is pictured here riding a horse-drawn hearse built in 1890. The hearse is in excellent condition today. This occasion is believed to be the centennial parade in 1969. Rouse followed in the footsteps of his father, working at the funeral home for 65 years. Phil Rouse served in the US Army Air Corps in World War II. (Courtesy of Sonny Herring.)

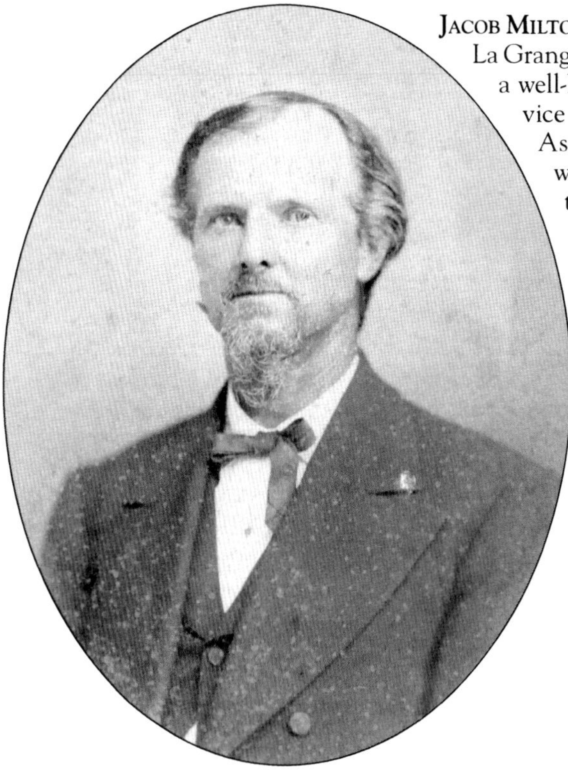

Jacob Milton Hadley, c. 1878. Dr. Hadley moved to La Grange in 1867, following the Civil War. He was a well-known physician in North Carolina and vice president of the North Carolina Medical Association. He and George F. Whitfield were behind the effort in 1869 to change the town's name to La Grange. (Courtesy of John Roy and Alice Croom.)

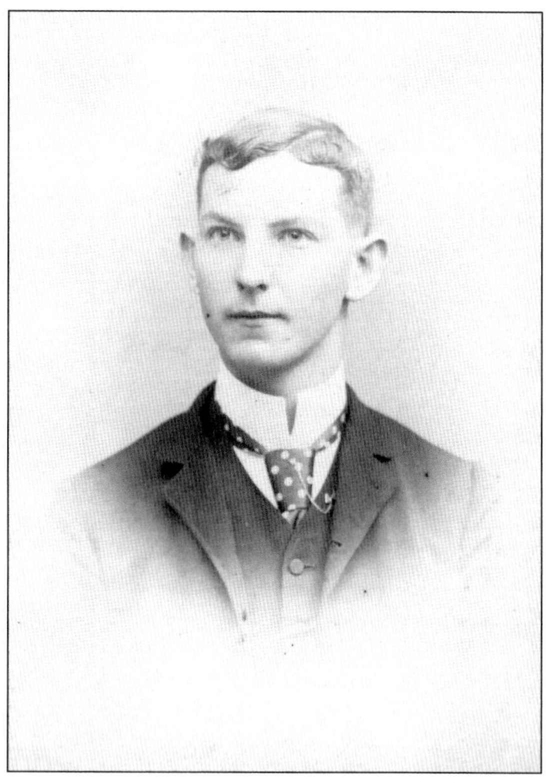

George Bacon Wood Hadley, c. 1878. The son of Dr. Jacob M. Hadley, George Hadley owned over 1,000 acres of La Grange farmland and eventually settled in Greenville, North Carolina. He was a professor of mathematics and former director of the Rouse Banking Company. He moved to Greenville sometime after 1902. (Courtesy of John Roy and Alice Croom.)

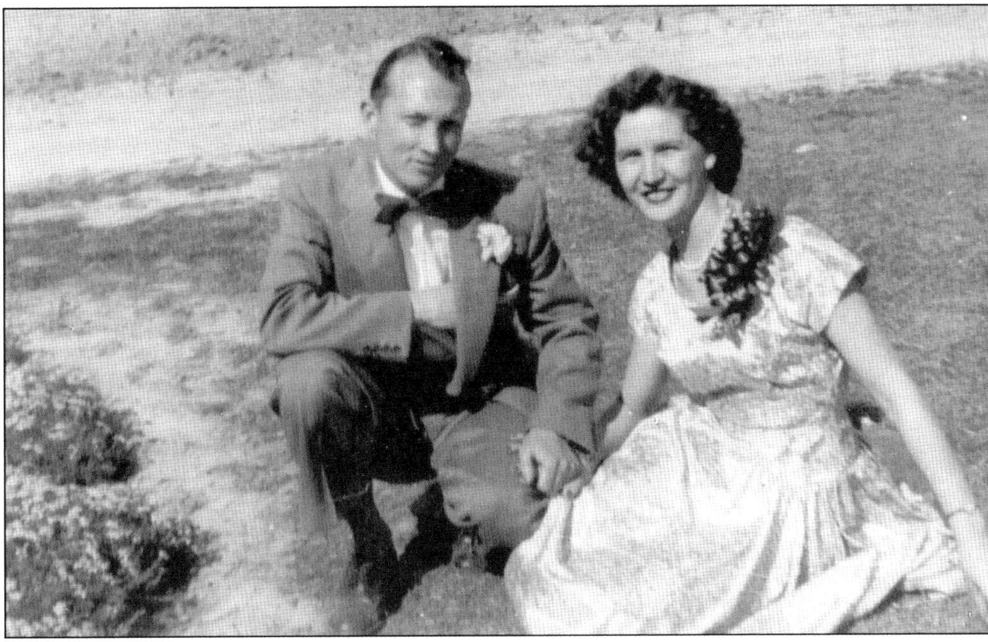

Cecil and Grace Burke, 1955. This photograph was taken in April for Easter. Grace was the former Grace Sugg of Greene County. The Suggs had six children and lived one mile from Snow Hill. At one time, Grace's father was the register of deeds for Greene County. Grace and Cecil met at the First Baptist Church of Snow Hill in 1954. (Courtesy of Grace Burke.)

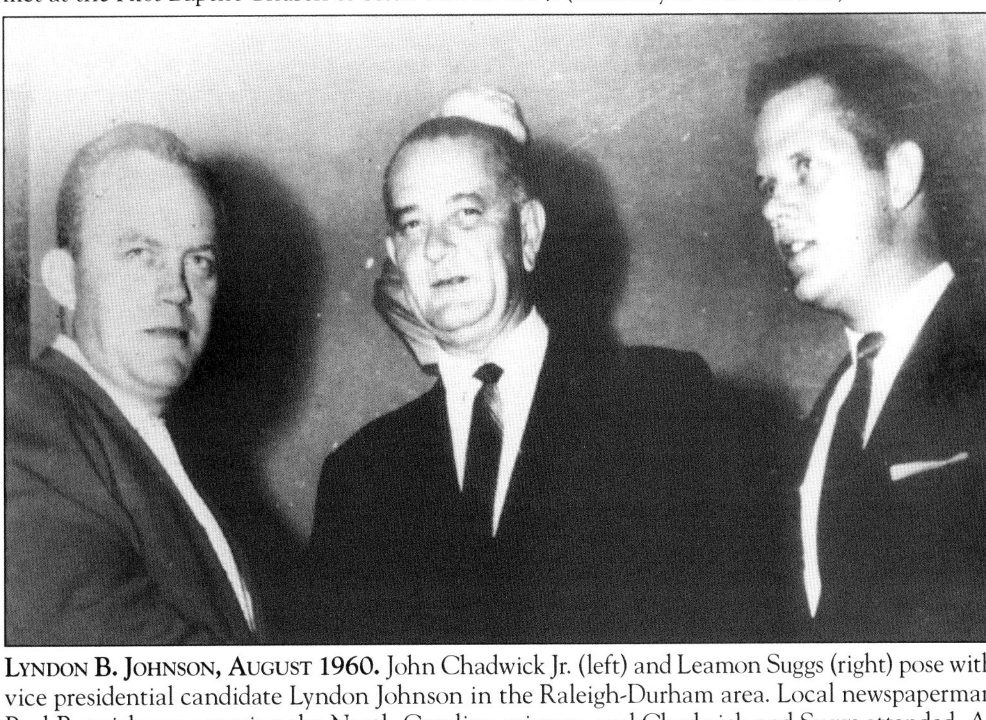

Lyndon B. Johnson, August 1960. John Chadwick Jr. (left) and Leamon Suggs (right) pose with vice presidential candidate Lyndon Johnson in the Raleigh-Durham area. Local newspaperman Paul Barwick was covering the North Carolina primary, and Chadwick and Suggs attended. At this time, Suggs was a student at Duke University. Johnson said of John Chadwick that he was "a lot of fun to be around." (Courtesy of Penny Dawson.)

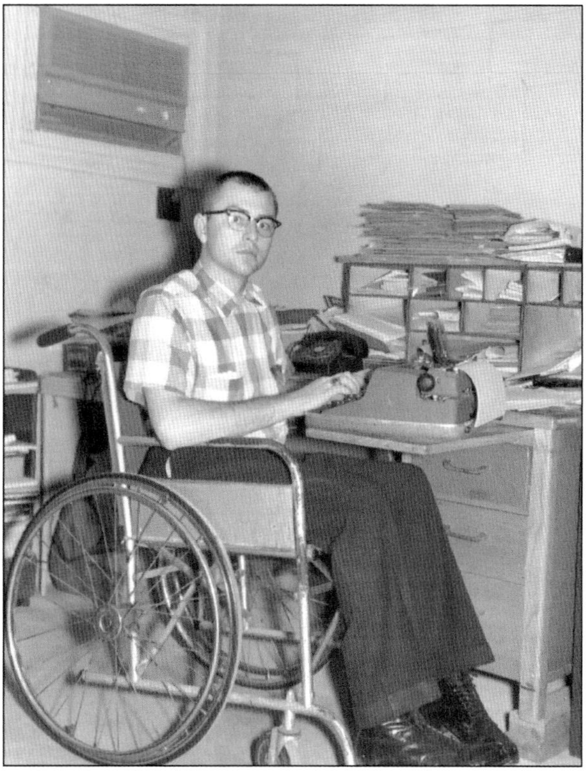

PAUL BARWICK, C. 1970. Barwick was the owner of the local newspaper, the *Weekly Gazette*. That paper was preceded by the *Sentinel*. The *Gazette* was established in 1953. According to many, Barwick was a giant of a man. He headed up La Grange's centennial celebration. (Courtesy of Sonny Herring.)

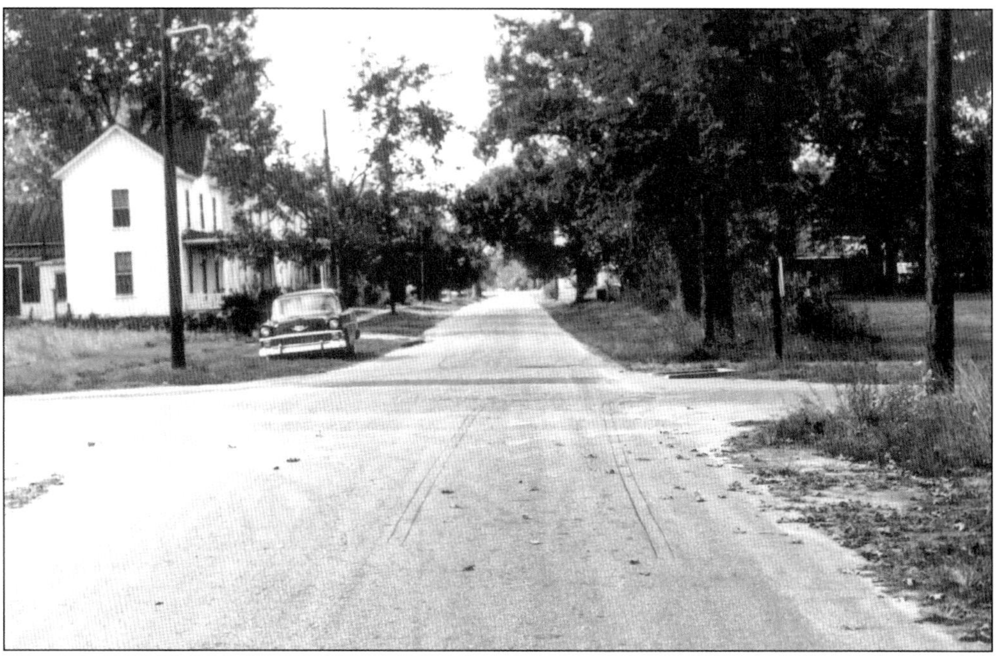

WASHINGTON AND CHARLES STREETS, 1950S. James Rouse took this photograph in the middle or late 1950s. The home on the left was built by the Wooten family in the 1880s. For many years, this was the home of longtime La Grange residents Ed and Hazel Wooten. Hazel taught second grade at the local school. (Courtesy of Sonny Herring.)

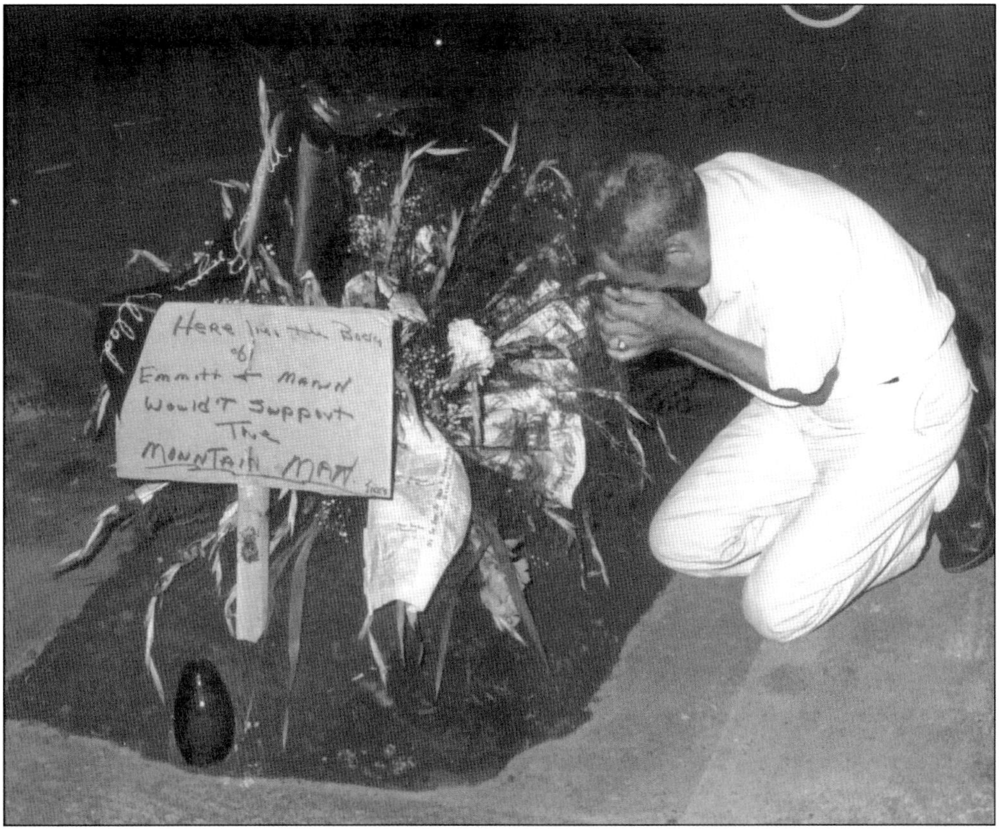

THE ELECTION GRAVEYARD, C. 1965. In the past, following elections in La Grange, the loser would be buried in effigy. The tradition has since died out. The losers of this particular election were Emmitt and Marvin. The poem was written by George "Jiggs" Anderson, who penned the epitaphs for the losers after each election. (Courtesy of Sonny Herring.)

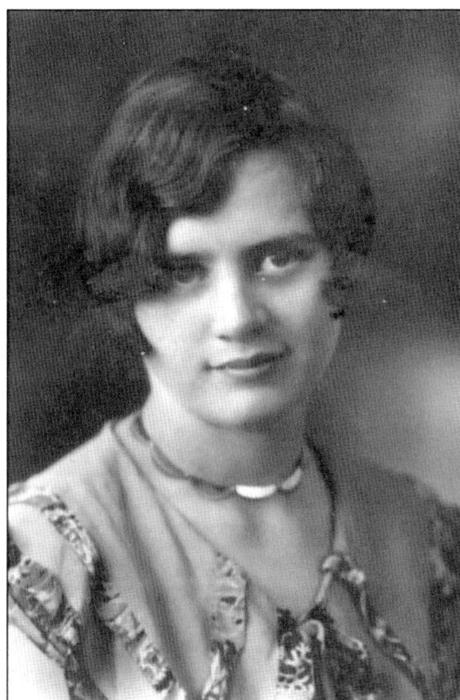

MELBA LOUISE MEWBORN CHADWICK, C. 1925. Melba Chadwick was a seamstress at Mewborn and Chadwick cleaners. She made alterations for virtually everyone in town. Her granddaughter, Penny Chadwick Dawson, would play with all of her buttons and imitate Melba Chadwick's sewing. Penny loved to visit her grandmother and play school. Melba was a member of First Missionary Baptist Church and served as its clerk for years. (Courtesy of Ann Cashwell and Penny Chadwick Dawson.)

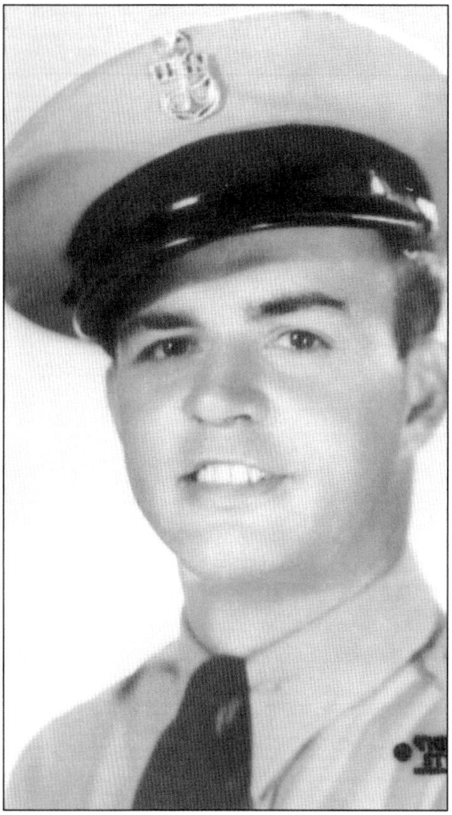

Jesse Leon Wilson, 1944. "J.L." Wilson, a Pearl Harbor survivor, was stationed on the USS *Dale*. An official report details a firefight involving the *Dale* and one enemy fighter and enemy dive-bombers. Wilson was the only man firing the .50-caliber machine gun on the ship, so it is assumed that he shot down the Japanese fighter. No one aboard the *Dale* was injured. (Courtesy of J.L. Wilson.)

John F. Kennedy, August 1960. Leamon Suggs (center) and John Chadwick Jr. (right) are seen here with presidential candidate John F. Kennedy. At this North Carolina primary speech, there were about 40 members of the state's Democratic delegation in attendance. Suggs and Chadwick had a front-row seat and met with the future president. According to Suggs, JFK was a shy man. (Courtesy of Penny Dawson.)

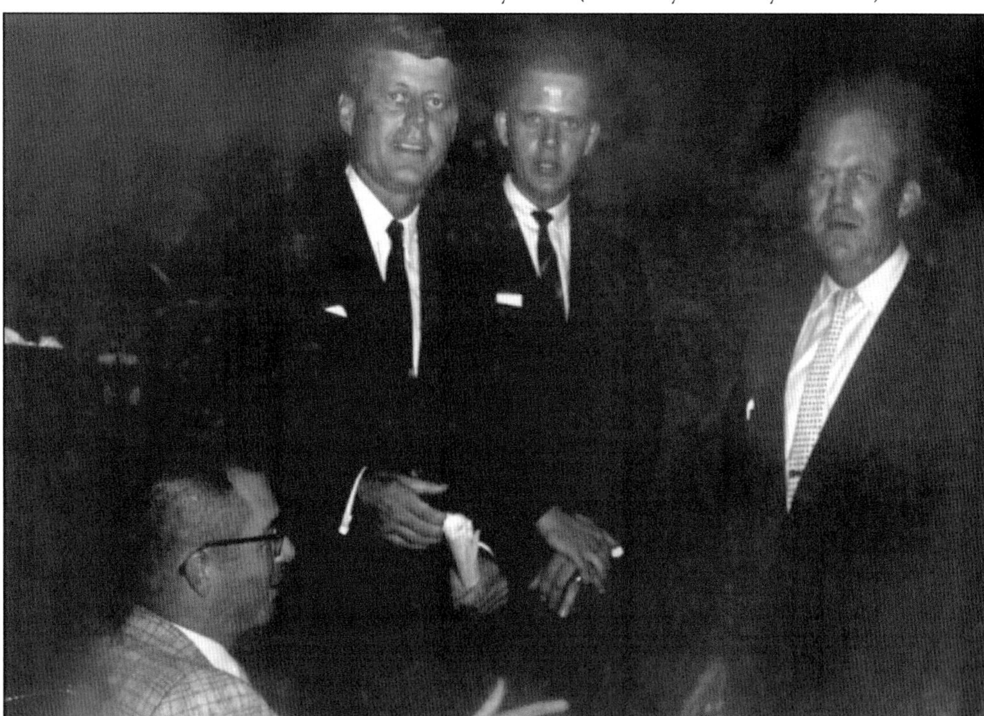

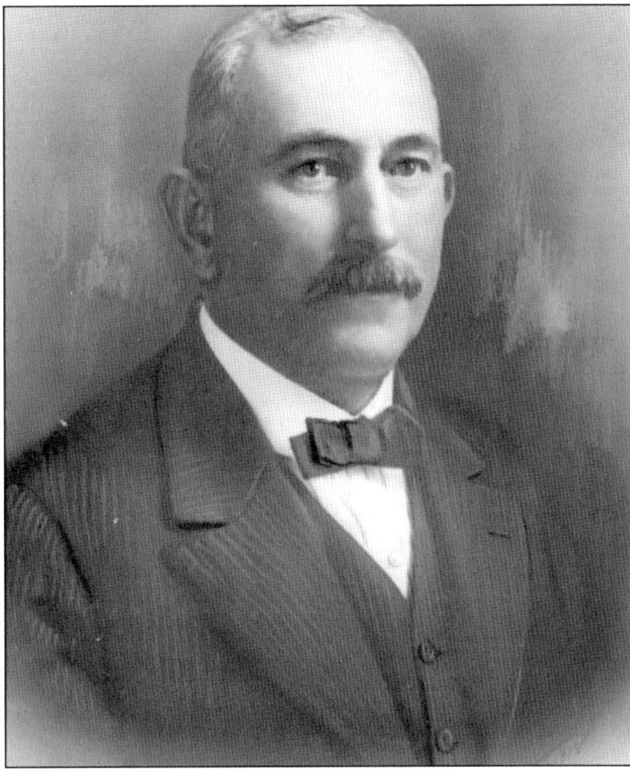

JOHN R. WOOTEN, 1918. Wooten was the president of the Bank of La Grange in 1910. He was known to give liberally to his church, First Missionary Baptist. The largest Sunday school classroom was named in his honor. The cost to build the addition to the church was $1,000. His portrait still hangs on the church's wall. (Courtesy of First Missionary Baptist Church.)

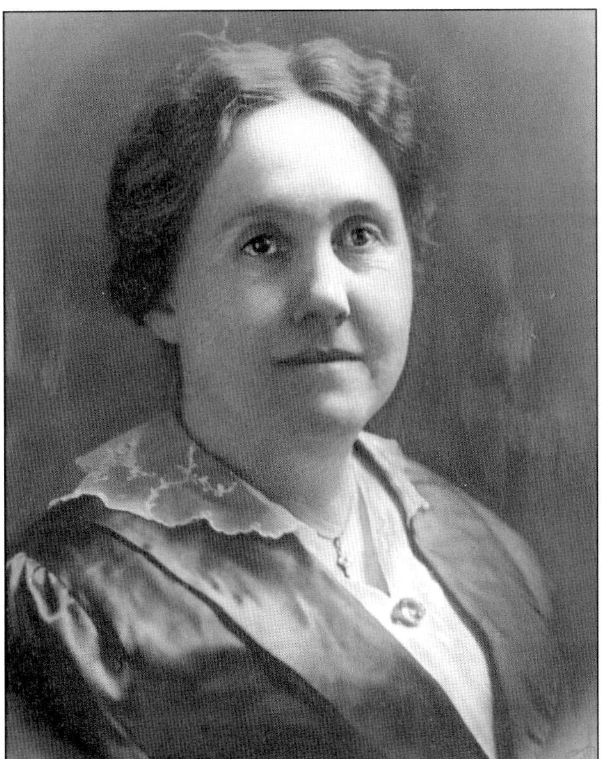

FRANCINE HALL WOOTEN, 1918. Like her husband, John Wooten, Francine was known to be a giving citizen. She taught Sunday school. The Wootens lived across the street from the church, just behind the Methodist church. (Courtesy of First Missionary Baptist Church.)

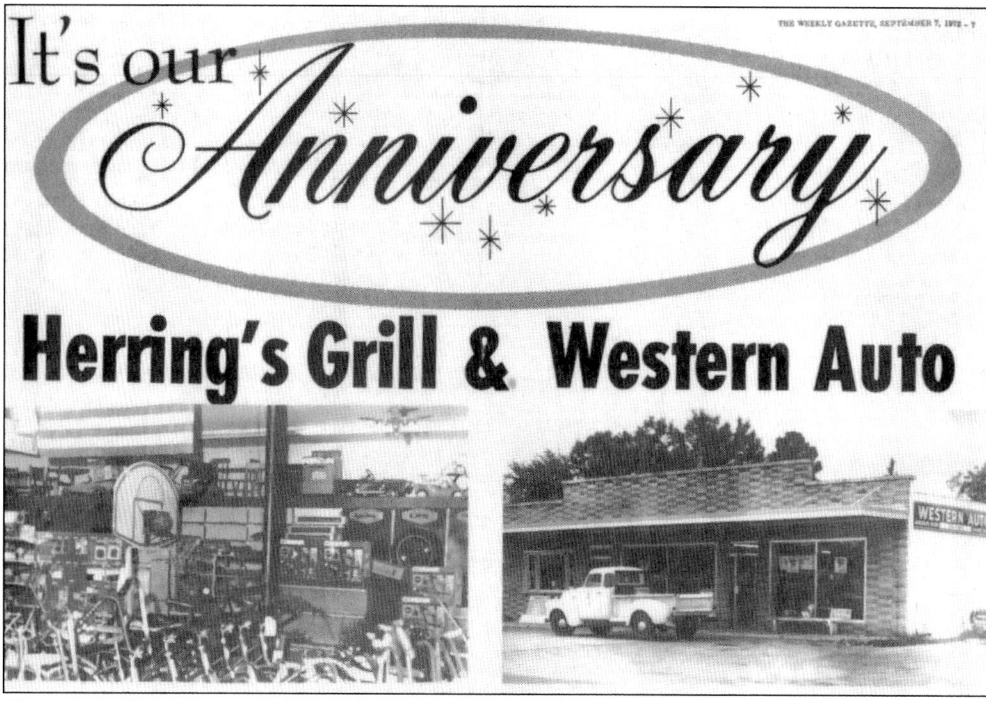

HERRING'S GRILL, 1972. The grill was a mainstay in La Grange for years. The restaurant also had the town's Western Auto store. The left side of the building housed the grill. (Courtesy of Harold and Annie Ruth Herring.)

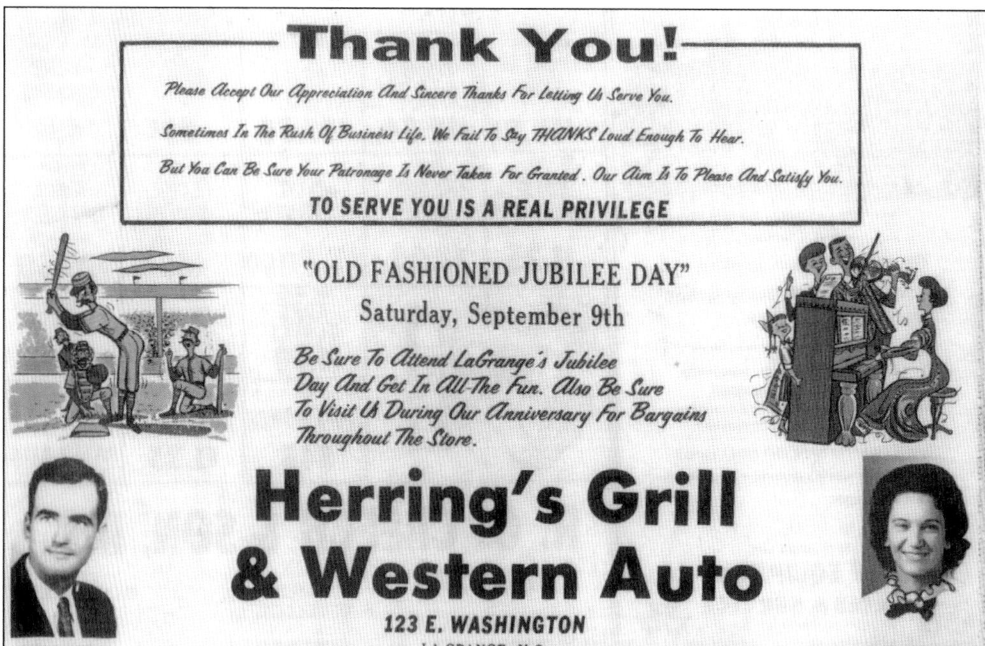

HERRING'S GRILL AND WESTERN AUTO, 1972. It is said that one can never ask the Herrings "How are you?" without them responding, "Blessed. I hope you are, too." They embody all that is good about La Grange. (Courtesy of Harold and Annie Ruth Herring.)

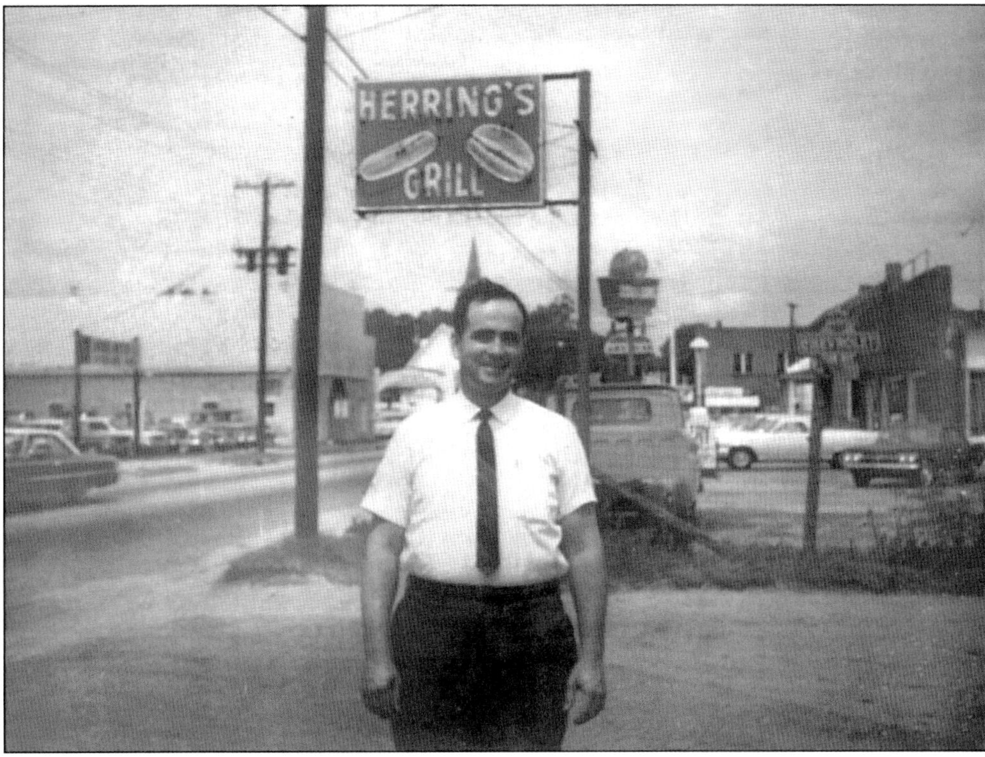

HAROLD HERRING, C. 1965. Herring stands in front of Herring's Grill. Behind him is Y.Z. Foss's Chevrolet dealership. Today, this lot is the site of the La Grange Public Library. The next Chevrolet dealership of note in La Grange was Dan Wise Chevrolet. Wise, a local bank executive, bought his Chevrolet dealership in 1982. (Courtesy of Harold and Annie Ruth Herring.)

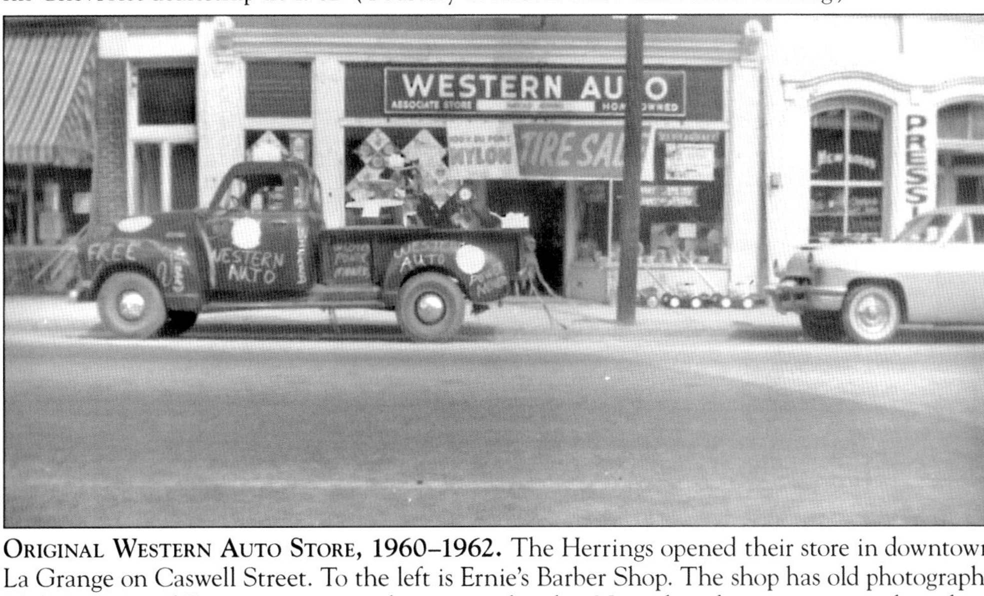

ORIGINAL WESTERN AUTO STORE, 1960–1962. The Herrings opened their store in downtown La Grange on Caswell Street. To the left is Ernie's Barber Shop. The shop has old photographs of the town, and Ernie gives a great haircut to this day. Note the advertisement on the side of the truck for "Wizard Power Mowers." The Wizard mower was popular in the 1960s. (Courtesy of Harold and Annie Ruth Herring.)

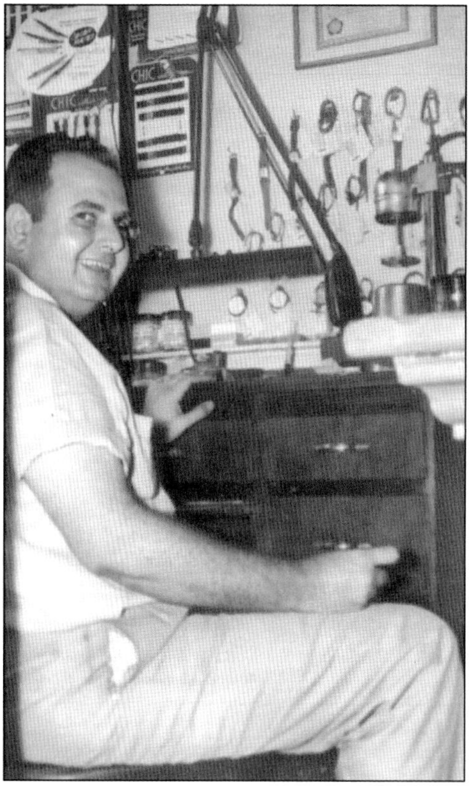

BEN S. HOLLOMAN, 1954. "Nick" Holloman began his jewelry business in Ernie's Barber Shop. Nick's jewelry space was located in the front section of the shop. He also had a jewelry section in Aldridge's Hardware Store. He moved to Aldridge's in 1950. Holloman eventually moved across the street from Ernie's, opening Holloman's Jewelry. (Courtesy of Ben S. Jr. and Deborah Holloman.)

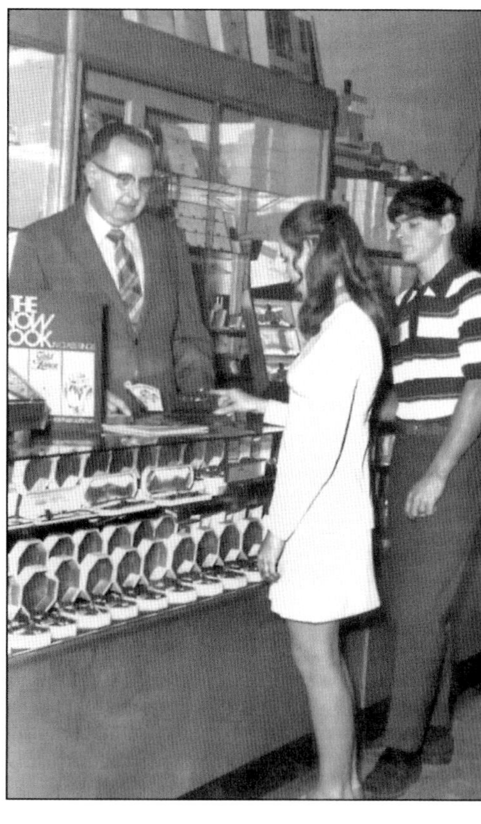

HOLLOMAN'S JEWELRY, 1971. J.E. Harrell and Vickie Hamilton look at graduation rings while Nick Holloman offers assistance. Holloman was a well-respected La Grange citizen. He was known to privately give money and assistance to those in need. Once, he gave money to a local college-bound student. (Courtesy of Ben S. Jr. and Deborah Holloman.)

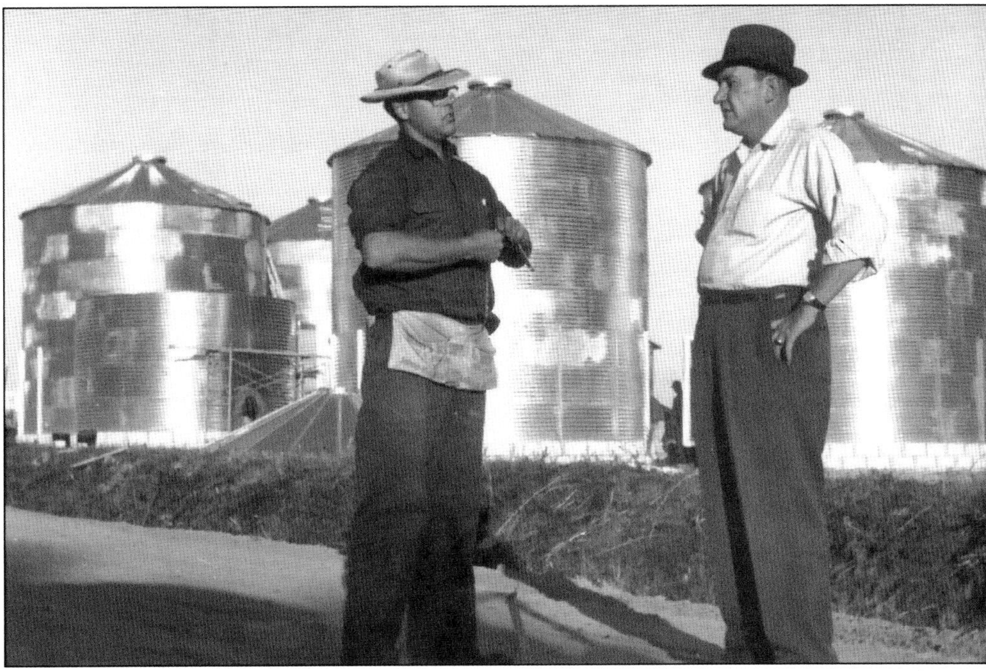

La Grange Agriculture, 1965–1969. Jack Crews (right) discusses matters of business with Lewis Herring. Since the late 1800s, La Grange has been a strong contributor to the farming industry of North Carolina. Historically, cash crops have included tobacco, corn, and soybeans. The area is still engaged with farming these crops on a major scale. (Courtesy of Sonny Herring.)

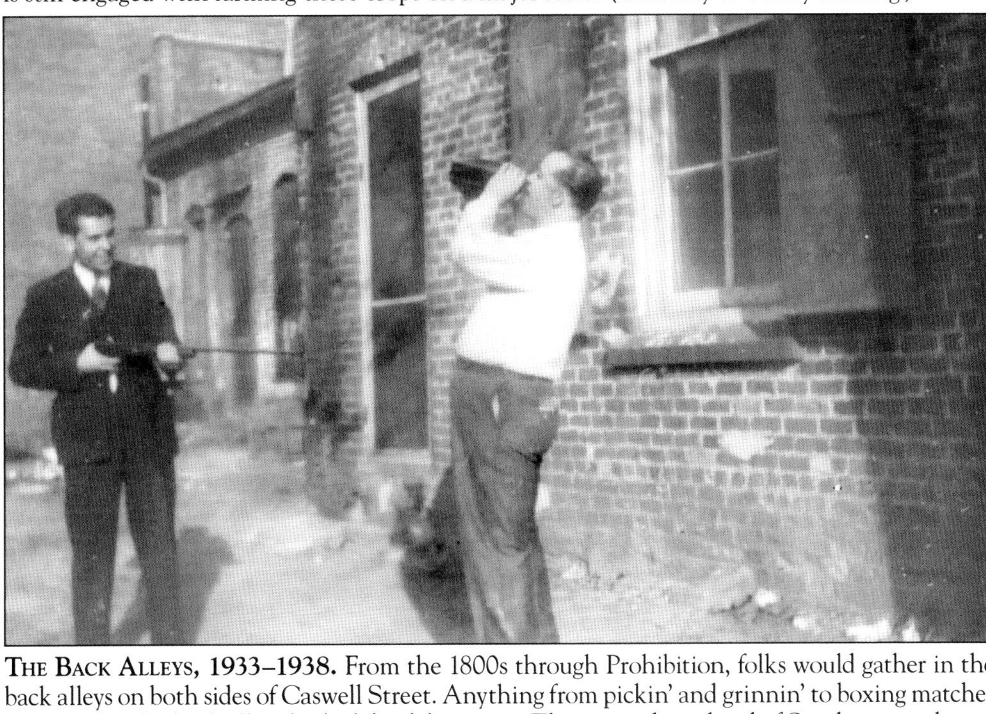

The Back Alleys, 1933–1938. From the 1800s through Prohibition, folks would gather in the back alleys on both sides of Caswell Street. Anything from pickin' and grinnin' to boxing matches took place. The back alleys had a life of their own. They served as a kind of Southern speakeasy. (Courtesy of Jim Dail, the Miller Woodard Collection.)

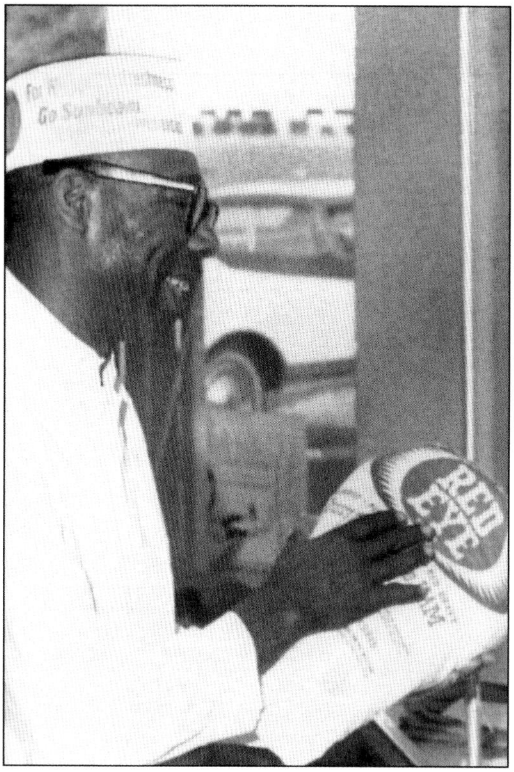

BRANCH'S STORE, 1967. Ira and Dorethea Branch came to La Grange in the early 1940s. Ira was a wonderful and well-respected businessman. It was common to find the mayor, councilmen, and businessmen sitting in Branch's Store, talking politics and other matters of business. Ira became the first African American elected to the town council. (Courtesy of Dorethea Branch.)

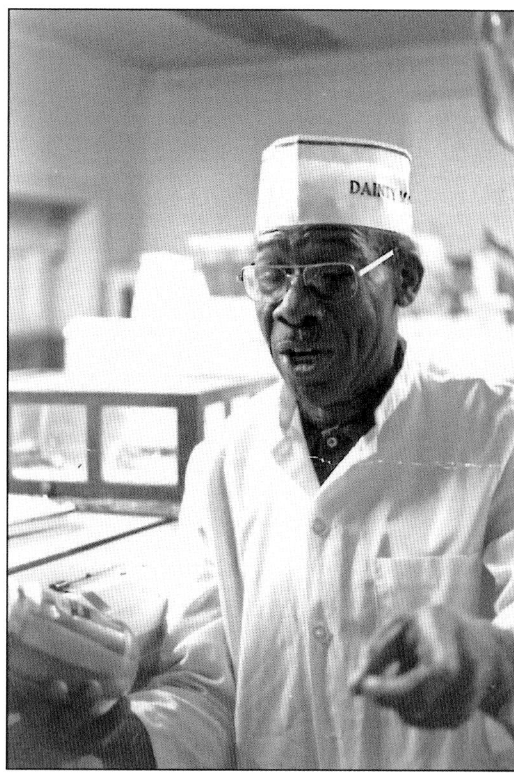

IRA BRANCH, 1978. Ira is wearing a Dainty Maid Bread hat. The bakery was located in nearby Kinston, North Carolina. Branch also had a pickle business of sorts. Many of the Frink school students would come across the street and purchase the pickles as well as other items. Dorethea would sell them to the children in the morning and afternoon. (Courtesy of Dorethea Branch.)

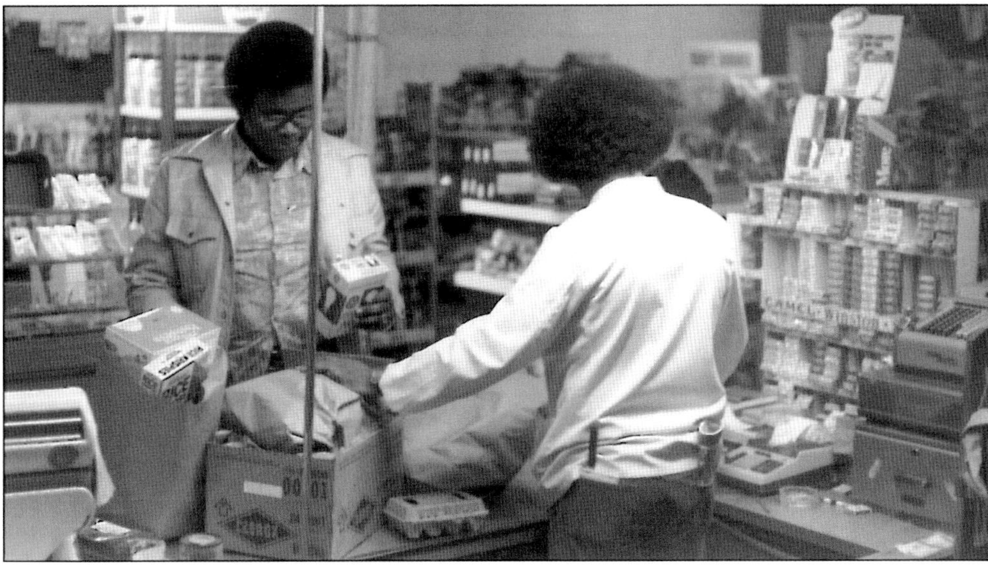

Dennis Branch, 1968. Dennis Branch, standing at the checkout counter examining a container of light bulbs, was the son of Ira and Dorethea. This photograph shows the inside of Branch's Store. Dennis worked at the store for a number of years. In 1981, he attended Trinity University in San Antonio, Texas, where he earned his master of arts degree. (Courtesy of Dorethea Branch.)

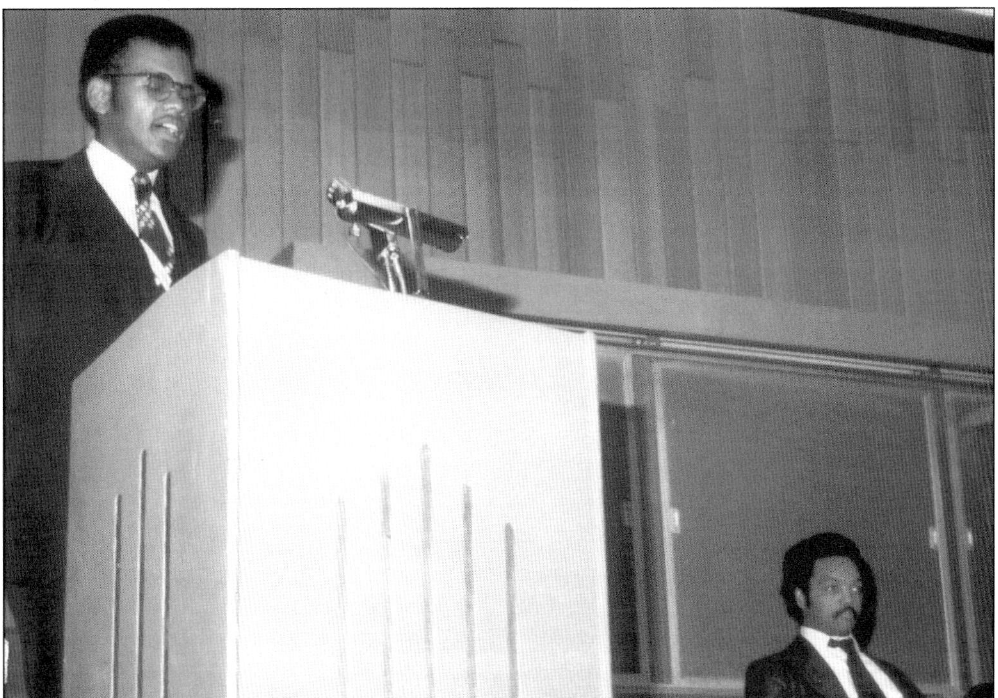

Dennis Branch and Jesse Jackson, 1982. Dennis Branch is seen here introducing the Reverend Jesse Jackson. Branch was selected by the university faculty to do so, Prof. Dr. Earl Lewis having recommended him. Dr. Lewis was a very active political leader in the San Antonio area. According to Branch, Dr. Lewis literally flipped a coin among three of his graduate students, and Dennis won. (Courtesy of Dorethea Branch.)

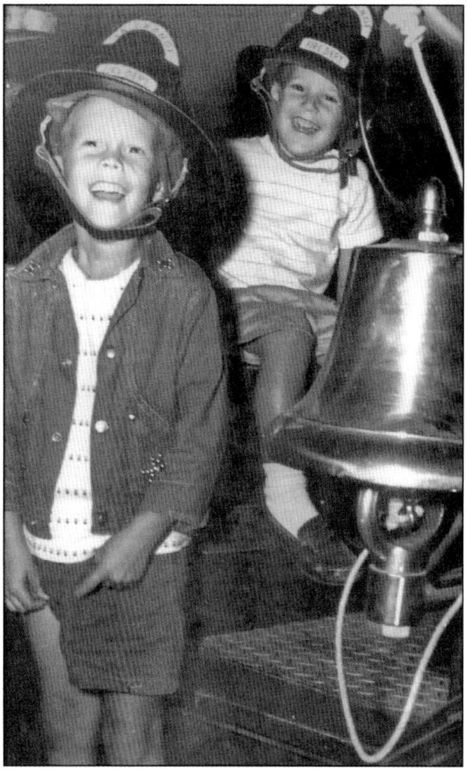

Ray and Mike Burke, 1961. The Burke boys are proudly wearing La Grange fire engine hats. Firefighting ran in the family, as their great-grandfather Cecil served the fire department for years. Today, Ray (left) is the town's pharmacist. This photograph, taken by his father, is one of Ray's favorite pictures. Mike is a well-known building contractor in Lenoir County. (Courtesy of Grace Burke.)

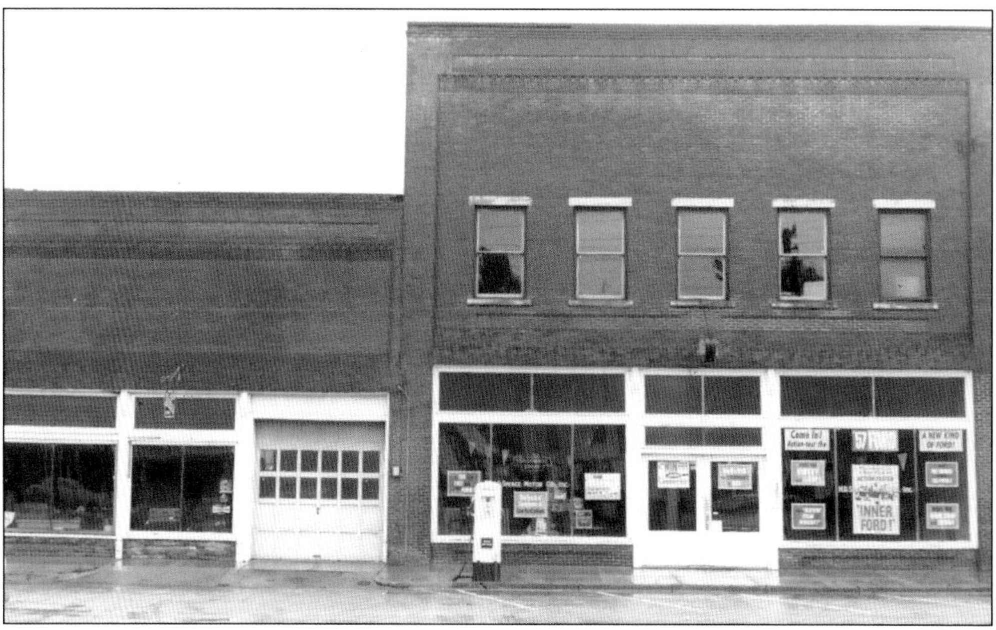

Herbert "H.D." Spence Motor Company, Ford Dealership, 1957. The dealership was active by the early 1940s. In later years, the La Grange fire engine was housed in the garage. John H. Rouse was one of the first residents to own a car dealership. He was offered but rejected a dealership for Oakland cars (Oakland Motor Company, 1907–1909). Oakland eventually became Oldsmobile. (Courtesy of Sonny Herring.)

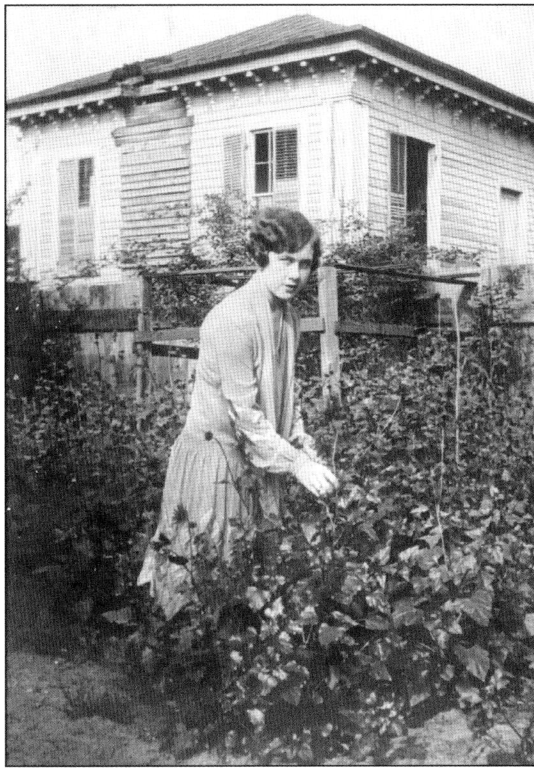

George F. Whitfield House, c. 1923. Melba Louise Mewborn Chadwick is seen here. This house was moved in the early 1920s. Originally, it was located on the current site of the Wells Fargo Bank. The house was among the first residences built in La Grange, sometime between 1855 and 1858. Currently, it is the oldest existing house in La Grange. (Courtesy of Ann Cashwell and Penny Chadwick Dawson.)

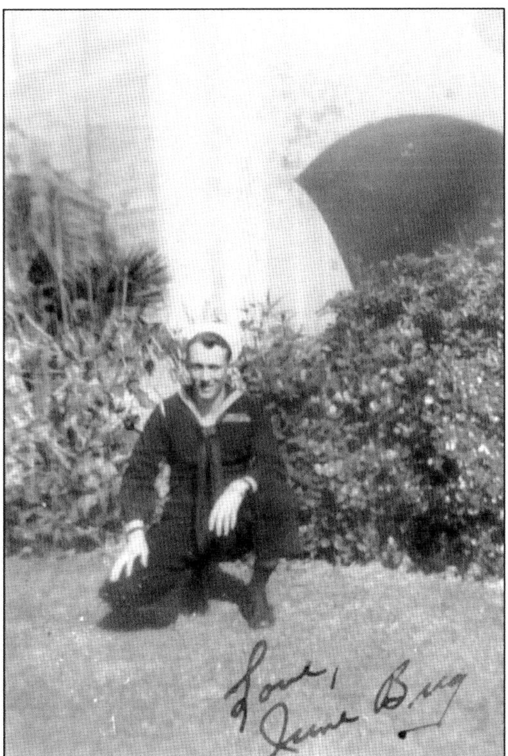

Cecil Raymond Burke Jr., 1942. The ever-entertaining "June Bug" Burke (1924–2010) served in the US Navy during World War II. He was a gunner aboard the USS *Alabama*. After his successful grill closed, Cecil opened Burke's Advertising, which thrived for 29 years. (Courtesy of Grace Burke.)

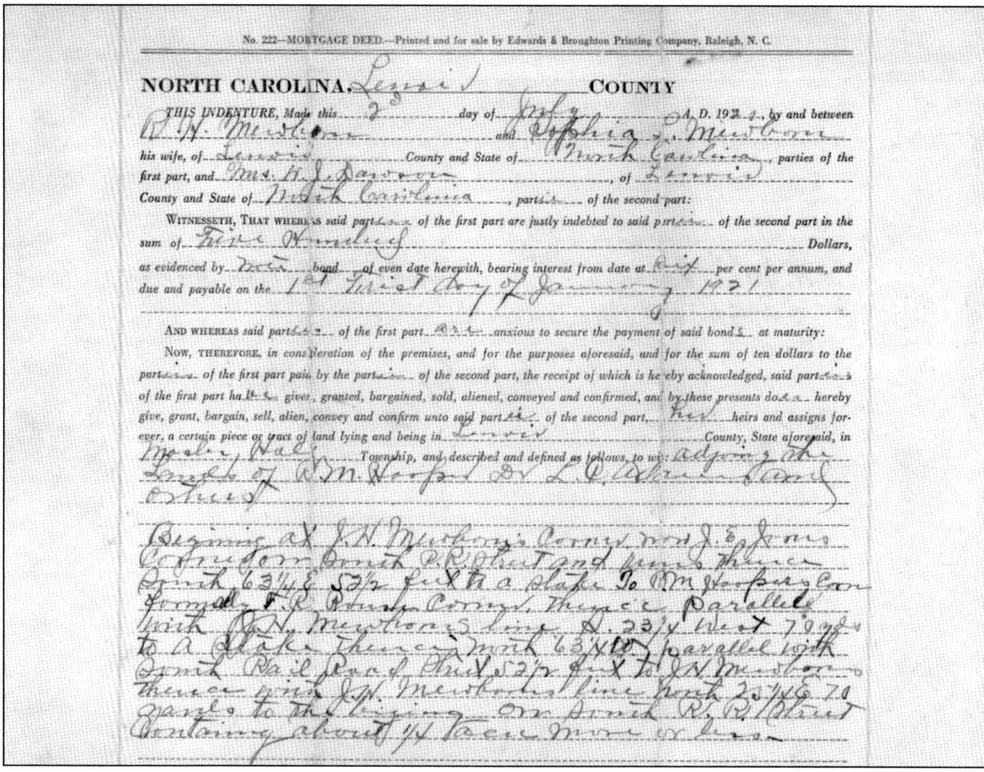

No. 222—MORTGAGE DEED.—Printed and for sale by Edwards & Broughton Printing Company, Raleigh, N. C.

NORTH CAROLINA, Lenoir COUNTY

THIS INDENTURE, Made this 2 *day of* July *A. D. 192*[illegible], *by and between* R. H. Mewborn *and* Sophia L. Mewborn *his wife, of* Lenoir *County and State of* North Carolina, *parties of the first part, and* Mrs. [illegible] *, of* Lenoir *County and State of* North Carolina *, part*[illegible] *of the second part:*

WITNESSETH, THAT WHEREAS *said part*[illegible] *of the first part are justly indebted to said part*[illegible] *of the second part in the sum of* Five Hundred *Dollars, as evidenced by* [illegible] *bond of even date herewith, bearing interest from date at* six *per cent per annum, and due and payable on the* 1st first day of January 1921

AND WHEREAS *said part*[illegible] *of the first part* are *anxious to secure the payment of said bond*[illegible] *at maturity:*

NOW, THEREFORE, *in consideration of the premises, and for the purposes aforesaid, and for the sum of ten dollars to the part*[illegible] *of the first part paid by the part*[illegible] *of the second part, the receipt of which is hereby acknowledged, said part*[illegible] *of the first part ha*[illegible] *given, granted, bargained, sold, aliened, conveyed and confirmed, and by these presents do*[illegible] *hereby give, grant, bargain, sell, alien, convey and confirm unto said part*[illegible] *of the second part,* [illegible] *heirs and assigns forever, a certain piece or tract of land lying and being in* Lenoir *County, State aforesaid, in* [illegible] *Township, and described and defined as follows, to wit:* [illegible]

[illegible]

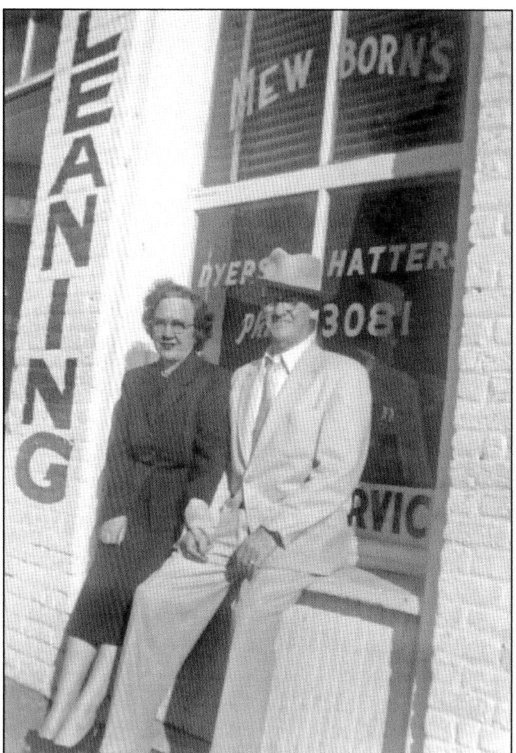

MEWBORN'S CLEANERS DEED. This deed shows that the original date of the signing of the cleaners was July 1920. Mewborn's Dry Cleaning was originally purchased by Rufus Hardy Mewborn (1870–1939) and his wife, Sophia Luna Mewborn (1881–1962.) Mewborn Cleaners eventually became Chadwick Cleaners. John Chadwick Jr. renamed the establishment. (Courtesy of Ann Cashwell and Penny Chadwick Dawson.)

RUFUS "R.H." AND SOPHIA MEWBORN. This photograph was taken in the late 1930s or early 1940s. Note the phone number, 3081, in the window. It was years later before La Grange would have the prefix 566. After the passing of Sophia, the cleaners remained in the family. It was run by John P. Chadwick (1926–1965) and Betsy Chadwick (1928–2001.) John was a decorated US Navy veteran of World War II. (Courtesy of Ann Cashwell and Penny Chadwick Dawson.)

JAKE HERRING JR., 1985. Herring was the first mail carrier in La Grange's postal history. "Mr. Jake," as he was called, was a big man, standing six feet, six inches tall. He loved La Grange, its people, and its history. Herring could tell stories of days gone by for hours. Once, while carrying mail, Jake was treed by a dog for over an hour. (Courtesy of Sonny Herring.)

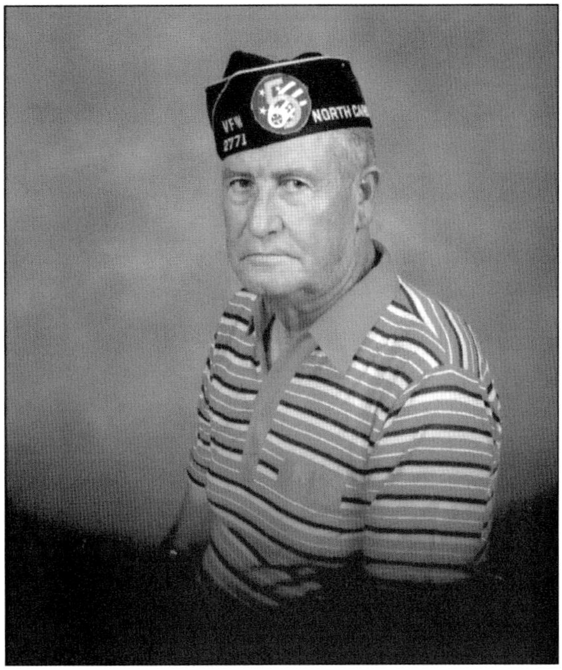

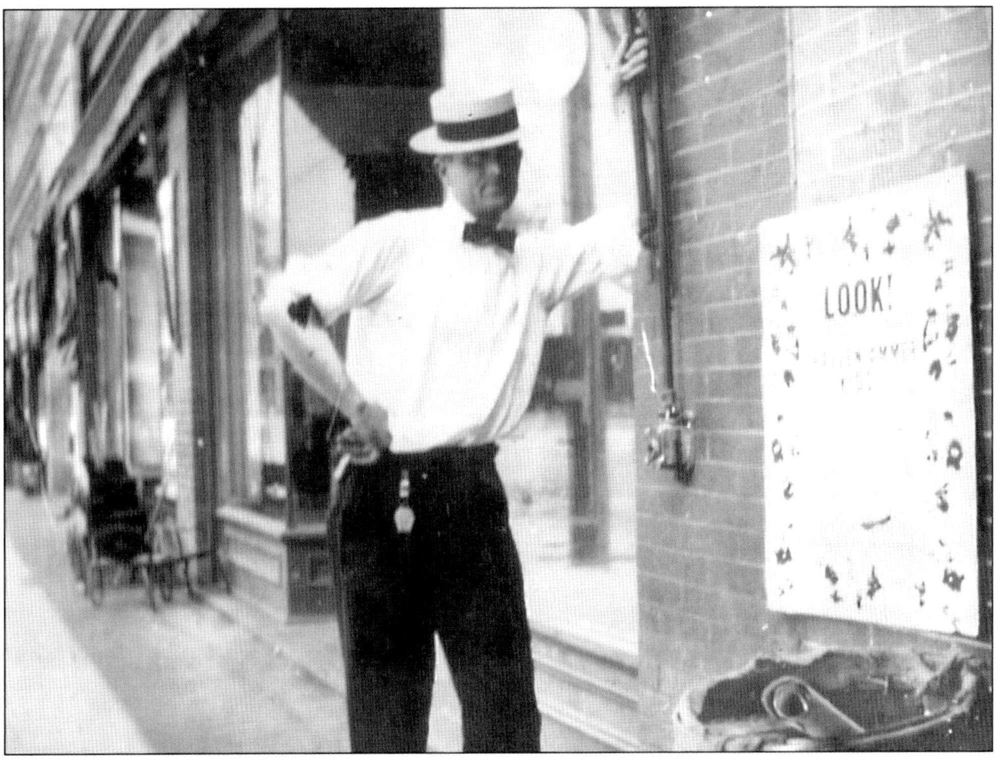

LA GRANGE BUSINESSMAN, C. 1913. A general merchandise businessman stands next to an advertisement that reads, "Look! Katzenjammer Kids." This was a reference to a cartoon created in 1897 by Rudolph Dirks. After 1903, there were animated motion pictures of the Katzenjammer Kids. (Courtesy of the Bob Rouse family.)

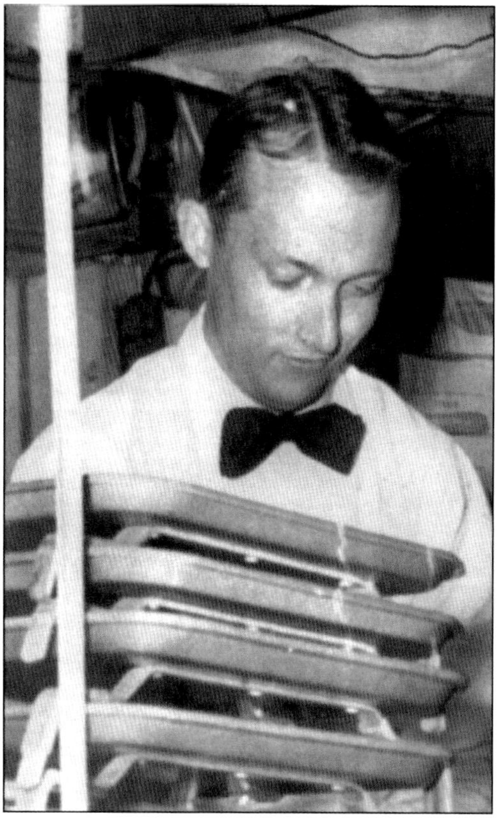

Cecil Burke Jr. and the S.O. Grill, 1951. It was once said that, "The best hot dog and cheeseburger in the South is sold on a little corner in a little town in North Carolina called the S.O. grill." Many train passengers would walk to the grill and have lunch. The word spread, and a sensation was born. (Courtesy of Grace Burke.)

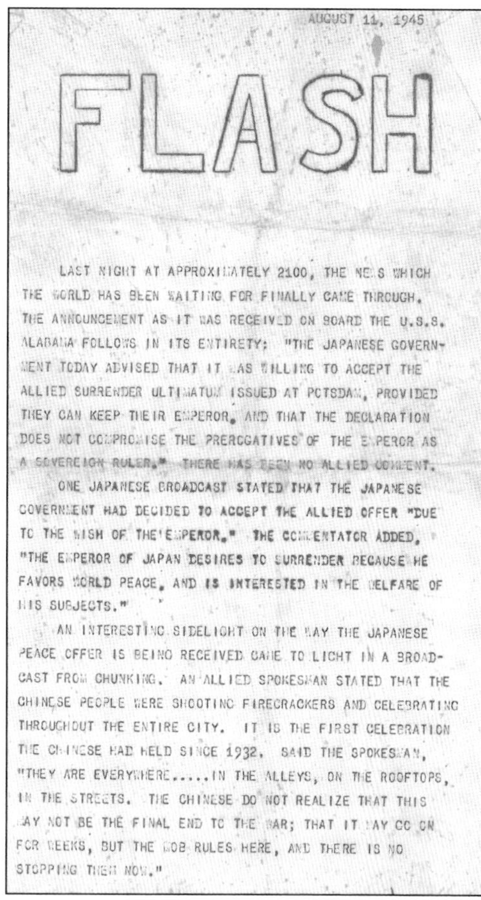

AUGUST 11, 1945

FLASH

LAST NIGHT AT APPROXIMATELY 2100, THE NEWS WHICH THE WORLD HAS BEEN WAITING FOR FINALLY CAME THROUGH. THE ANNOUNCEMENT AS IT WAS RECEIVED ON BOARD THE U.S.S. ALABAMA FOLLOWS IN ITS ENTIRETY: "THE JAPANESE GOVERNMENT TODAY ADVISED THAT IT WAS WILLING TO ACCEPT THE ALLIED SURRENDER ULTIMATUM ISSUED AT POTSDAM, PROVIDED THEY CAN KEEP THEIR EMPEROR, AND THAT THE DECLARATION DOES NOT COMPROMISE THE PREROGATIVES OF THE EMPEROR AS A SOVEREIGN RULER." THERE HAS BEEN NO ALLIED COMMENT.

ONE JAPANESE BROADCAST STATED THAT THE JAPANESE GOVERNMENT HAD DECIDED TO ACCEPT THE ALLIED OFFER "DUE TO THE WISH OF THE EMPEROR." THE COMMENTATOR ADDED, "THE EMPEROR OF JAPAN DESIRES TO SURRENDER BECAUSE HE FAVORS WORLD PEACE, AND IS INTERESTED IN THE WELFARE OF HIS SUBJECTS."

AN INTERESTING SIDELIGHT ON THE WAY THE JAPANESE PEACE OFFER IS BEING RECEIVED CAME TO LIGHT IN A BROADCAST FROM CHUNKING. AN ALLIED SPOKESMAN STATED THAT THE CHINESE PEOPLE WERE SHOOTING FIRECRACKERS AND CELEBRATING THROUGHOUT THE ENTIRE CITY. IT IS THE FIRST CELEBRATION THE CHINESE HAD HELD SINCE 1932. SAID THE SPOKESMAN, "THEY ARE EVERYWHERE.....IN THE ALLEYS, ON THE ROOFTOPS, IN THE STREETS. THE CHINESE DO NOT REALIZE THAT THIS MAY NOT BE THE FINAL END TO THE WAR; THAT IT MAY GO ON FOR WEEKS, BUT THE MOB RULES HERE, AND THERE IS NO STOPPING THEM NOW."

***FLASH*, August 11, 1945.** The *FLASH* was an announcement that was given daily aboard the USS *Alabama*. Cecil Burke Jr. kept this memento, which reads, "The Japanese Government today advised that it was willing to accept the Allied surrender ultimatum issued at Potsdam, provided they can keep their Emperor." (Courtesy of Grace Burke).

CECIL BURKE JR., 1951. Here is a young Cecil Burke. What a welcome La Grange offered to passersby who came to the center of town, on the corners of Washington and Caswell Streets, to see and smell the delightful food of the S.O Grill. Cecil embodied that welcoming attitude, saying, "Welcome to La Grange." (Courtesy of Grace Burke.)

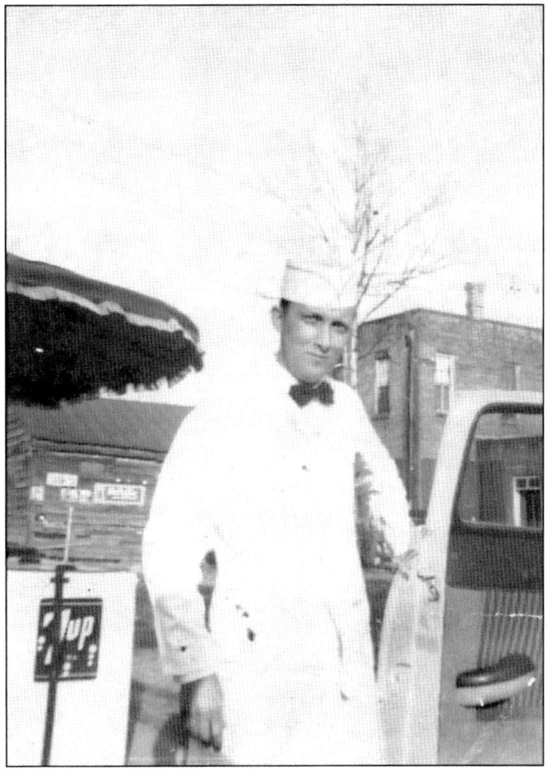

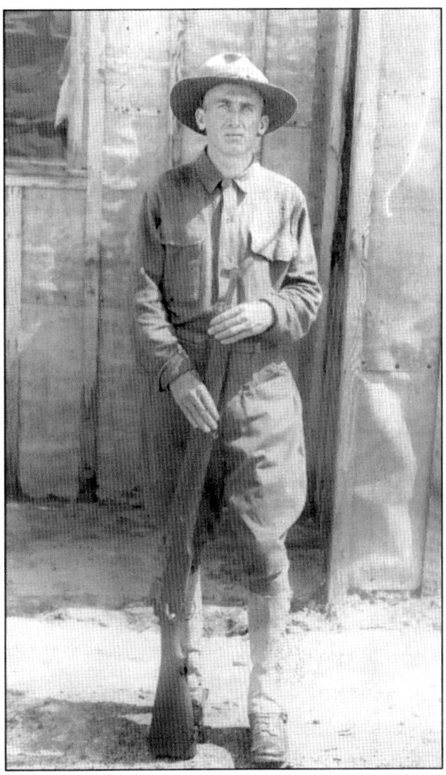

CECIL RAYMOND BURKE SR., 1917. Burke, a World War I veteran, was very involved in the town's volunteer fire department. He was known to be quite a pistol of a man, full of energy. His grandson, Cecil Raymond "Ray" Burke III, has been the town's pharmacist for the past several years. (Courtesy of Grace Burke.)

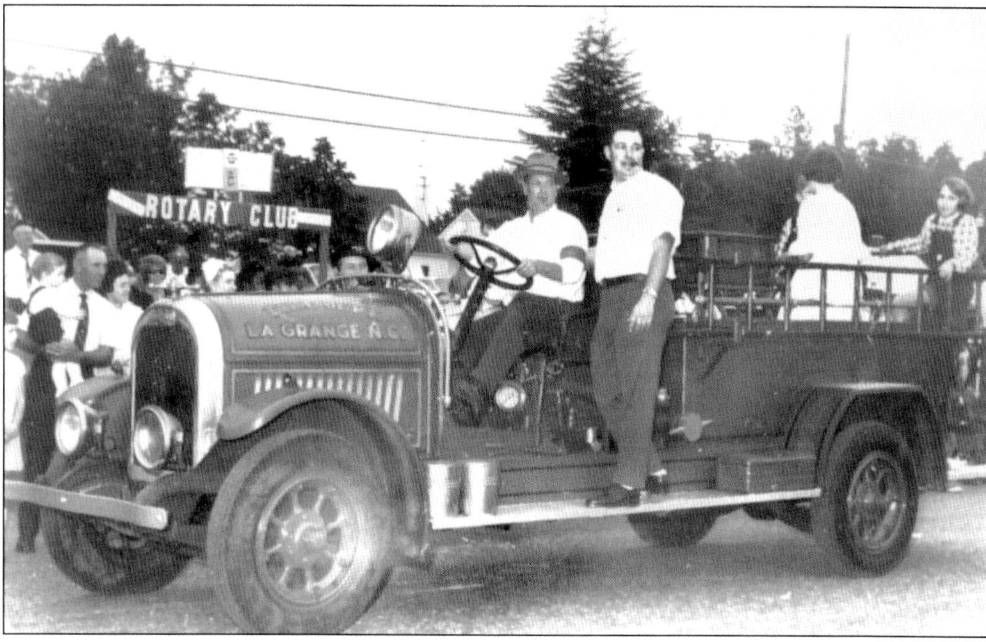

LA GRANGE FIRE TRUCK, 1976. Shown here is the 1976 centennial parade. Each year, the fire department rolls out its equipment and engines. The parade goes east up Railroad Street through the center of town and ends on the other side of West Railroad Street. Here is Peter Herring and S. Marvin Sawyer. Sawyer helped design the current fire station, located on Railroad Street. (Courtesy of Sonny Herring.)

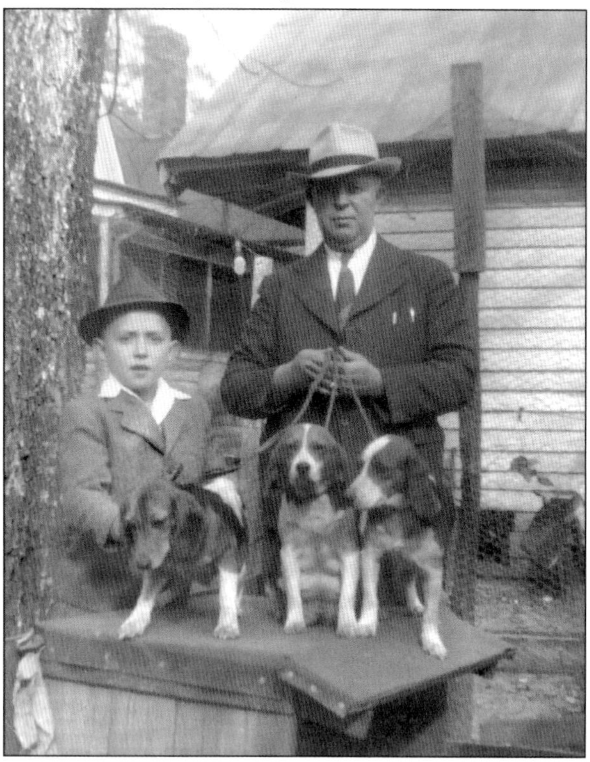

HENRY ABBOTT AND SON, 1947. Here is Henry and his son Henry Abbott Jr. showing off their prized beagles. Henry Jr. became a mail carrier and a farmer. He was very involved with Community Baptist Church and mission outreach programs. Henry and Jean have traveled all over the world on mission trips. (Courtesy of Jean Abbott.)

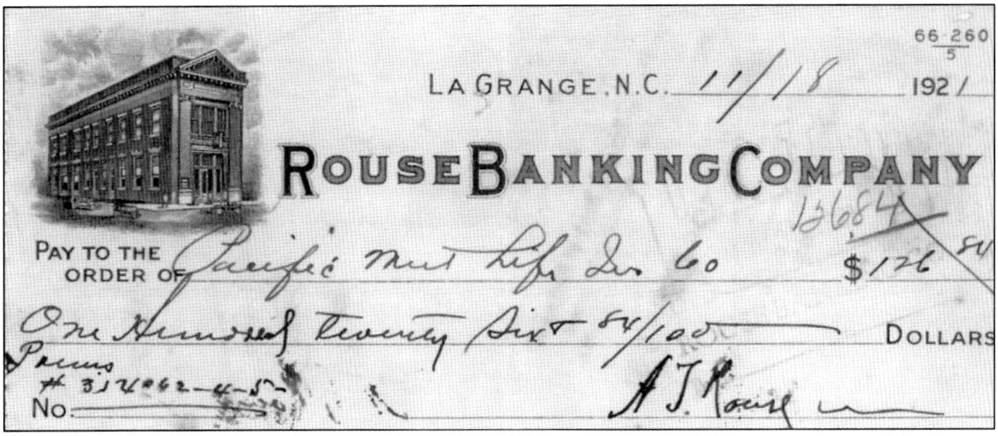

ROUSE BANKING COMPANY CHECK, 1921. Noah James Rouse was the president of the bank, established in 1908. In 1906, he was the president of the Citizens Bank of Kinston. Rouse was nominated for North Carolina attorney general in 1902. In 1903, Rouse was elected mayor of Kinston, North Carolina. The head cashier was Noah's brother Thomas Richard Rouse. (Courtesy of Grace Burke.)

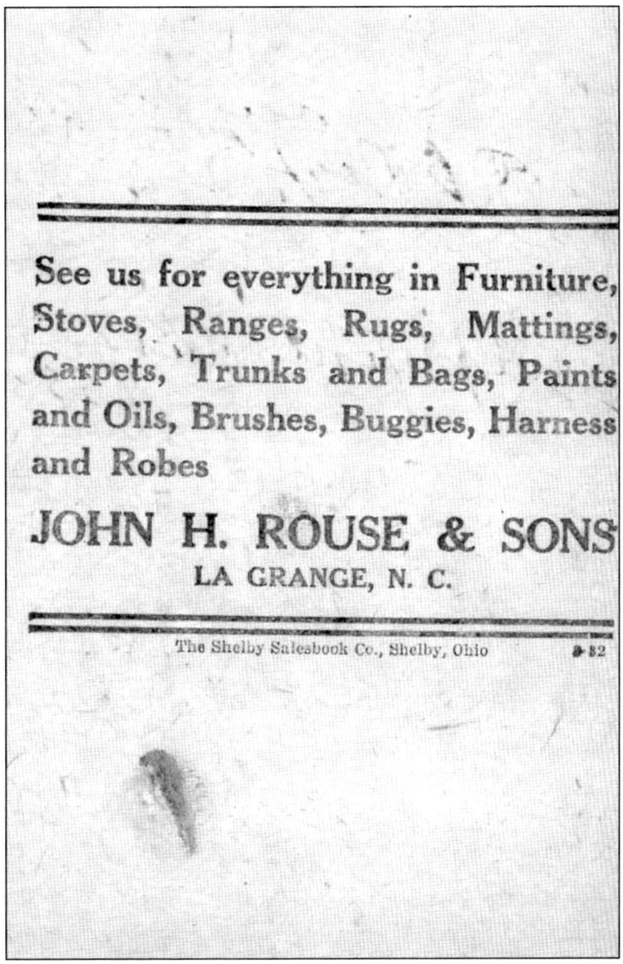

JOHN H. ROUSE & SONS, C. 1934. This advertisement was ordered from the Shelby Salesbook Company. The Rouses were entrepreneurial, owning many businesses in town and helping to start new businesses as opportunities presented themselves. The Rouses were also known for their gracious philanthropy. (Courtesy of Rouse Funeral Home.)

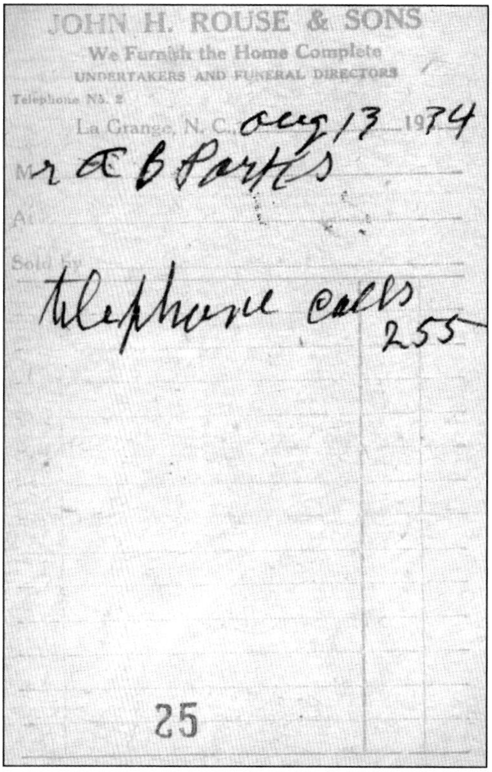

JOHN H. ROUSE & SONS
We Furnish the Home Complete
UNDERTAKERS AND FUNERAL DIRECTORS
Telephone No. 2
La Grange, N. C., aug 13 1934

telephone calls 255

25

RECEIPT, 1934. Note the letterhead offering funeral and undertaker services as well as home furnishing. John H. Rouse, according to his son Bob, tried out about every type of business possible. The phone numbers at the time, such as 255 here, were only three digits in length. (Courtesy Rouse Funeral Home.)

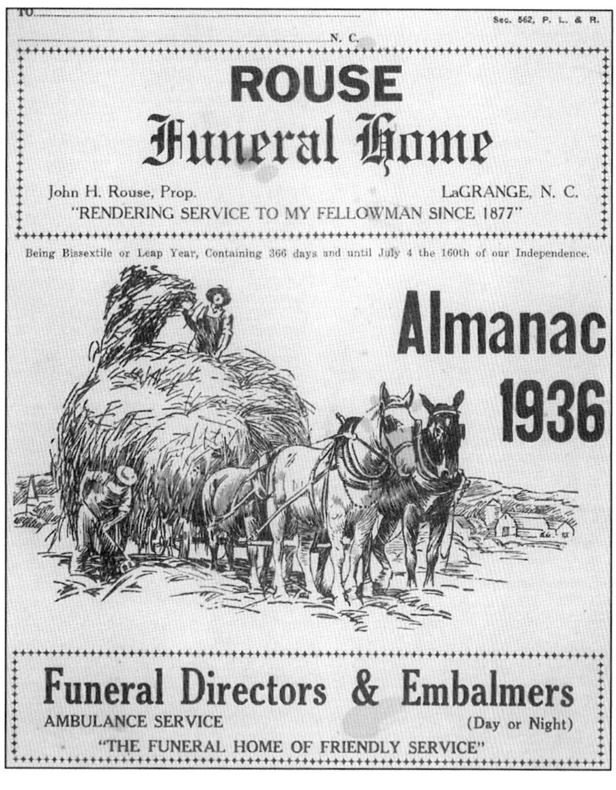

ALMANAC, 1936. The almanac was a popular way of advertising. In an agrarian community such as La Grange, the Almanac was read religiously by farmers and townspeople alike. The slogan "Rendering Service to My Fellowman Since 1877" is a reference to John H. Rouse's carpentry days. (Courtesy of Rouse Funeral Home.)

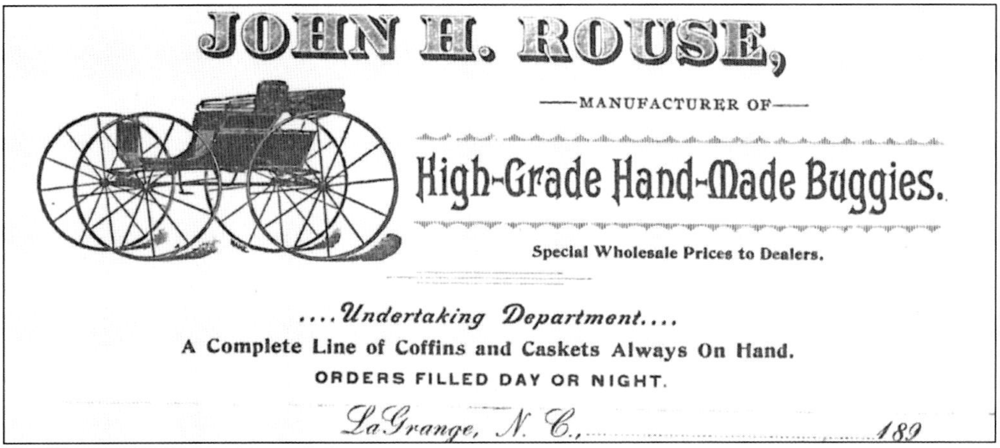

BUGGY ADVERTISEMENT, 1890. At one time, this factory employed nearly 100 people. It was a vital part of La Grange's industrial development. Due to his ability to work with wood, John H. Rouse made and designed coffins and also built furniture and homes in the town. (Courtesy of Rouse Funeral Home.)

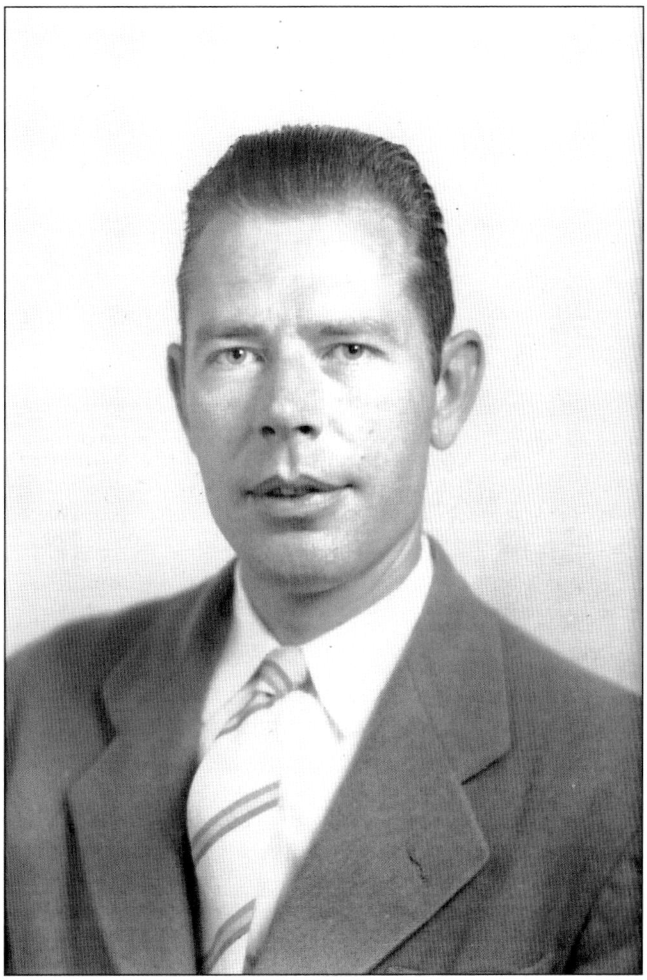

JOHN H. ROUSE JR., 1952. John Rouse Jr. was the funeral director and one of the Rouse Funeral Home ambulance drivers. He also taught at the high school and was active in local sports, coaching the La Grange High School football team. (Courtesy of Rouse Funeral Home.)

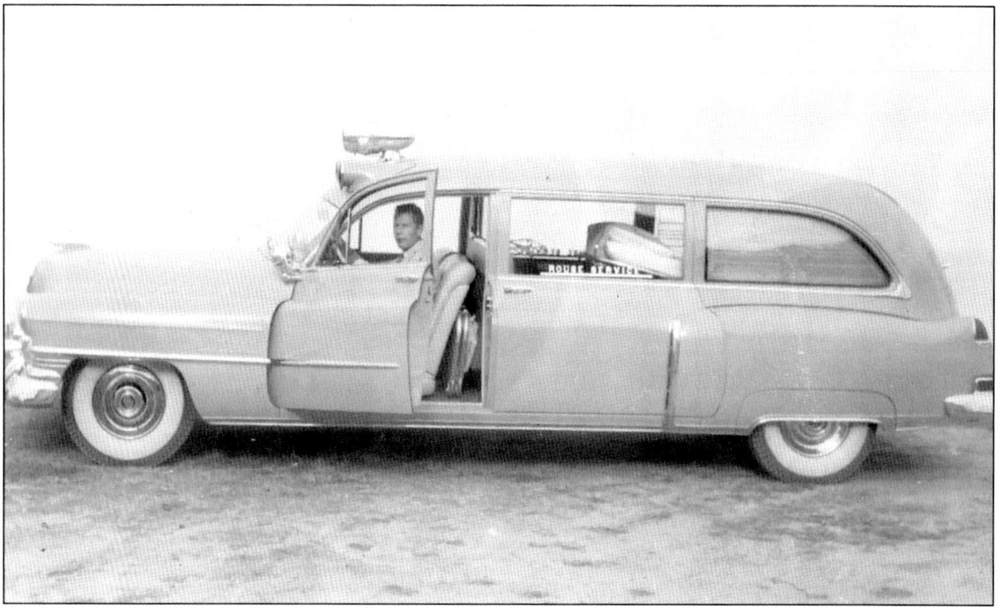

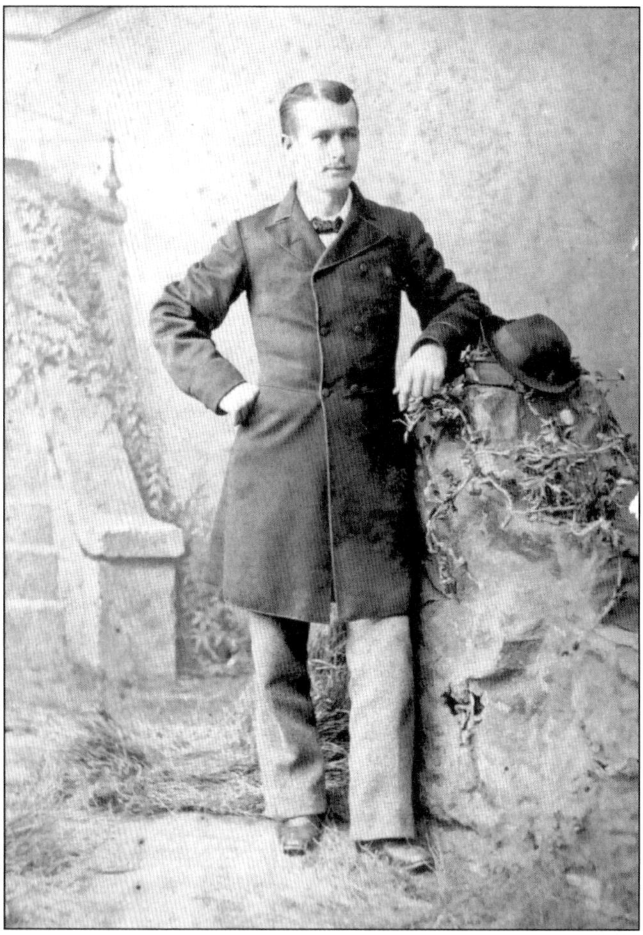

Town's First Ambulance, 1952. John H. Rouse Jr. is sitting in the ambulance, which was used to transport emergency patients and was also used during funerals. It was common at this time for funeral homes to also provide ambulance service for the surrounding areas. (Courtesy of Rouse Funeral Home.)

Dr. James M. Hodges, c. 1883. Dr. Hodges is pictured here at or near his graduation from Bellevue Hospital College in New York. After graduation, he came back home to La Grange. In the fall of 1883, he began his practice. He was well thought of and owned a 160-acre farm just outside of La Grange. (Courtesy of K.D. Kennedy Jr.)

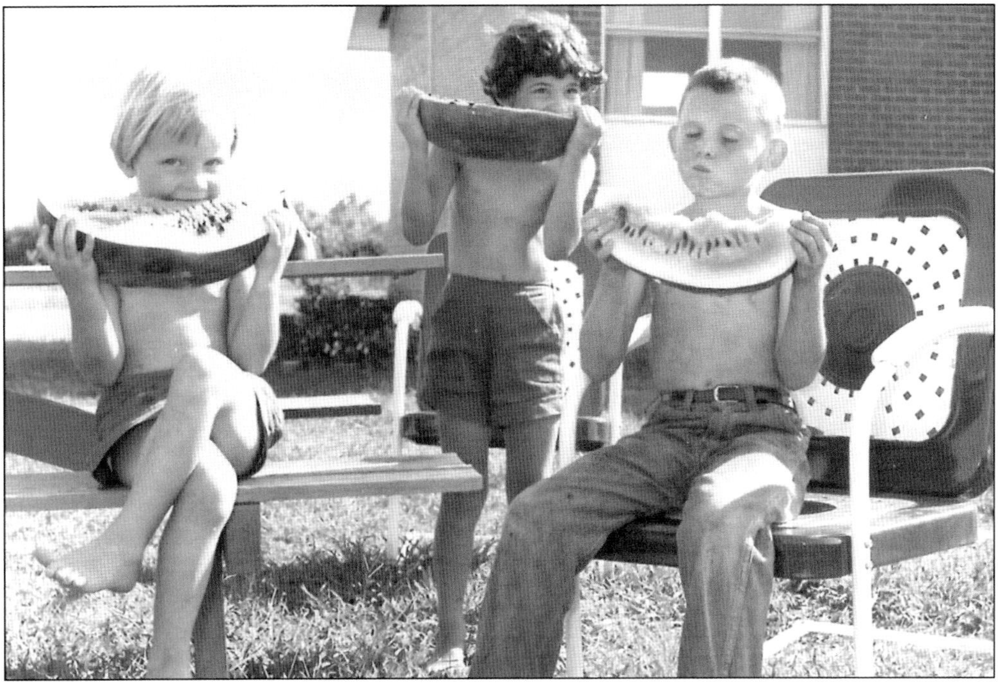

WATERMELON EATING, 1958. Mack Caulder and his two sisters enjoy a snack at the Barwick home. These children were adopted by the Paul Barwick family. The Barwicks ran their paper near their home on Railroad Street. The home still has the ramp that Paul Barwick used to enter and exit. The watermelon must have been perfect. Just take a look at Mack's expression. (Courtesy of Sonny Herring.)

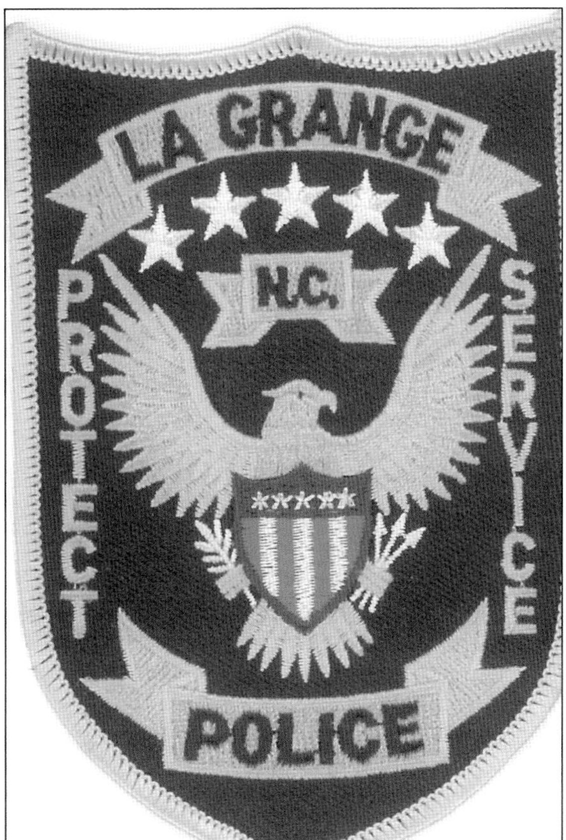

POLICE DEPARTMENT PATCH, C. 1997. This is one of the last patches of the La Grange Police Department. This patch was designed by the entire department, under Chief John Sullivan. All of the officers had input as to the design. The patch was worn on both sleeves of shirts and coats. (Courtesy of Jerry Davis.)

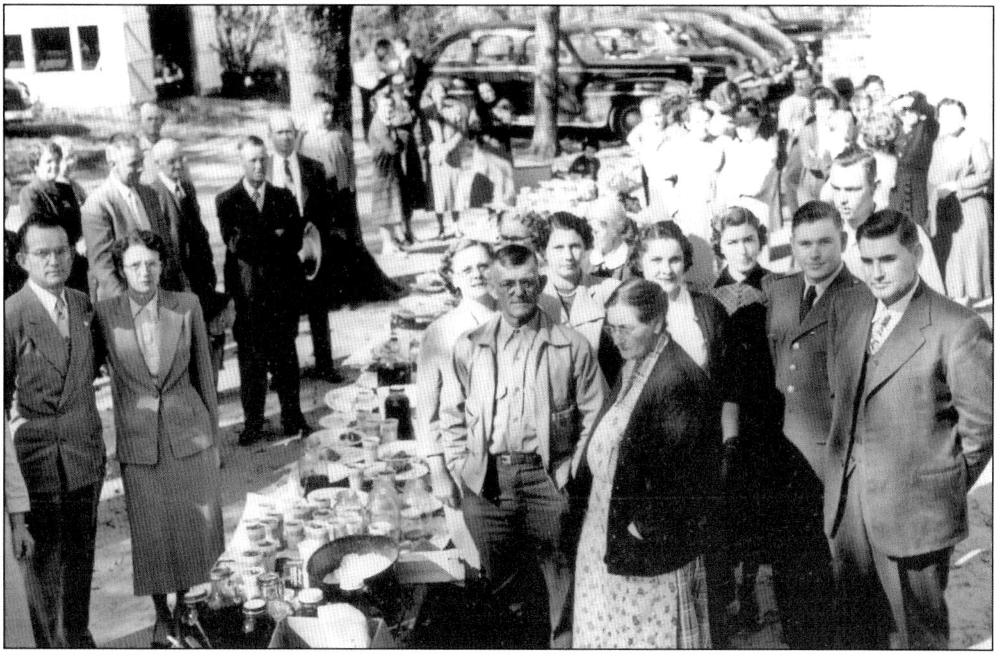

Creech Family Reunion, 1951. This family outing was an annual Creech family event. Among those in attendance are, on the left, Tyson and Laura Creech, Moses Mewborn, Lynn Rouse, Alton Sutton, and Kirby Sutton. Persons on the right include Leslie Creech Sr., Edna Creech Baker, Geneva Creech Hardy, Ester Ruth Creech Williams, Josie Creech Williams, Roger Creech, Raymond Creech, and Kenneth Creech. (Courtesy of Leslie Creech Sr. and Jr.)

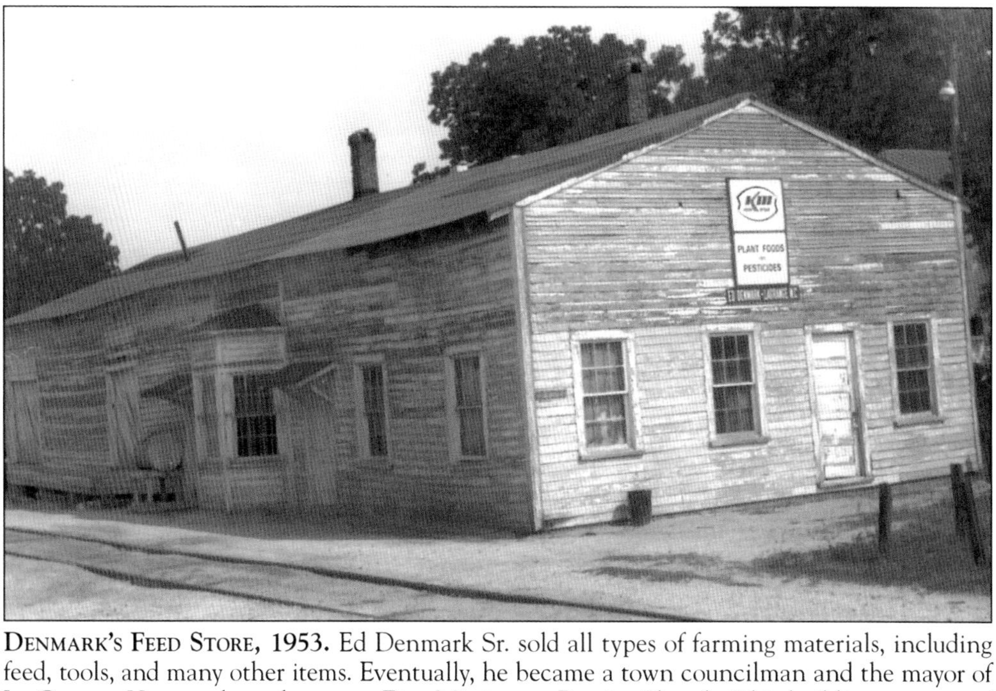

Denmark's Feed Store, 1953. Ed Denmark Sr. sold all types of farming materials, including feed, tools, and many other items. Eventually, he became a town councilman and the mayor of La Grange. He was also a deacon at First Missionary Baptist Church. This building was one of the original tobacco warehouses in the early 1900s. (Courtesy of Sonny Herring.)

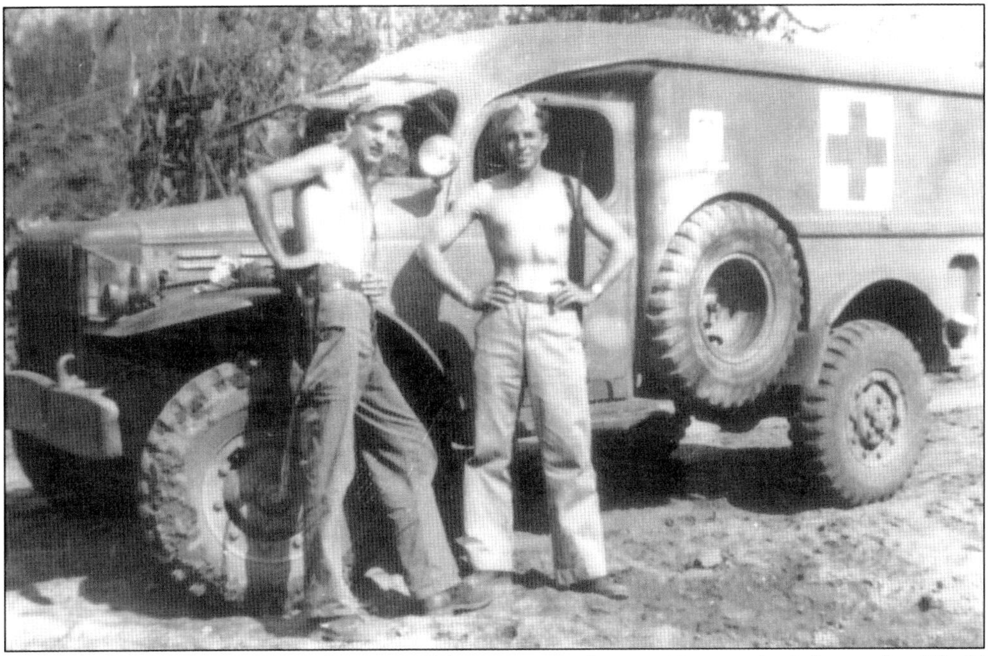

FLOYD DAWSON, 1942–1944. Like many of the men in La Grange, Dawson (right) served in World War II. Floyd was a local farmer outside of La Grange. His dad was "Bull" Dawson. Floyd made extra money sharpening saw blades for $2 a saw. (Courtesy of Sonny Herring.)

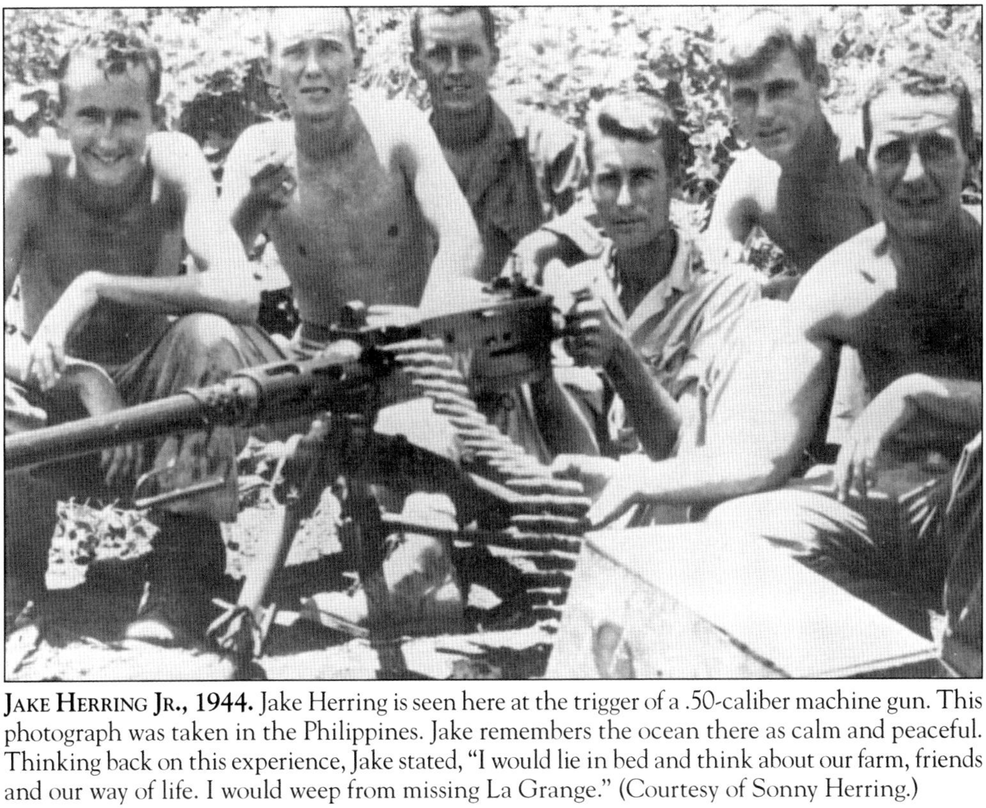

JAKE HERRING JR., 1944. Jake Herring is seen here at the trigger of a .50-caliber machine gun. This photograph was taken in the Philippines. Jake remembers the ocean there as calm and peaceful. Thinking back on this experience, Jake stated, "I would lie in bed and think about our farm, friends and our way of life. I would weep from missing La Grange." (Courtesy of Sonny Herring.)

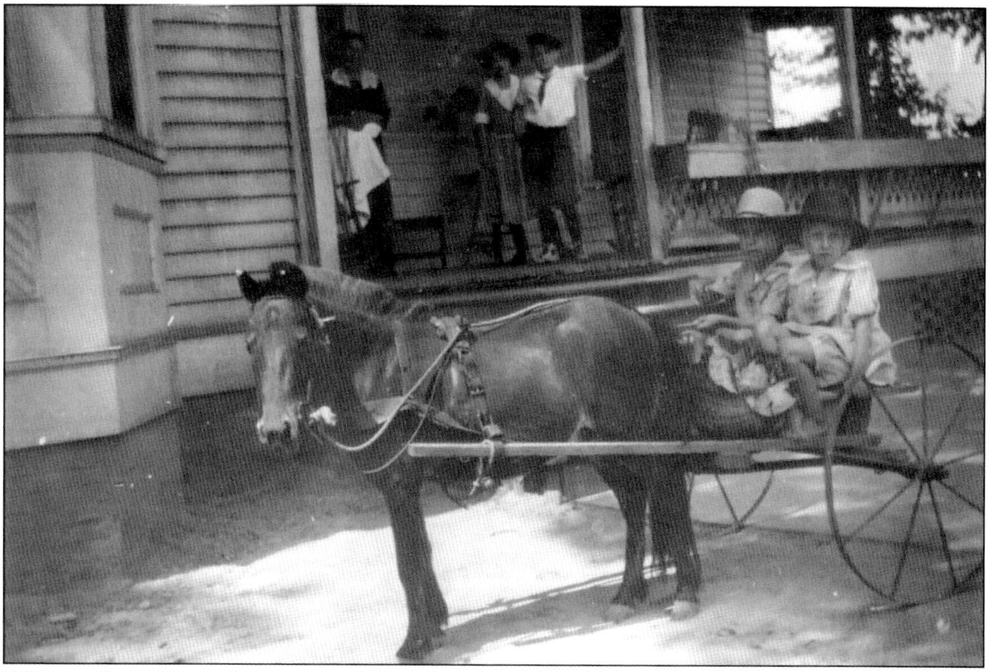

"Shorty" in a Pony Cart, 1923. The girl with Mark "Shorty" Hodges is Mary Emma Kennedy, Shorty's younger sister. This house is located across from the Christian church. The woman at left on the porch is Molly Dawson Kennedy, the youngsters' grandmother. The boy on the porch is Kenneth Durwood Kennedy, father of "K.D." Kennedy Jr. The house was built in 1886, and K.D. restored it between 2009 and 2012. The young woman on the porch is unidentified. (Courtesy of K.D. Kennedy Jr.)

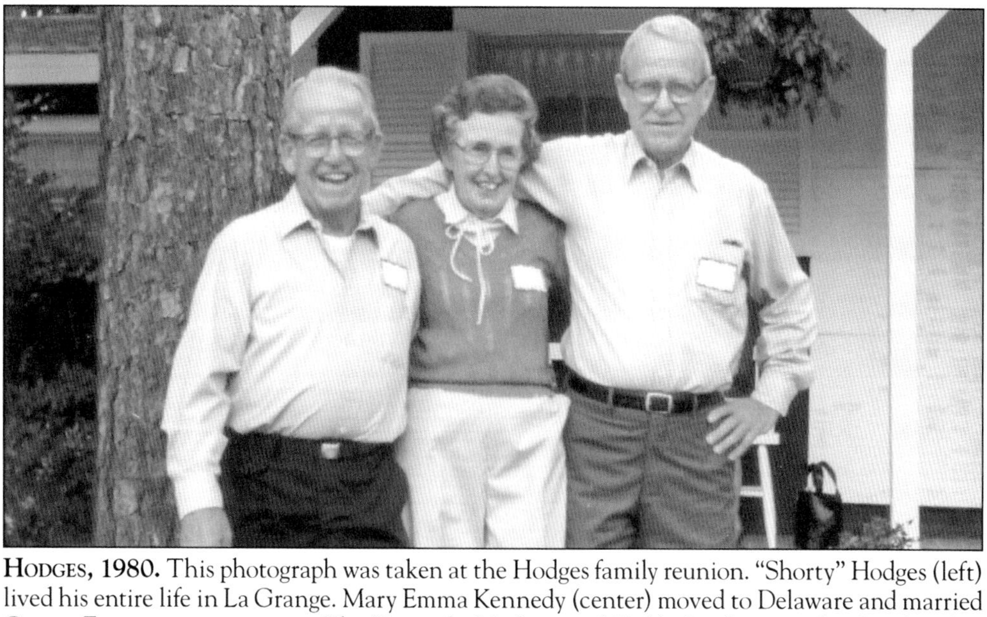

Hodges, 1980. This photograph was taken at the Hodges family reunion. "Shorty" Hodges (left) lived his entire life in La Grange. Mary Emma Kennedy (center) moved to Delaware and married Grover Foster, an accountant. The Kennedy, Hodges, and Fields families are closely related to one another. The Kennedy homesite is on Washington Street, across from the Christian church. (Courtesy of K.D. Kennedy Jr.)

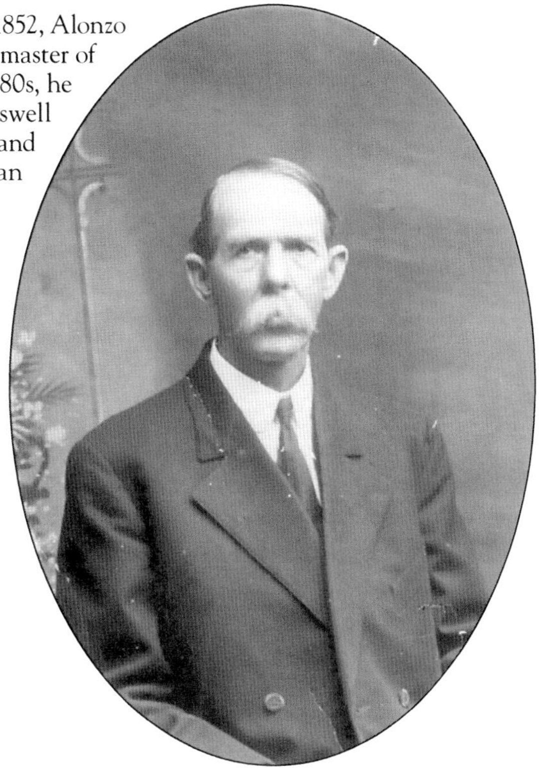

Alonzo Walter Kennedy, 1890. Born in 1852, Alonzo Kennedy was a farmer. He was the first postmaster of the neighboring town of Institute. In the 1880s, he owned a general merchandise store on Caswell Street. Kennedy, along with Shade Wooten and others, was a founder of the First Christian Church. (Courtesy of K.D. Kennedy Jr.)

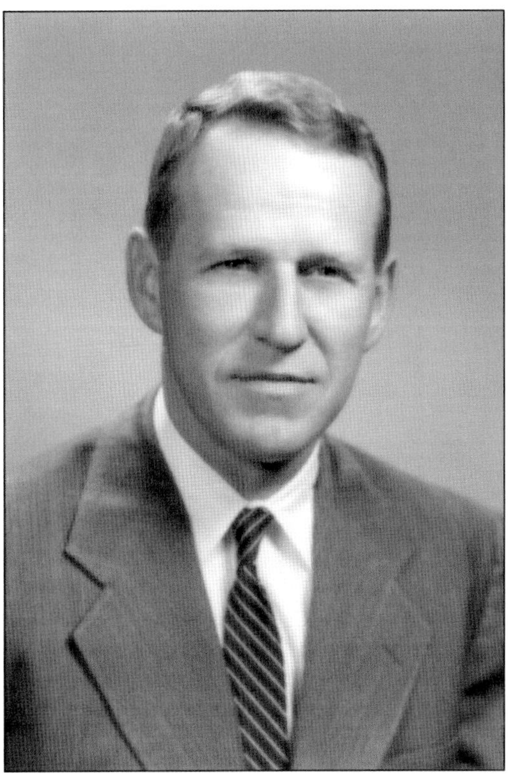

Kenneth Kennedy, 1955. During World War II, Kennedy worked at Fairchild Aircraft in Burlington, North Carolina, building Corsairs. He later opened an electrical supply wholesale distribution company. The company, Electric Supply Company, was based in Wilson. Currently, there are six branches throughout North Carolina. The company is still managed by the Kennedy family. (Courtesy of K.D. Kennedy Jr.)

CHICAGO
PHILADELPHIA
DETROIT
INDIANAPOLIS
PONTIAC, MICH.

OAKLAND MOTOR COMPANY

PONTIAC. MICH.

BOSTON
SAN FRANCISCO
KANSAS CITY
MINNEAPOLIS
SAN ANTONIO

May 24th, 1915.

Rouse Motor Car Co.,
La Grange, N. C.

Gentlemen:-

I regret very much to learn, upon my return home this morning from a business trip, that you have not replied to my letter of May 11th, in which I asked if you were in position to consider an offer from us to take the agency for our 1916 line.

I had hoped you would be interested and that by the time I got back home I would have some word from you on the subject so we could promptly get down to figuring out the details of the proposition. There are a number of very confidential things I want to say to you in regard to the new models we are bringing out which I can't say until I know you are at least in position to consider our offer.

I will say, however, that we have already accomplished certain things that are sure to make the Oakland one of the most easily sold lines of pleasure cars in the entire automobile industry. There will be two models particularly, that, both in character and price, will outdo anything thus far announced for 1916. We are already starting 1916 production and will be in position to make deliveries when you most need the cars.

When we finally make our formal public announcement of these models there are sure to be more applications from dealers than we can well take care of, even with our unusual facilities for large and quick production. I am giving you this advance opportunity to look into our proposition because I feel I would like to have your cooperation in handling the Oakland business in your territory.

As I stated in my letter of the 11th, we will offer our Family "Four" at $1050, completely equipped--a bigger and better car than we sold last year at $1200. I doubt very much if there will be on the market for 1916 as big a car as this--with so much power, such distinctive lines and such complete equipment--at anywhere near the price. It has already created a sensation among our own dealers and is but a forerunner of the surprise we have in store in the balance of our line.

I should like to hear from you in regard to this matter by return mail or by wire. The season is rapidly advancing and your courtesy in this respect will be helpful to me in working out our selling plans.

Very truly yours,

OAKLAND MOTOR COMPANY.

Fred W Warner

FWW/BA

General Sales Manager.

OAKLAND MOTOR COMPANY LETTER. This 1915 letter was written to John H. Rouse. He was being asked to take an automobile dealership from Oakland Motors. Rouse eventually turned down the offer to establish the Oakland dealership. This letter was written in an attempt to convince Rouse to purchase or open the dealership in the area. Rouse was not very impressed with vehicles, having sold them earlier. He believed that the automobile was unreliable and was going to eventually die out. He stated, "The car is a fad and will not replace the horse-drawn buggy." At this time, Oakland Automobiles had existed for a mere seven years. In its first year, Oakland produced 278 cars. The company lasted until 1928. (Courtesy of the Bob Rouse family.)

Dr. J.Y. Joyner Day, 1947. This program insert details the ceremony honoring La Grange citizen James Yadkin Joyner, affectionately referred to as "J.Y." At this time, Dr. Joyner had retired from education and was being recognized for his contributions to the community. He was once named the "Tar Heel of the Week" by the *News and Observer*. (Courtesy of Speck and Sister Fields.)

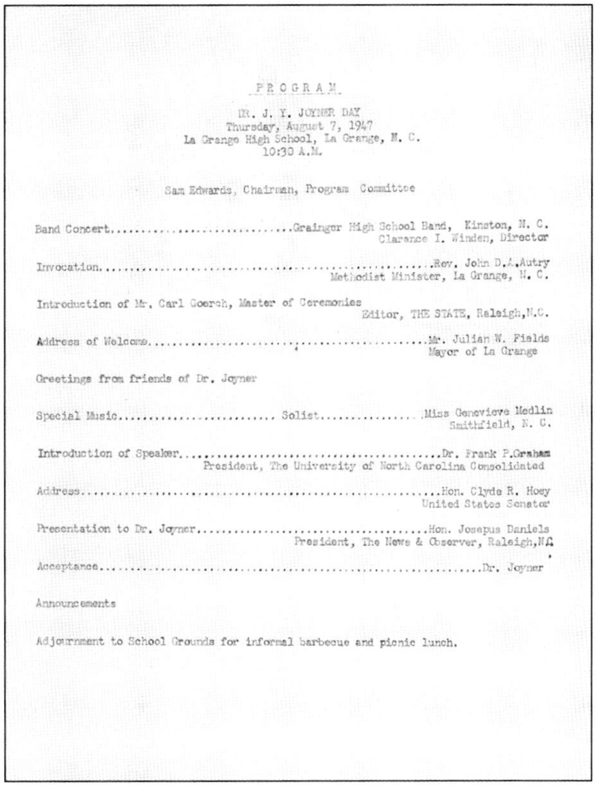

PROGRAM

DR. J. Y. JOYNER DAY
Thursday, August 7, 1947
La Grange High School, La Grange, N. C.
10:30 A.M.

Sam Edwards, Chairman, Program Committee

Band Concert........................Grainger High School Band, Kinston, N. C.
Clarance I. Winden, Director

Invocation........................Rev. John D.A.Autry
Methodist Minister, La Grange, N. C.

Introduction of Mr. Carl Goerch, Master of Ceremonies
Editor, THE STATE, Raleigh,N.C.

Address of Welcome........................Mr. Julian W. Fields
Mayor of La Grange

Greetings from friends of Dr. Joyner

Special Music........................ Solist........................Miss Genevieve Medlin
Smithfield, N. C.

Introduction of Speaker........................Dr. Frank P.Graham
President, The University of North Carolina Consolidated

Address........................Hon. Clyde R. Hoey
United States Senator

Presentation to Dr. Joyner........................Hon. Josepus Daniels
President, The News & Observer, Raleigh,N.C.

Acceptance........................Dr. Joyner

Announcements

Adjournment to School Grounds for informal barbecue and picnic lunch.

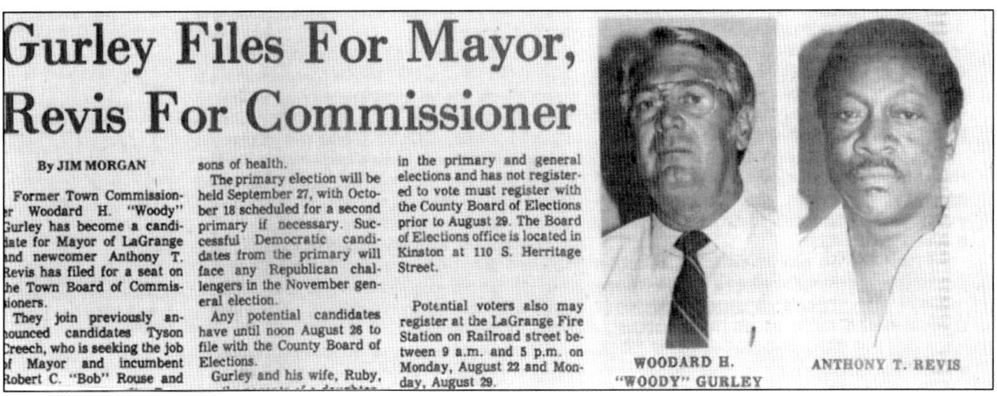

Gurley Files For Mayor, Revis For Commissioner

By JIM MORGAN

Former Town Commissioner Woodard H. "Woody" Gurley has become a candidate for Mayor of LaGrange and newcomer Anthony T. Revis has filed for a seat on the Town Board of Commissioners.

They join previously announced candidates Tyson Creech, who is seeking the job of Mayor and incumbent Robert C. "Bob" Rouse and

sons of health.

The primary election will be held September 27, with October 18 scheduled for a second primary if necessary. Successful Democratic candidates from the primary will face any Republican challengers in the November general election.

Any potential candidates have until noon August 26 to file with the County Board of Elections.

Gurley and his wife, Ruby,

in the primary and general elections and has not registered to vote must register with the County Board of Elections prior to August 29. The Board of Elections office is located in Kinston at 110 S. Herritage Street.

Potential voters also may register at the LaGrange Fire Station on Railroad street between 9 a.m. and 5 p.m. on Monday, August 22 and Monday, August 29.

WOODARD H. "WOODY" GURLEY

ANTHONY T. REVIS

Woodard H. Gurley Runs for Mayor, 1983. Prior to running for mayor, "Woody" Gurley served as a town commissioner from 1979 to 1983. In 1983, Gurley stated that he wanted to "make La Grange a better place to live, work and play." He won the election and went on to serve from 1984 to 1988 and from 1992 to the present. Woody is one of the most respected mayors in La Grange's history and is the friend of former governors. (Courtesy of Grace Burke.)

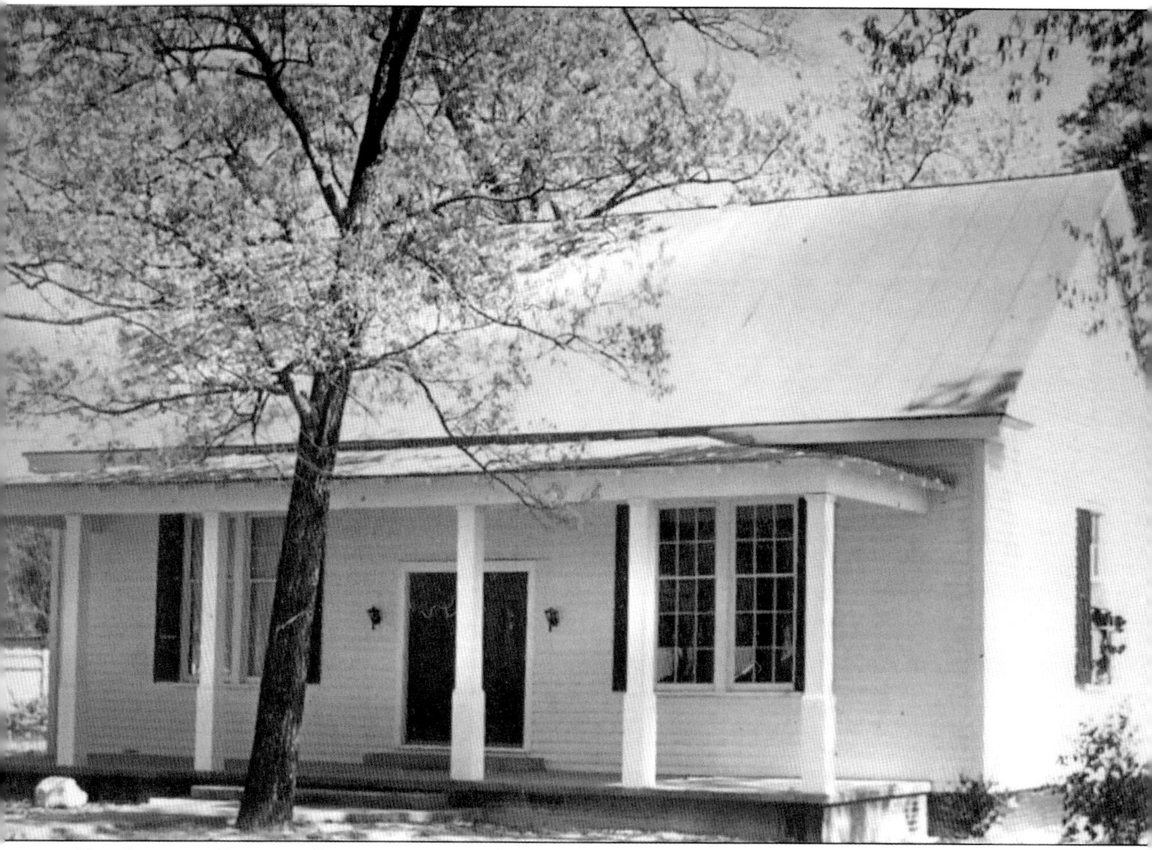

La Grange Garden Club, c. 1930. This building was moved from the Bear Creek district in 1857. The building has been for more than 70 years the Garden Club. Prior to that, it was the town's community center. At the time the building was moved to this area, there were very few structures in the town of La Grange. Council Wooten Sr. was expanding his property and began to build. This church was originally a Primitive Baptist Church. Many have speculated as to why the congregation had an internal split at Bear Creek. The most common story is that the church split over how money was being distributed to the mission field. La Grange citizens met here in 1869 to discuss the town's name change, from Moseley Hall to La Grange. (Courtesy of the Heritage Place, Lenoir Community College.)

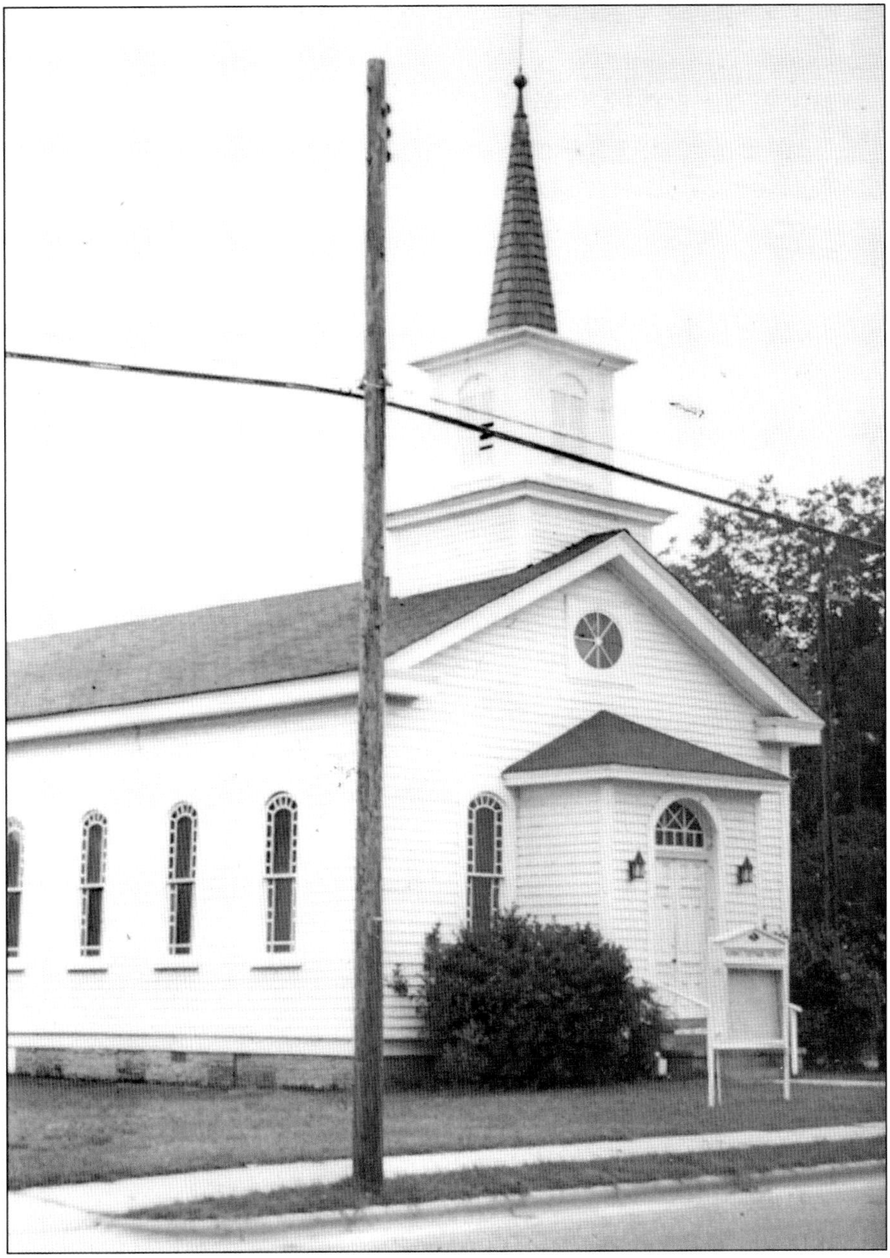

First Missionary Baptist Church, c. 1935. This is the oldest church in La Grange. It was financed in 1857 by Council Wooten Sr., who deeded the land and the building to the church. Originally, this church was a part of Joshua Herring's Bear Creek Church in the mid- to late 1700s. The church moved to its current location in 1857 because of a split in the congregation. During the Civil War, the building was used as a hospital. The town came under fire in March 1865. Gen. John Scofield was moving to meet up with Gen. William Sherman in Goldsboro. Scofield communicated to Gen. Darius Couch to shut down the gunfire on the railroad in Moseley Hall. During the buildup to rid the railroad of the agitators, there was a skirmish in which two Union soldiers were killed and a few were wounded. (Courtesy of the Heritage Place, Lenoir Community College.)

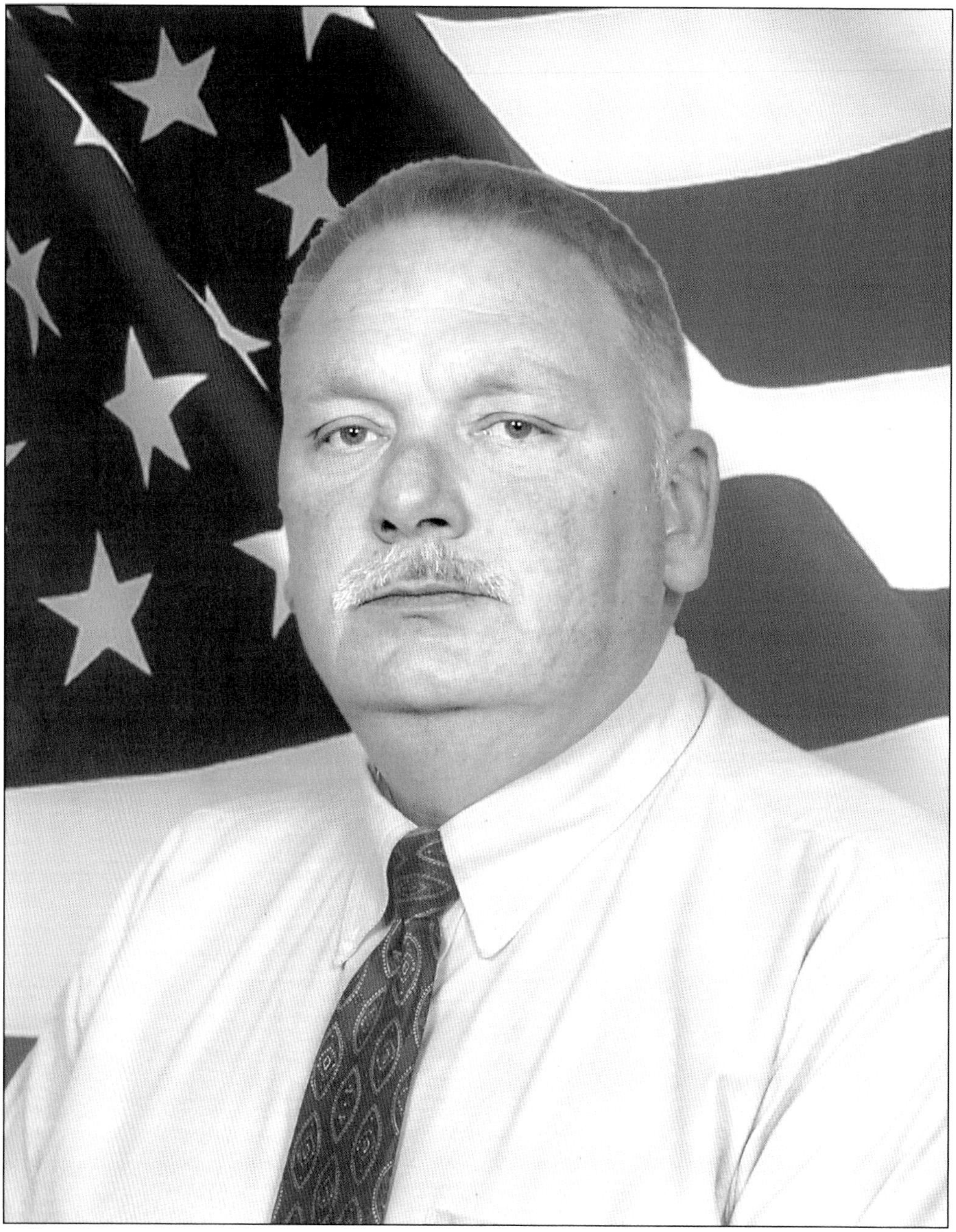

John Sullivan, 2009. Sullivan was the last police chief in La Grange. In 2009, the town voted to end the La Grange Police Department and have the Lenoir County sheriff patrol in La Grange. The Lenoir County deputy sheriff's office is located in the old police station today. Lt. Jerry Davis (former assistant police chief under Sullivan) is the supervisor of that station. Prior to coming to La Grange, Sullivan was the police chief of Fremont, North Carolina. The headquarters at the time was located by the Hardy Newsome buildings. The old jail cell is also in that area. At one time, there was a small booth in town that was used as a mini depot. It is now the concession stand at the La Grange Elementary ballpark. While Sullivan was chief, the police department relocated to its current Railroad Street facility. (Courtesy of John Sullivan.)

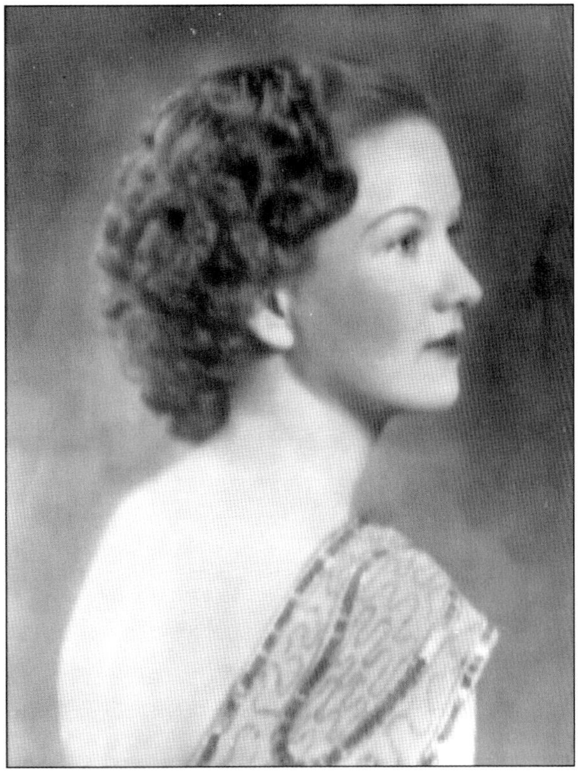

Frances Earle Walters, 1932. The town does not hold beauty pageants any longer, but Frances Walters was crowned the first Miss La Grange in 1931. The pageant was short-lived. Frances's son Speck Fields still has the white Miss La Grange sash. Frances married Spot Fields, future mayor of La Grange, in 1937. (Courtesy of Speck and Sister Fields.)

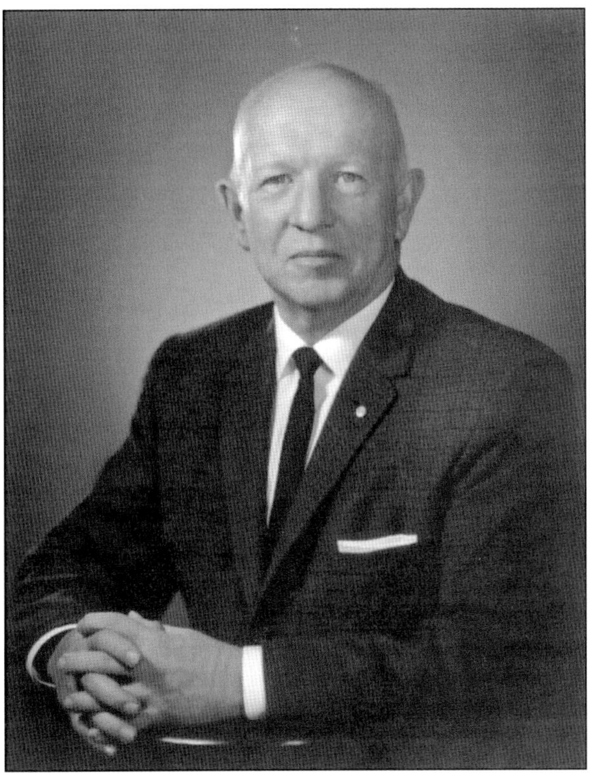

Julian William Fields, 1961. This photograph was taken when Julian "Spot" Fields ran for the North Carolina House. He was the mayor of La Grange in the 1950s. The nickname "Spot" came about during his baseball playing days. He was known as a great batter and had a talent for getting the team out of a bad spot. (Courtesy of Speck and Sister Fields.)

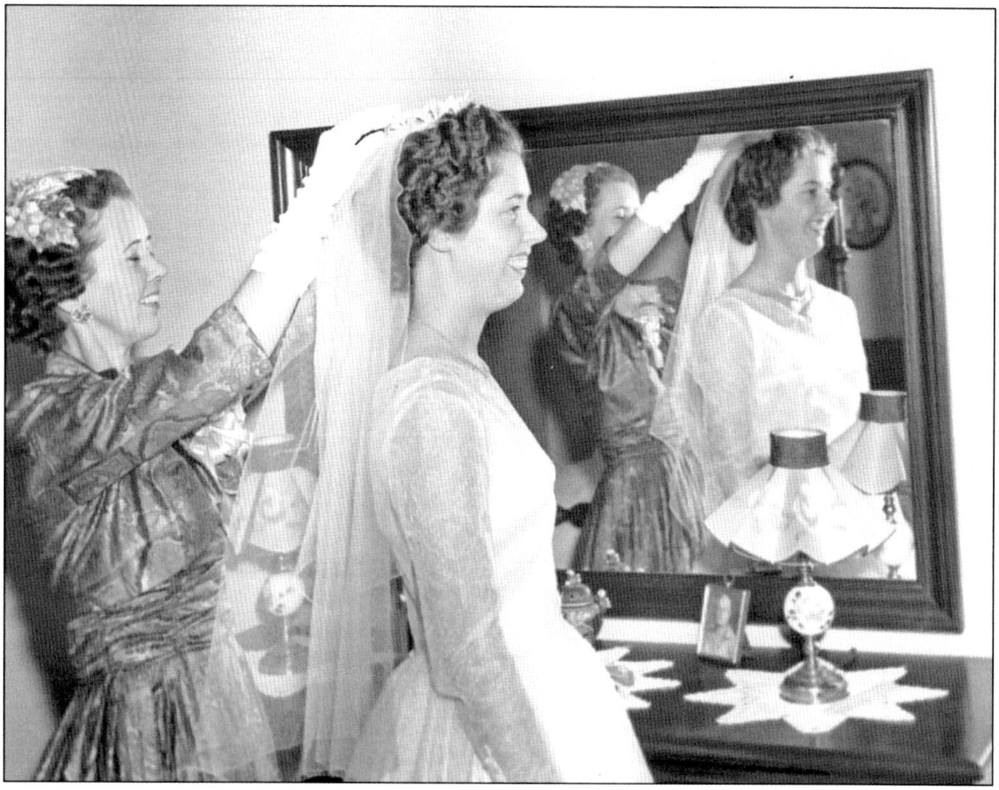

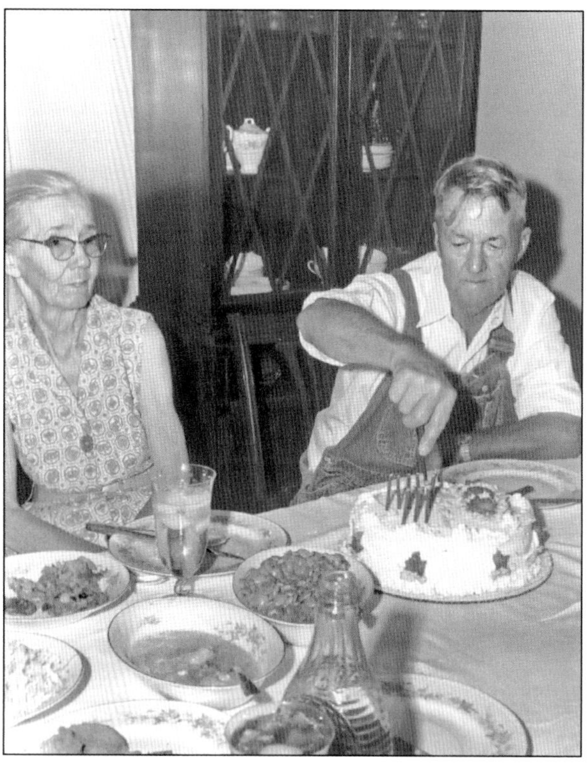

DOROTHY ALDRIDGE, 1962. In this photograph on her wedding day, Dorothy Aldridge is having her veil placed on her head by her mother, Thelma Aldridge. Dorothy married Leamon Suggs, former teacher and assistant principal at North Lenoir High School. Her father, Harry Aldridge, was a well-respected homebuilder who constructed many of the homes in the Lake Pine area of La Grange. (Courtesy of Sonny Herring.)

LEON AND GERTIE ROUSE, C. 1967. The Rouses here are celebrating a child's ninth birthday. Some of the food on display is still popular today, including butter beans, baked apples, and fried chicken. The Rouses were from the Bucklesberry area. (Courtesy of Sonny Herring.)

ORDINANCES, 1943. One town ordinance, at Section 47, reads as follows: "That a fine of one dollar . . . spitting on the sidewalks, or on the floor of any public building." Section 48 reads, "That in driving or riding in and out of alley ways, across sidewalks, all team shall walk and all motor vehicles shall stop and sound horn before crossing sidewalk under a penalty of one dollar for each . . . offense." (Courtesy of Speck and Sister Fields.)

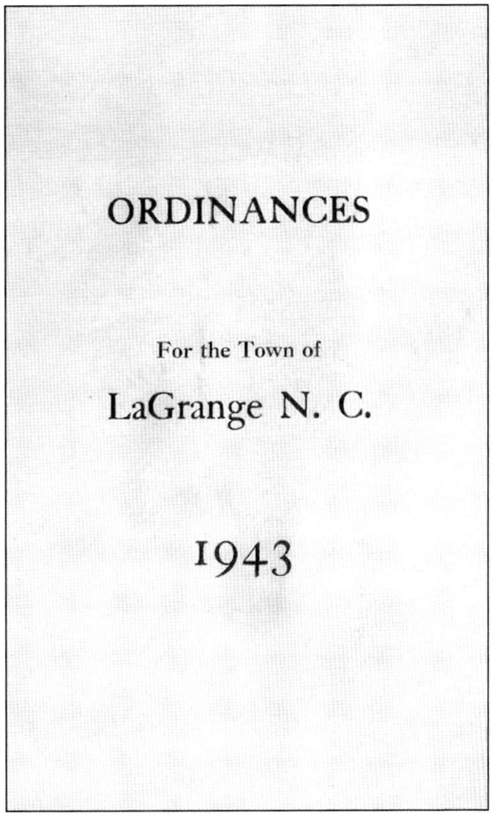

ORDINANCES

For the Town of

LaGrange N. C.

1943

SECTIONS OF ORDINANCES, 1945. On these pages are a few notable ordinances. Section 15 has a fine for not having a light on a bicycle at night. Section 16 requires bicycle riders to dismount when they meet someone in a crosswalk. Section 13 calls for fining owners of bulldogs $20 if their dogs are not leashed. (Courtesy of Speck and Sister Fields.)

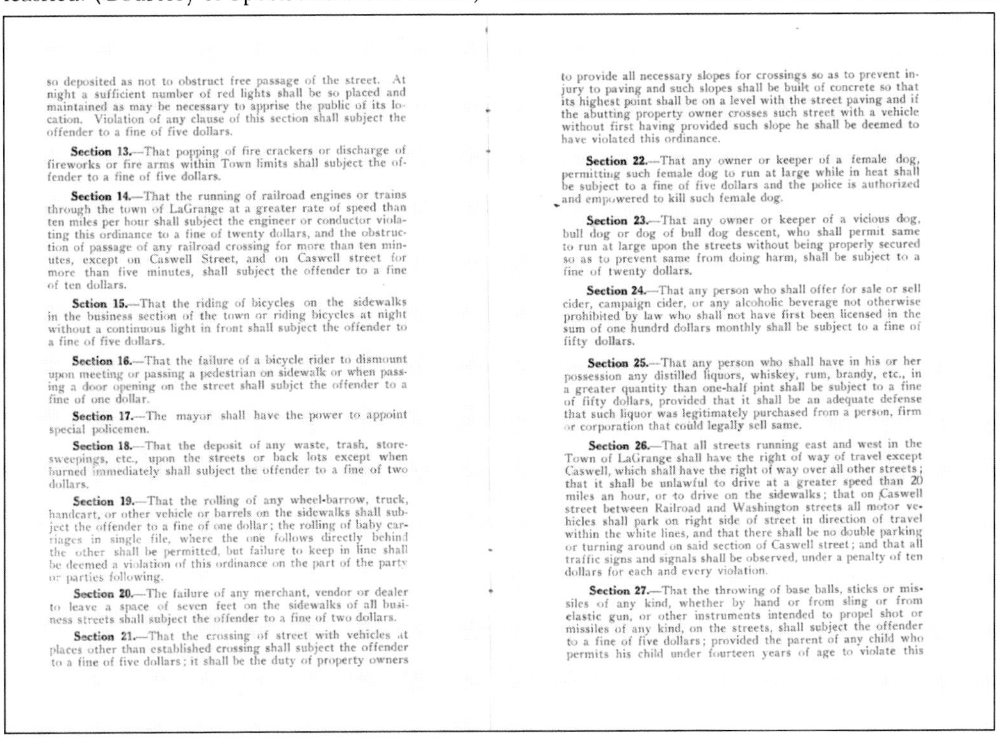

so deposited as not to obstruct free passage of the street. At night a sufficient number of red lights shall be so placed and maintained as may be necessary to apprise the public of its location. Violation of any clause of this section shall subject the offender to a fine of five dollars.

Section 13.—That popping of fire crackers or discharge of fireworks or fire arms within Town limits shall subject the offender to a fine of five dollars.

Section 14.—That the running of railroad engines or trains through the town of LaGrange at a greater rate of speed than ten miles per hour shall subject the engineer or conductor violating this ordinance to a fine of twenty dollars, and the obstruction of passage of any railroad crossing for more than ten minutes, except on Caswell Street, and on Caswell street for more than five minutes, shall subject the offender to a fine of ten dollars.

Sction 15.—That the riding of bicycles on the sidewalks in the business section of the town or riding bicycles at night without a continuous light in front shall subject the offender to a fine of five dollars.

Section 16.—That the failure of a bicycle rider to dismount upon meeting or passing a pedestrian on sidewalk or when passing a door opening on the street shall subjct the offender to a fine of one dollar.

Section 17.—The mayor shall have the power to appoint special policemen.

Section 18.—That the deposit of any waste, trash, storesweepings, etc., upon the streets or back lots except when burned immediately shall subject the offender to a fine of two dollars.

Section 19.—That the rolling of any wheel-barrow, truck, handcart, or other vehicle or barrels on the sidewalks shall subject the offender to a fine of one dollar; the rolling of baby carriages in single file, where the one follows directly behind the other shall be permitted, but failure to keep in line shall be deemed a violation of this ordinance on the part of the party or parties following.

Section 20.—The failure of any merchant, vendor or dealer to leave a space of seven feet on the sidewalks of all business streets shall subject the offender to a fine of two dollars.

Section 21.—That the crossing of street with vehicles at places other than established crossing shall subject the offender to a fine of five dollars; it shall be the duty of property owners to provide all necessary slopes for crossings so as to prevent injury to paving and such slopes shall be built of concrete so that its highest point shall be on a level with the street paving and if the abutting property owner crosses such street with a vehicle without first having provided such slope he shall be deemed to have violated this ordinance.

Section 22.—That any owner or keeper of a female dog, permitting such female dog to run at large while in heat shall be subject to a fine of five dollars and the police is authorized and empowered to kill such female dog.

Section 23.—That any owner or keeper of a vicious dog, bull dog or dog of bull dog descent, who shall permit same to run at large upon the streets without being properly secured so as to prevent same from doing harm, shall be subject to a fine of twenty dollars.

Section 24.—That any person who shall offer for sale or sell cider, campaign cider, or any alcoholic beverage not otherwise prohibited by law who shall not have first been licensed in the sum of one hundrd dollars monthly shall be subject to a fine of fifty dollars.

Section 25.—That any person who shall have in his or her possession any distilled liquors, whiskey, rum, brandy, etc., in a greater quantity than one-half pint shall be subject to a fine of fifty dollars, provided that it shall be an adequate defense that such liquor was legitimately purchased from a person, firm or corporation that could legally sell same.

Section 26.—That all streets running east and west in the Town of LaGrange shall have the right of way of travel except Caswell, which shall have the right of way over all other streets; that it shall be unlawful to drive at a greater speed than 20 miles an hour, or to drive on the sidewalks; that on Caswell street between Railroad and Washington streets all motor vehicles shall park on right side of street in direction of travel within the white lines, and that there shall be no double parking or turning around on said section of Caswell street; and that all traffic signs and signals shall be observed, under a penalty of ten dollars for each and every violation.

Section 27.—That the throwing of base balls, sticks or missiles of any kind, whether by hand or from sling or from elastic gun, or other instruments intended to propel shot or missiles of any kind, on the streets, shall subject the offender to a fine of five dollars; provided the parent of any child who permits his child under fourteen years of age to violate this

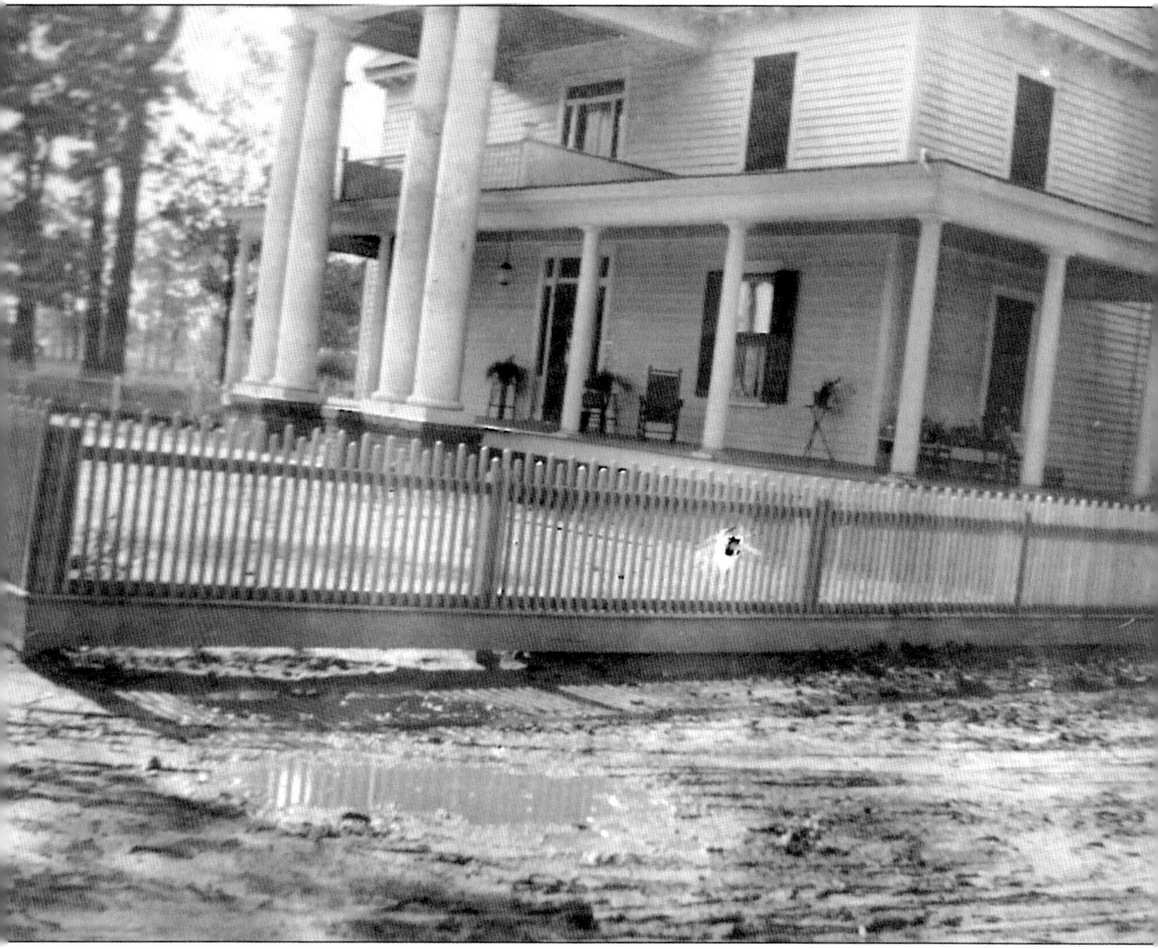

The Drew Murphy House/Pitt Hotel, c. 1960. Drew Murphy was a successful businessman in the 1850s. This house was one of the first three homes in La Grange (Moseley Hall). It was built by Murphy about 1855. Local historian Nannie Braxton Herring stated that, by 1858, the house was one "of the first three homes in Moseley Hall." The building has an interesting story. R.G. Creech and a Mrs. Pitts swapped houses. The story is that both Mrs. Pitts and Creech wanted one another's home. Pitts had converted this home into a hotel, but she no longer wanted to run the establishment and thereby offered the swap to Creech. He took the deal, which brought an end to the Pitt Hotel. By 1919, Tyson Creech owned and was living in the house. The only original portion of the Drew Murphy house still remaining is the foundation. George Foss is undertaking an extensive renovation of the home. (Courtesy of the Bob Rouse family.)

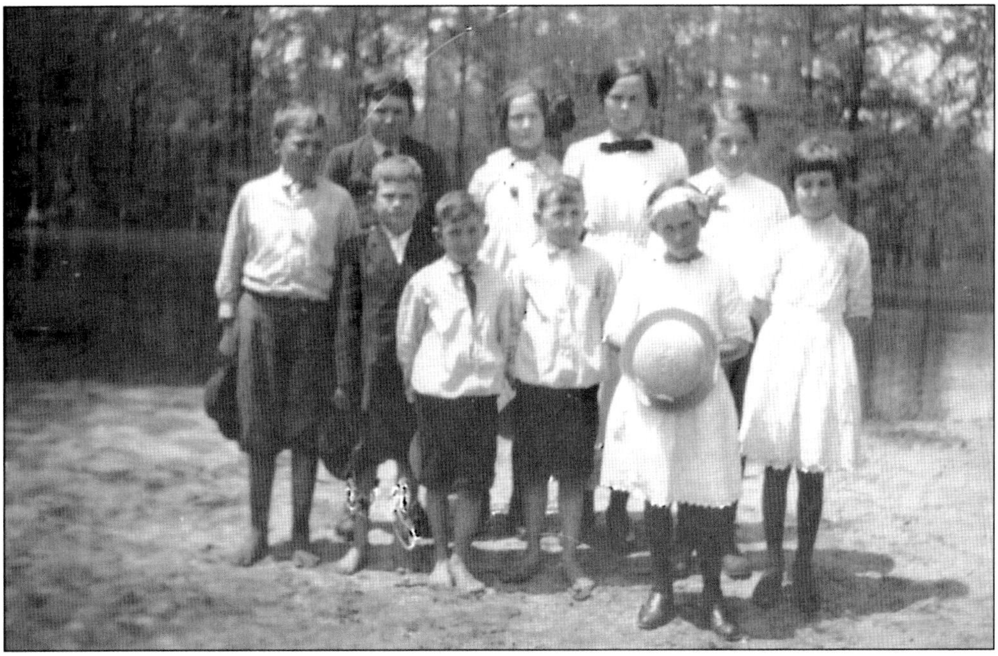

Children at the Mill, 1905–1910. These local children pose at Walters Mill, which was a popular recreational gathering place for local families. Here, the children are wearing their Sunday best. As was common for the day, boys are wearing hats and knickers. (Courtesy of the Bob Rouse family.)

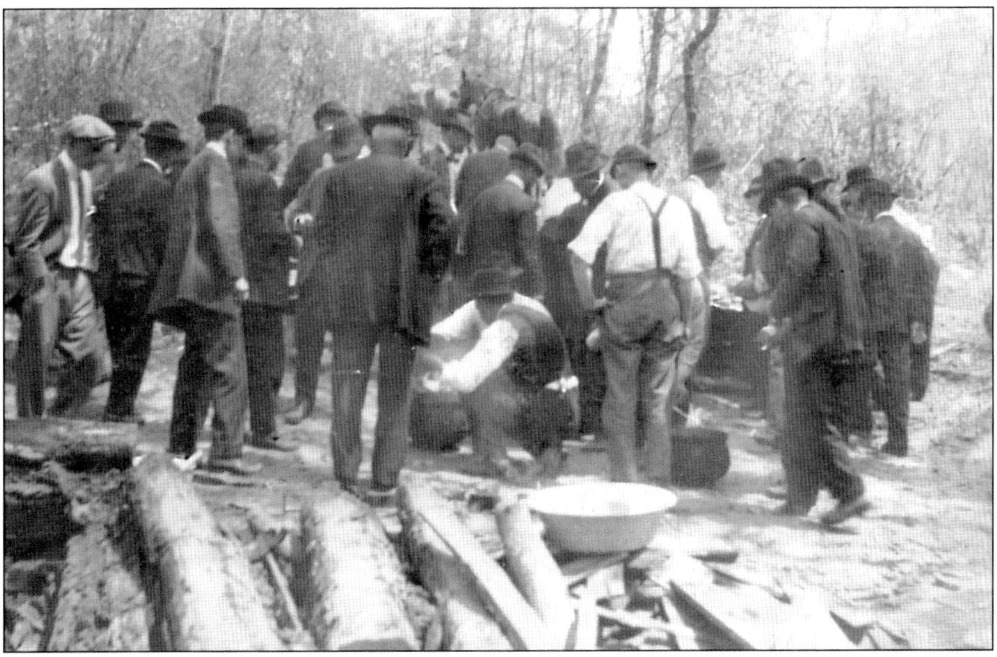

Clearing, 1905–1910. A common town occurrence was to have many of the men participate in clearings or barn raisings. This was generally an all-day event. Note the stew cooking. Strangely, the men are wearing their good clothes. A traditional food item in La Grange is fish stew and boiled eggs. (Courtesy of the Bob Rouse family.)

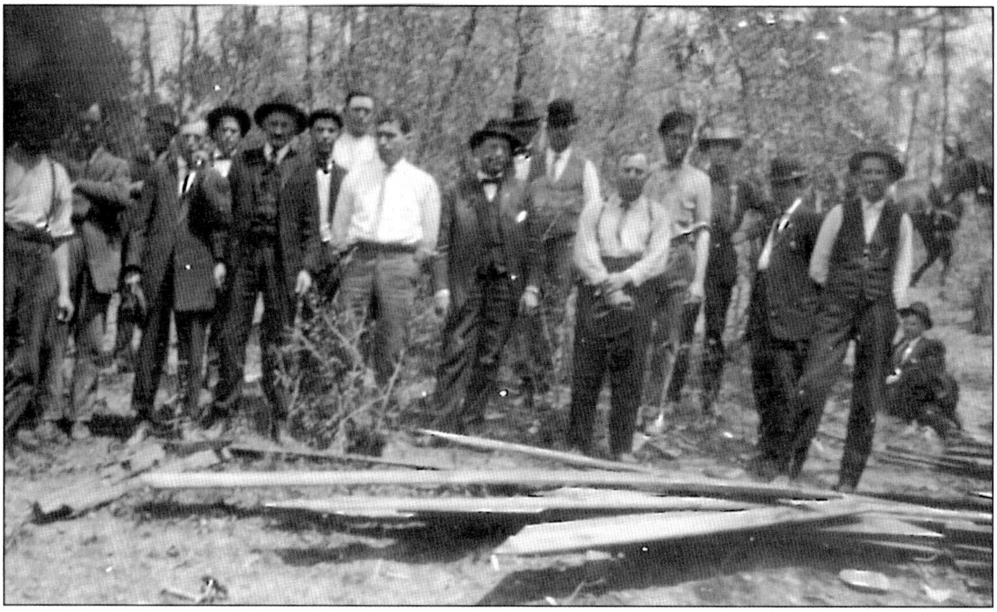

WAITING TO BUILD, 1905–1910. This is another gathering of the men of La Grange. In the center, wearing a bow tie, is John H. Rouse. He was well known for his carpentry work, and, more than likely, he supervised this construction site. It is amazing how items and circumstances of dress have changed since the time of this photograph. How many men today would do hard labor in a shirt and tie? (Courtesy of the Bob Rouse family.)

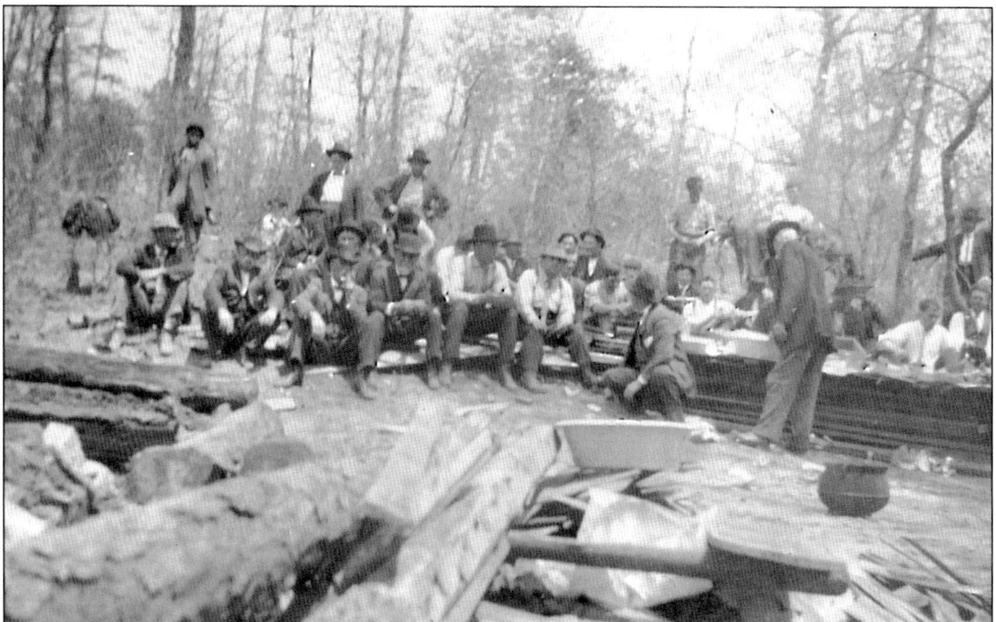

CLEAR AND BUILD, 1905–1910. This photograph shows that the men had cleared a portion of the land. A stack of lumber has been stored for the new build. Prior to 1911, the town built almost exclusively with wood. When the men of the town pitched in like this, it was usually of some benefit for someone. (Courtesy of the Bob Rouse family.)

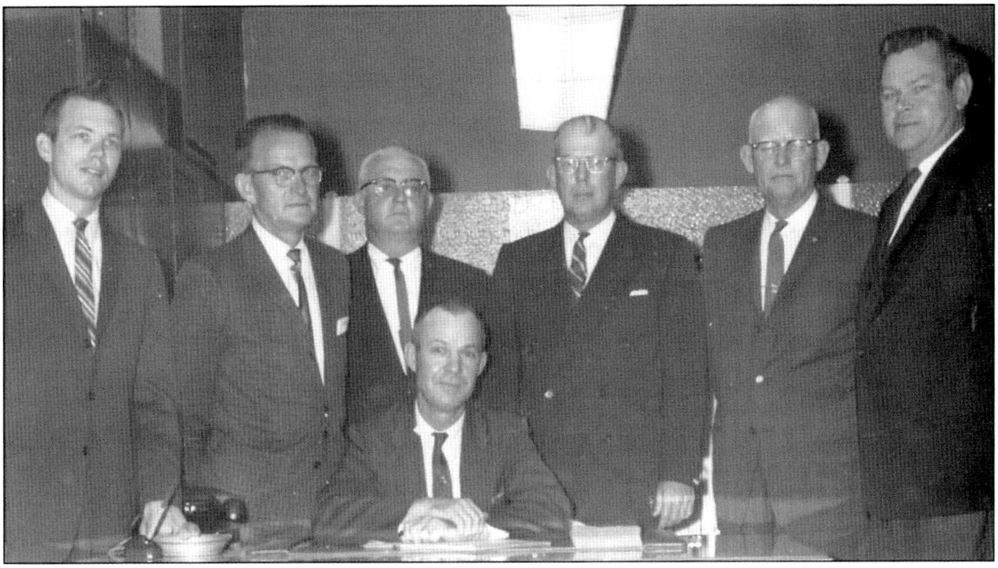

La Grange Board of Commissioners, 1960s. Some of the most well-known men in La Grange's recent history are E.B. Walters, Mayor Hal Williams (sitting), Ed Denmark (standing to right of mayor), Roy Rouse, Sid Meyers, Tyson Creech, and Lee Carr Sutton. Denmark served as mayor for two terms in the 1970s, and he later became the county commissioner, serving in that capacity until his death in 1984. (Courtesy of Grace Burke.)

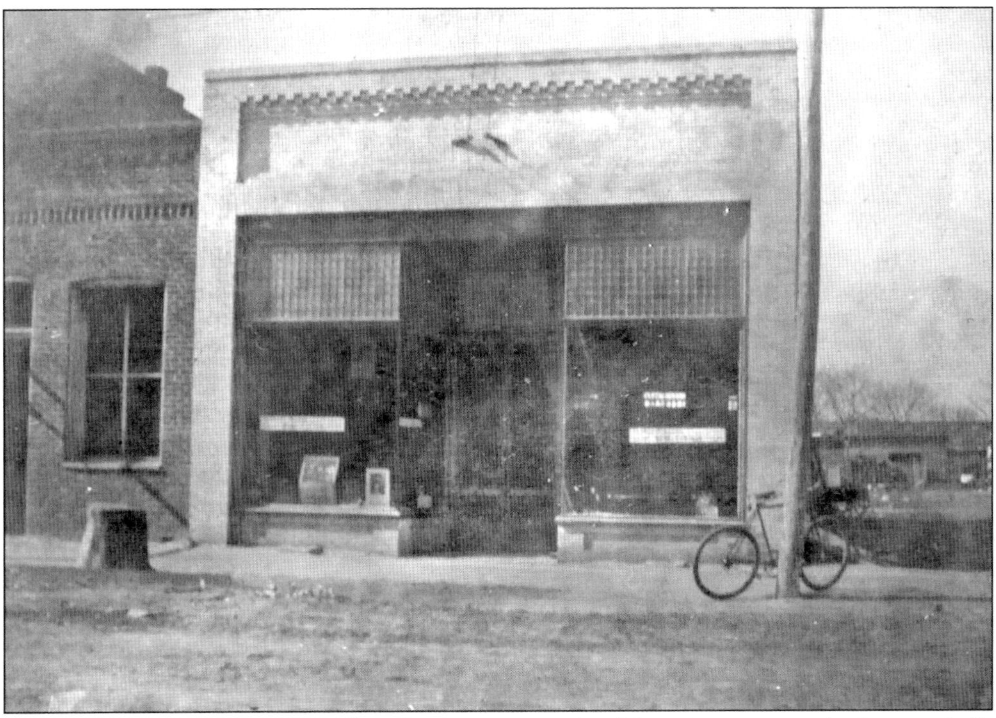

La Grange, 1912. The streets of La Grange were made of dirt. At times, crushed oyster shells were applied to the main streets (Caswell, Washington, and Railroad). This is a photograph of the town after the fire of 1911. The blaze destroyed all of the wood buildings in La Grange. This building today is a local business, Harrison's Accounting. (Courtesy of the Bob Rouse family.)

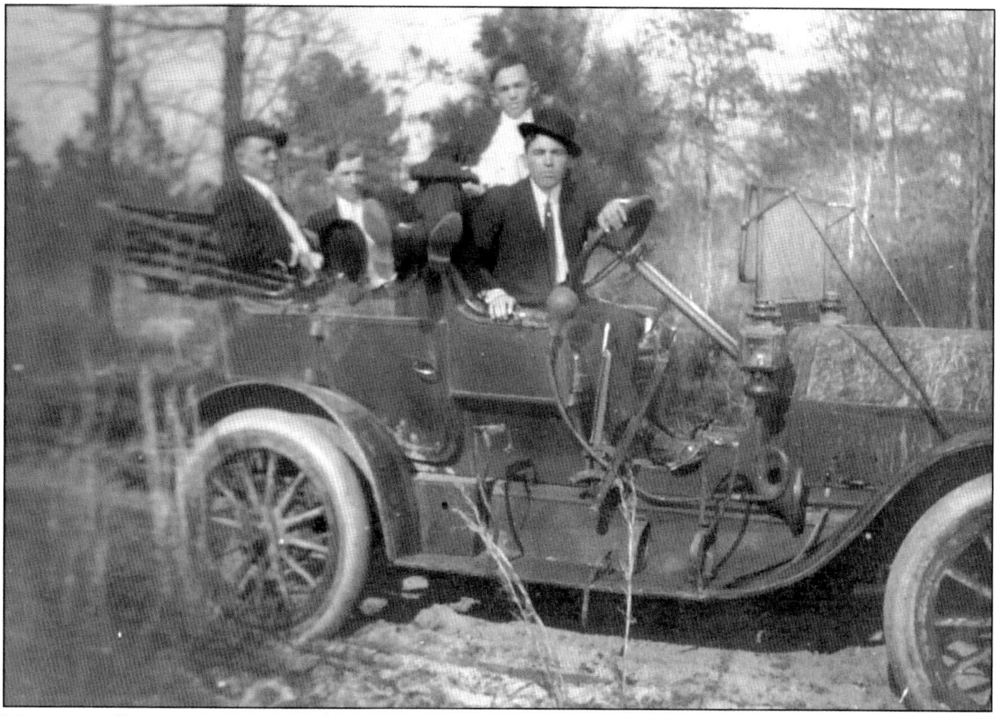

Mitchell Car, about 1910. These men are posing in a 1906 Mitchell automobile. The Mitchell car company was in business until 1923. Automobiles in La Grange were rare because most residents were farmers and did not travel much. (Courtesy of the Bob Rouse family.)

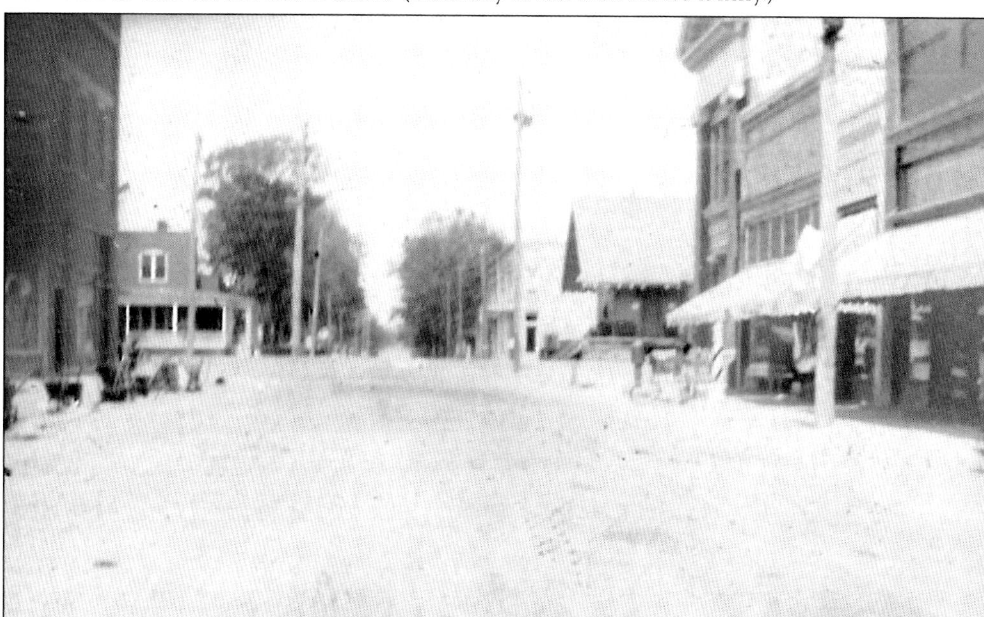

Downtown, c. 1912. The main street in La Grange is actually Caswell Street, named after the first state governor, Richard Caswell. This photograph shows some of the businesses that survived the fire of 1911. The buildings in view were erected of stone prior to the fire. The train depot and the buggy factory did not burn down. (Courtesy of the Bob Rouse family.)

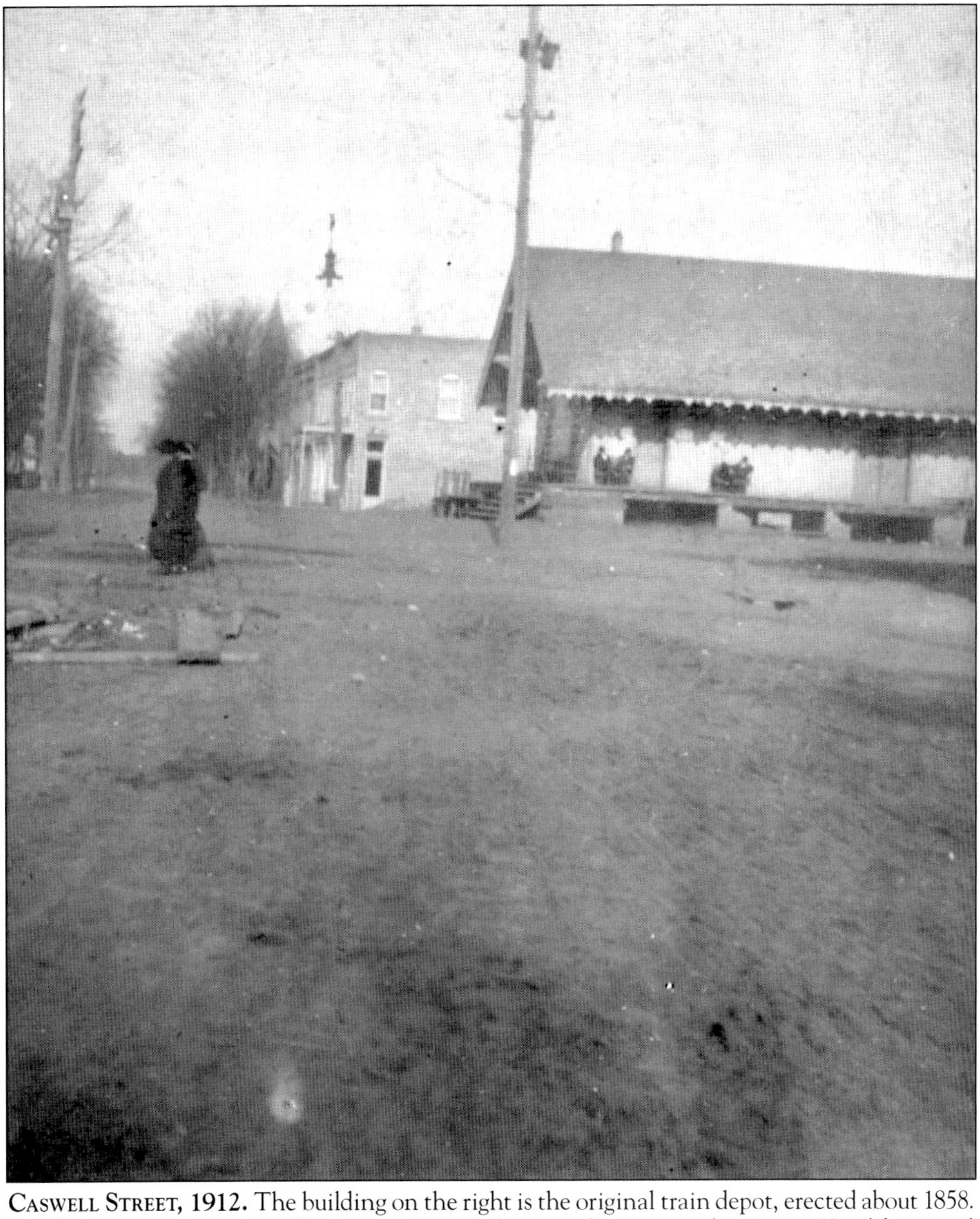

Caswell Street, 1912. The building on the right is the original train depot, erected about 1858. The ladies are walking down Railroad Street, perhaps on their way to the Harper Hotel for a meal or social activity. (Courtesy of the Bob Rouse family.)

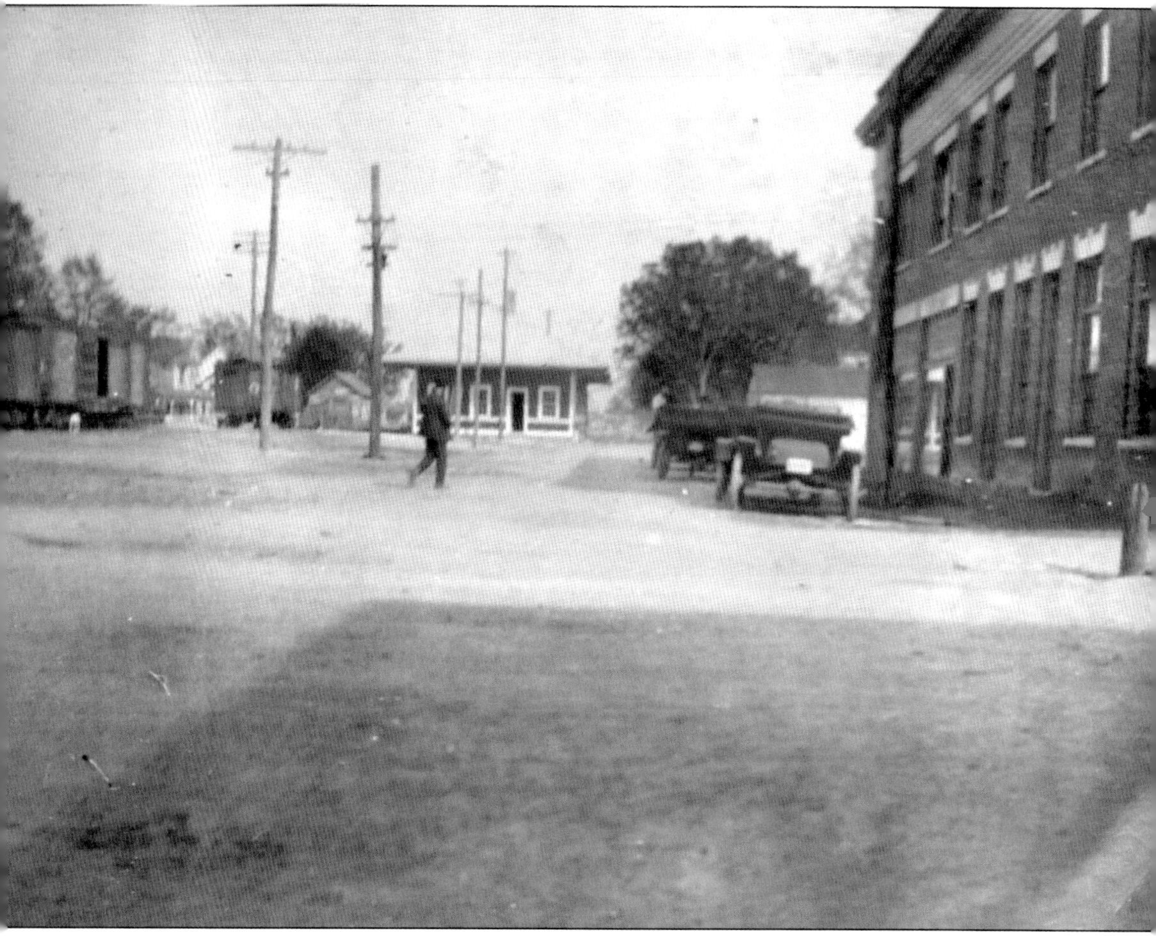

RAILROAD STREET, 1912. A few early automobiles line Railroad Street. The building on the right is the Rouse Bank. At one time, it was the Fields Hotel. The train stopped in La Grange because it was a major supply depot. Now, however, the railroad does not stop in La Grange. (Courtesy of the Bob Rouse family.)

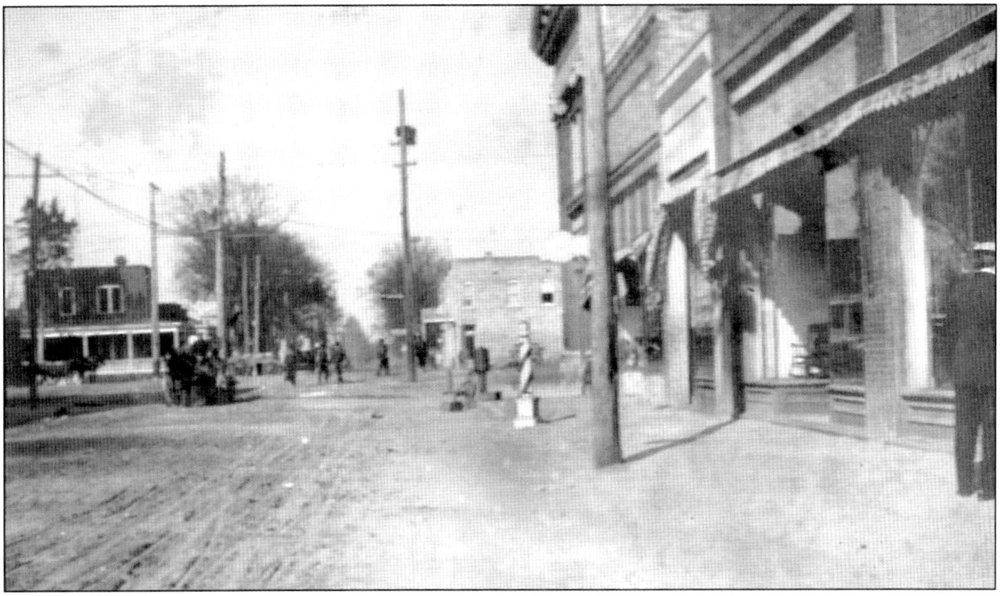

Breaking for Lunch, 1912. It would appear that these are workers breaking for lunch from the Rouse Buggy factory. In the left foreground is the home of Commodore Barrow. The carriage in front of his home is a Rouse buggy. John H. Rouse built this home after the 1911 fire. It was one of the first brick homes in town. (Courtesy of the Bob Rouse family.)

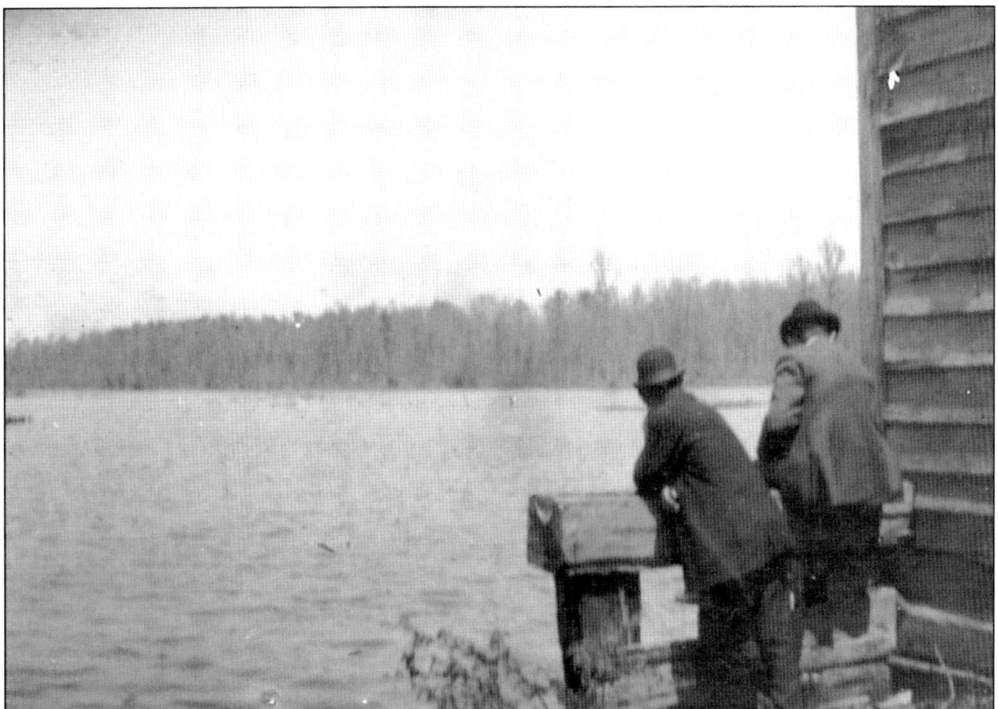

Walters Mill, 1910. Two men relax as they stand by the mill. The facility was a gristmill, used to grind many of the farmers' corn and wheat. The mill was the site for making flour and grinding meal. (Courtesy of the Bob Rouse family.)

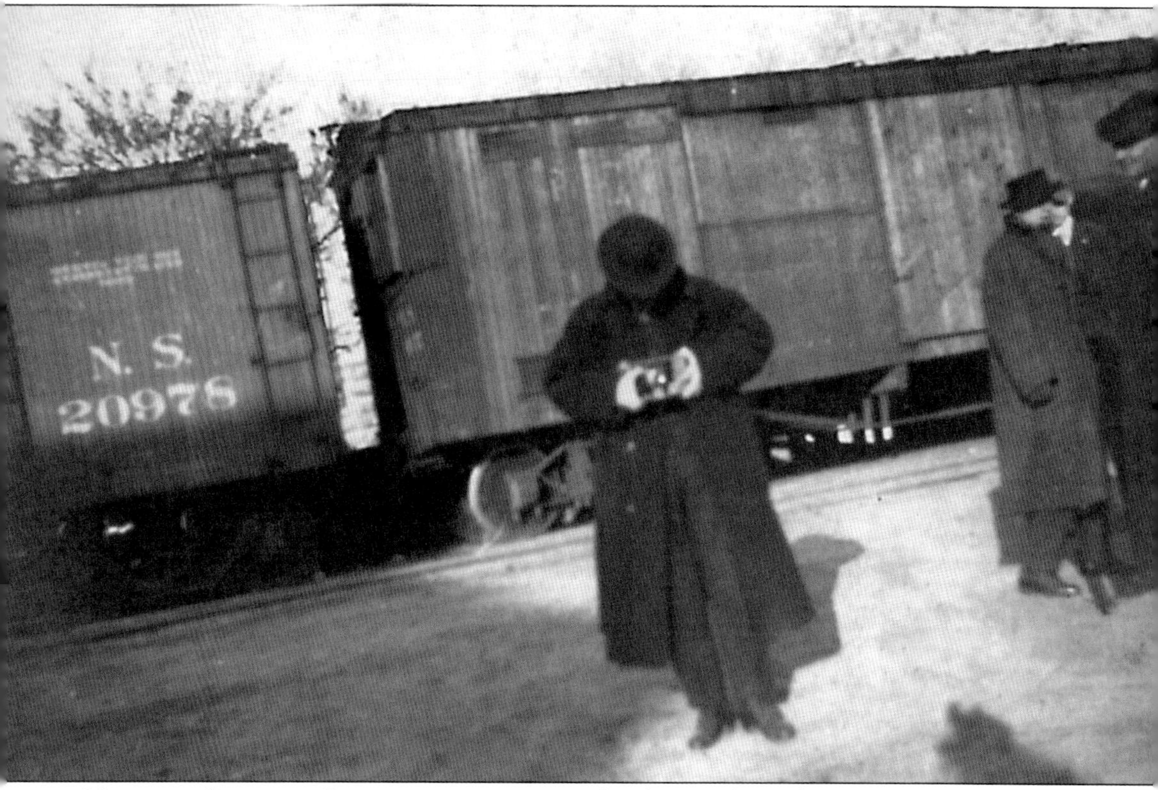

Northern Southern Railroad, 1910–1912. A local man takes a photograph in front of what is believed to be a boxcar from the Northern Southern Railroad. The Northern Southern was formed in 1883. The camera appears to be either a Seneca or Kodak. Both had an attached viewing lens so the photograph could be shot from the waist. (Courtesy of the Bob Rouse family.)

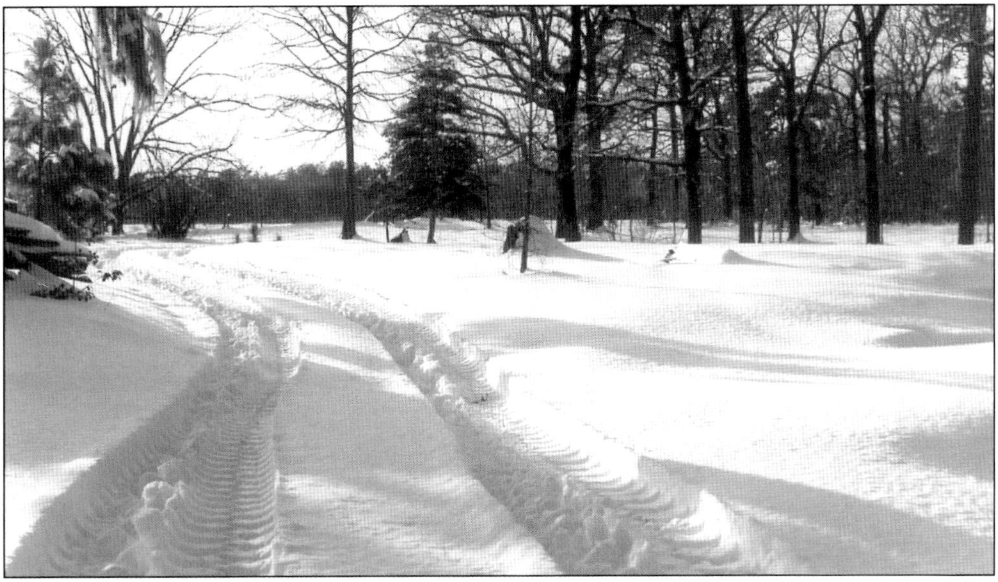

SNOW IN BUCKLESBERRY, 1958. Among James Rouse's collection of images are nature photographs. He captured many pictures in the La Grange area. Here is the Bucklesberry area after a tremendous snowstorm. On this occasion, Rouse shot several photographs of the snowstorm, many of which have not been previously published. (Courtesy of Sonny Herring.)

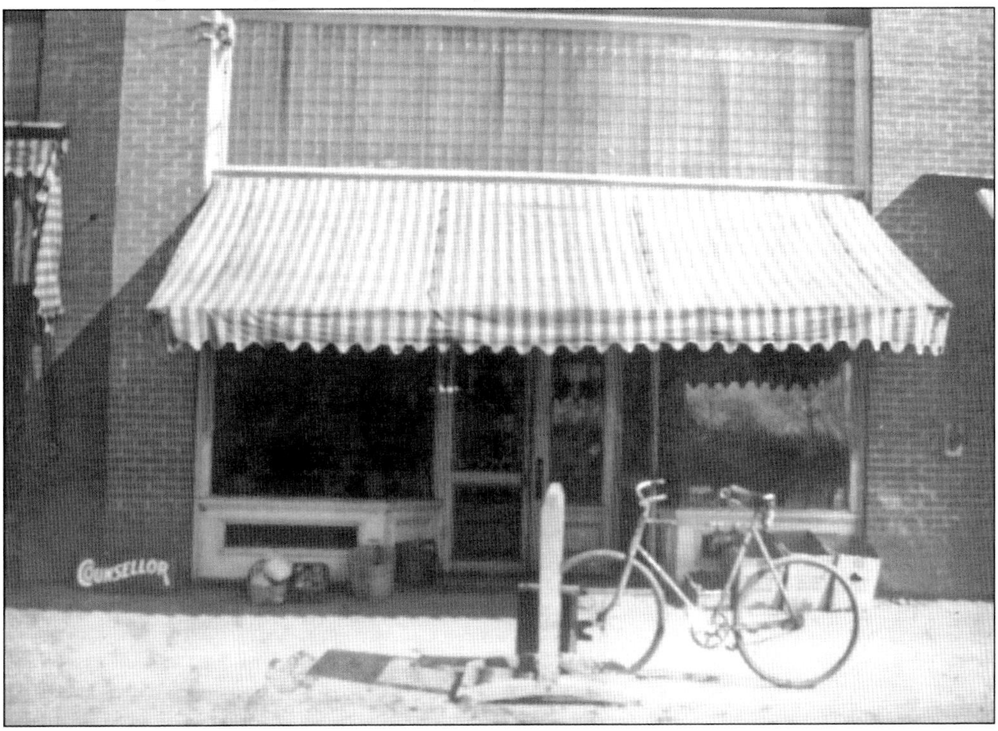

STOREFRONT, 1912–1914. A bicycle stand has been installed in front of a general merchandise store. The "Counsellor" sign indicates a cigar made by the J.C. Winters Company of Red Lion, Pennsylvania. This cigar was a very popular brand throughout North Carolina. Tobacco use was widespread and socially accepted. (Courtesy of the Bob Rouse family.)

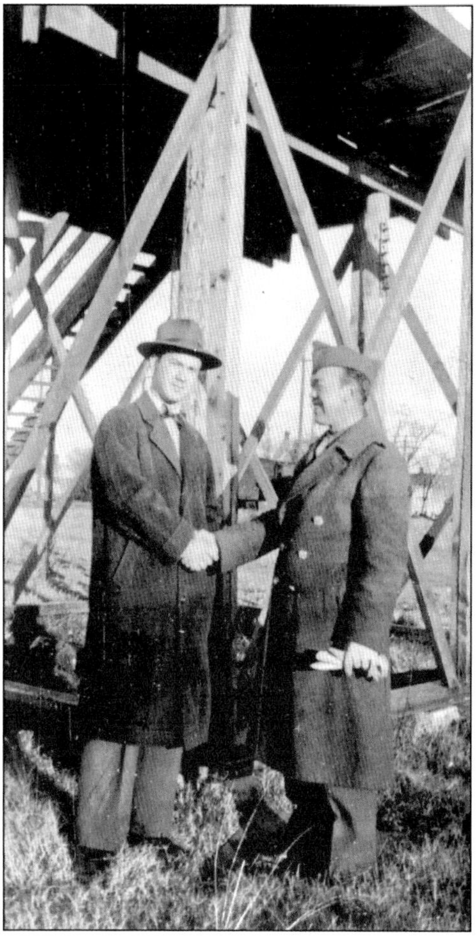

LOOKOUT TOWER, 1943. Here is a rare photograph of the lookout tower in La Grange during World War II. Shown here are John Parrott Walters Jr. (left) with his cousin Thomas Haywood Walters. A well-known insurance agent in La Grange, John Walters was also associated with the Export Leaf Tobacco Company of Richmond, Virginia. (Courtesy of J.P. Walters III.)

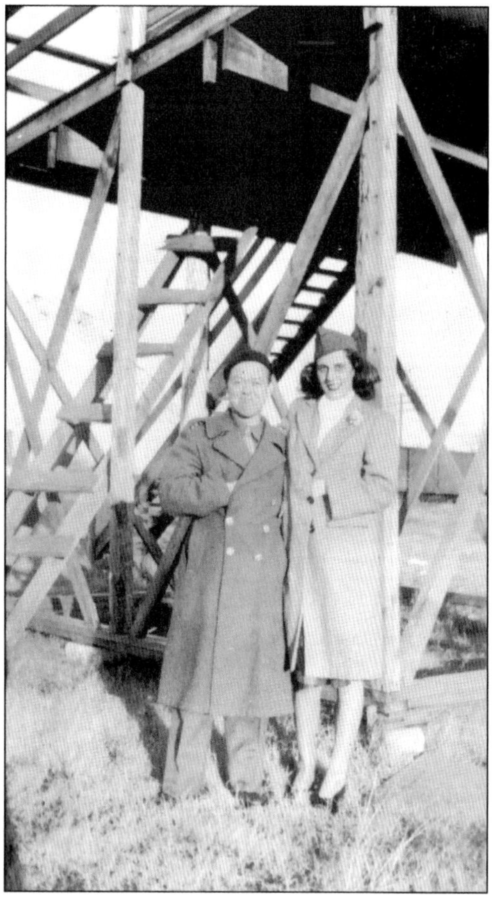

THE WALTERS AT THE LOOKOUT TOWER, 1943. Thomas Walters and Mahala Edwards Walters pose at the lookout tower. During the war, the tower was used to search the skies for enemy aircraft in an effort to keep La Grange safe. Many of the citizens voluntarily stood duty, looking into the skies. Mahala Walters worked at her family's business, J.P. Walters Insurance Agency, from 1948 to 1998. (Courtesy of J.P. Walters III.)

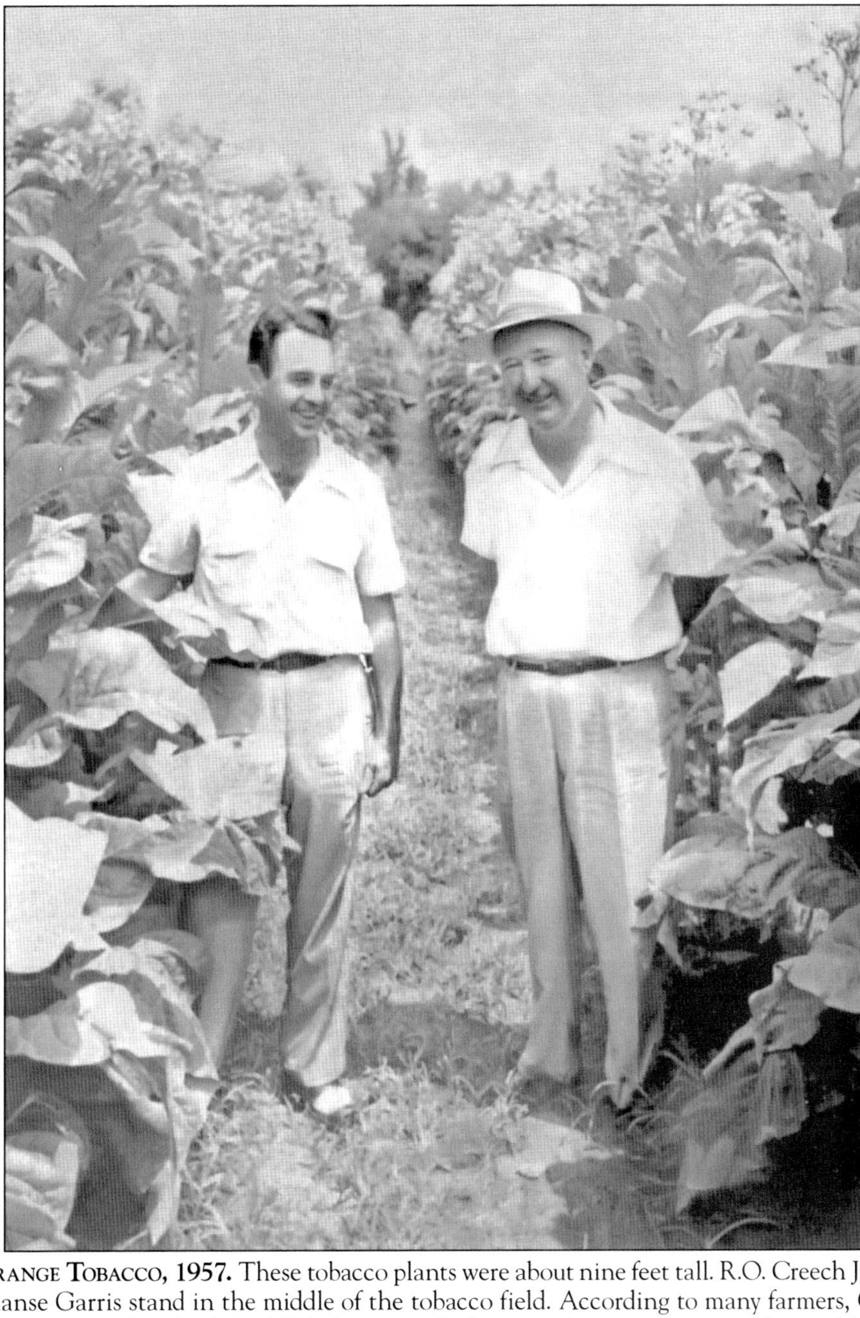

La Grange Tobacco, 1957. These tobacco plants were about nine feet tall. R.O. Creech Jr. (left) and Ranse Garris stand in the middle of the tobacco field. According to many farmers, Croker 39 was easy to work with. After 1956, this type of tobacco and seven others were banned because of strict government guidelines. The plants seen here are nearing harvest time. The process for harvest begins near the end of July and continues to early to mid-August. Once the tobacco plants are picked, they are taken to the curing barns, where they are tied onto sticks. Soon after this process, the tobacco is "put up" into barns. The barns are heated in order to turn the tobacco to a golden brown. Once the tobacco cures, the barns are opened. Eventually, the tobacco is placed in the pack house for final absorption of moisture, grading, and bundling. The tobacco is then pressed flat and loaded for shipping. (Courtesy of Speck and Sister Fields.)

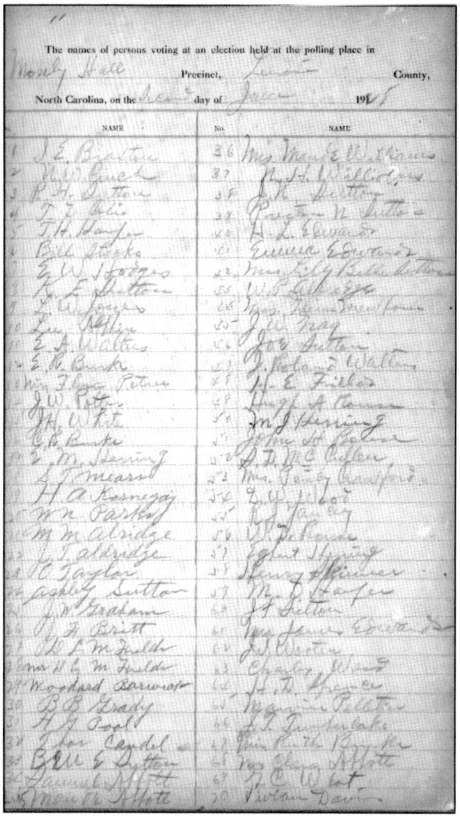
The names of persons voting at an election held at the polling place in Mosely Hall Precinct, Lenoir County, North Carolina, on the ___ day of June 1918

NAME | No. | NAME

Moseley Hall Polling Records, 1918. The Moseley Hall Township poll workers wrote down every voter's name. The voting process was much like it is today. More than likely, the town's residents voted at the community building or in one of the larger buildings. The votes would have been counted by hand and taken to Kinston for the final precinct counts. (Courtesy of Speck and Sister Fields.)

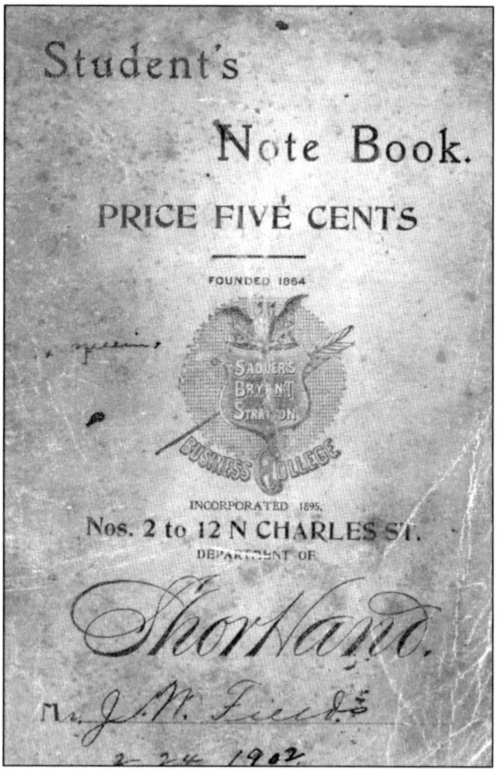

J.W. Fields Notebook, 1902. J.W. Fields Sr. owned a general merchandise store in La Grange. This notebook was a ledger, or account book. Fields daily recorded the items he sold and the items he purchased. Many ledgers of this sort still exist in La Grange. They were the best available method of bookkeeping. (Courtesy of Speck and Sister Fields.)

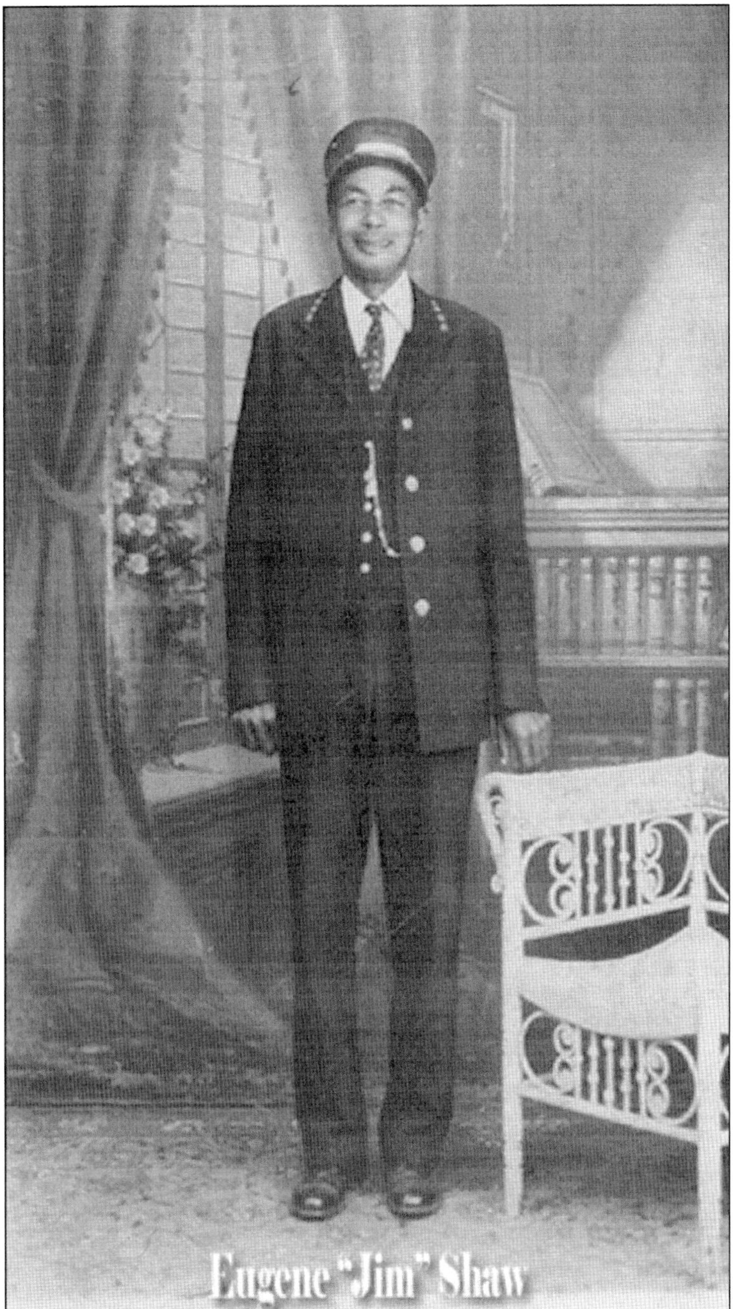

EUGENE SHAW, 1935. One of La Grange's most beloved citizens, "Jim" Shaw was the man who gave La Grange its nickname, "The Garden Spot." He was a porter for the Atlantic & North Carolina Railroad. The route, referred to as the "Shoofly," would at times change, so it was considered a temporary route. Those working the line were thus always ready for it to change. The term "shoofly" meant a temporary bypass, or a temporary road. Shaw was the first African American in town to own an automobile and to have indoor plumbing. (Courtesy of Eugene Jim Shaw family.)

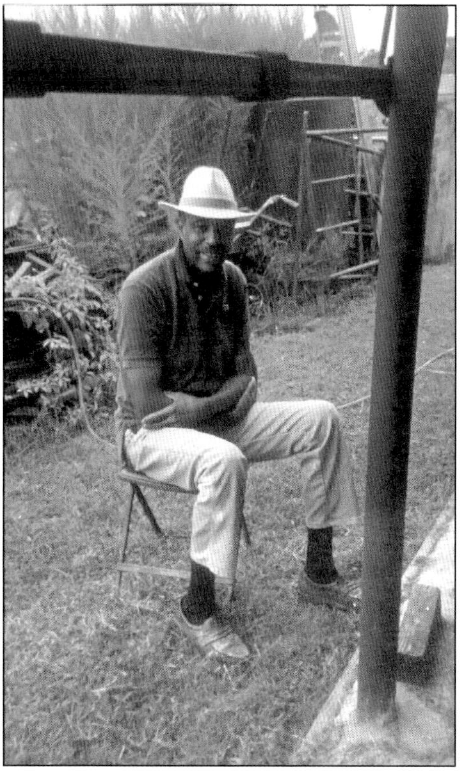

Jurden Wooten, 2002. "Chick" Wooten was a very well-known artist in La Grange. His paintings were very well known in Lenoir County. Today, Wooten's paintings can cost over $500. He also authored a book, *Pa Pa Tracks Days Back Yonder.* A self-taught painter, Wooten depicted the days of his Southern youth. (Courtesy of Edward and Murthis Wooten.)

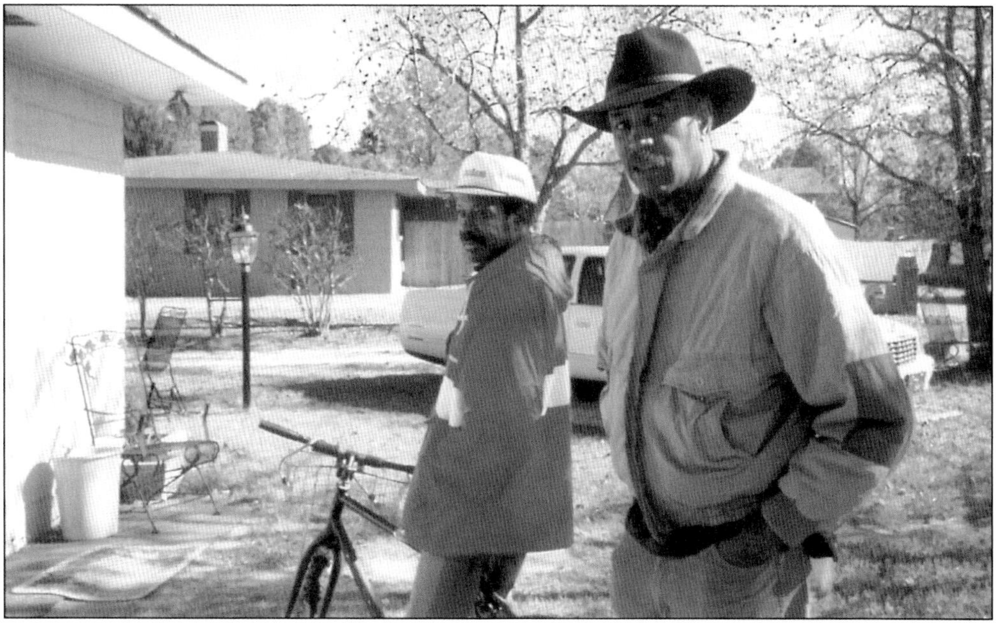

Chick and George Wooten, 2001. Chick (right) is seen here with his brother George. Many of Chick's paintings depicted the farm life of eastern North Carolina. He worked for many years at the Howell Day Care Center and painted one of his best murals there and for the Howell's Center in New Bern. George Wooten used to sing for the successful La Grange–based singing group the Corsairs. (Courtesy of Edward and Murthis Wooten.)

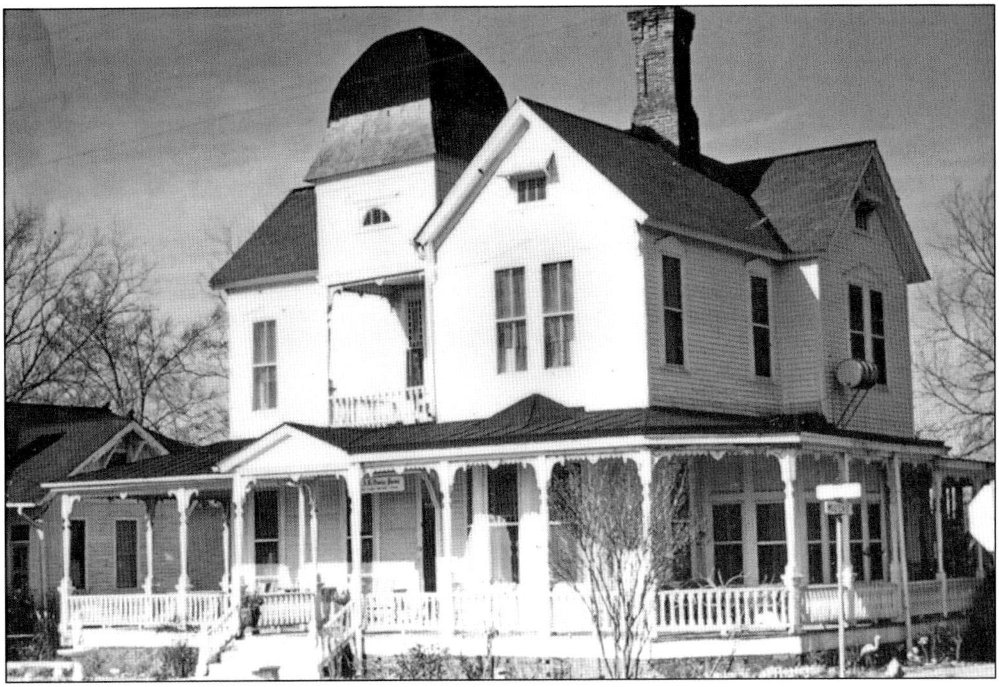

A.C. Davis House, c. 1938. This was the main building and residence of the founder of the Davis Military School, A.C. Davis. The school was founded in La Grange in 1880 by A.C. Davis and his brother Jefferson "Jeff." Davis lived here until the school moved to Winston Salem. (Courtesy of the Heritage Place, Lenoir Community College.)

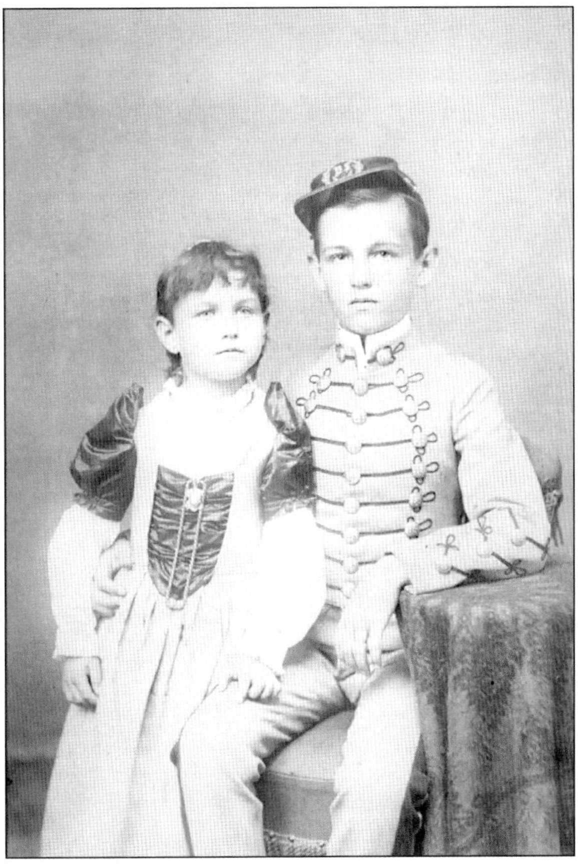

Davis Military School Cadet, c. 1885. This photograph shows a young cadet in full uniform. The "DS" can be seen on his cap. Local historian Gary Fields owns one of the original uniforms, which is currently on loan to the present-day Davis Military School in Winston Salem, North Carolina. (Courtesy of the Heritage Place, Lenoir Community College.)

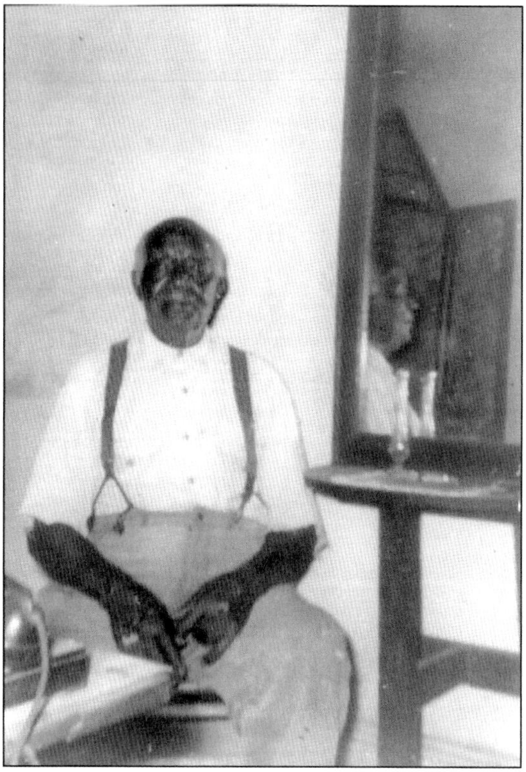

George Palmer, c. 1950. From the 1920s to the 1950s, Palmer was an influential businessman in La Grange. He moved back to La Grange in the 1920s after working in the Philadelphia naval yards. Palmer built many homes in the area, which came to be called Palmer Town. The houses that Palmer built were called shotgun houses. Palmer Street was named in his honor. (Courtesy of Murthis Wooten.)

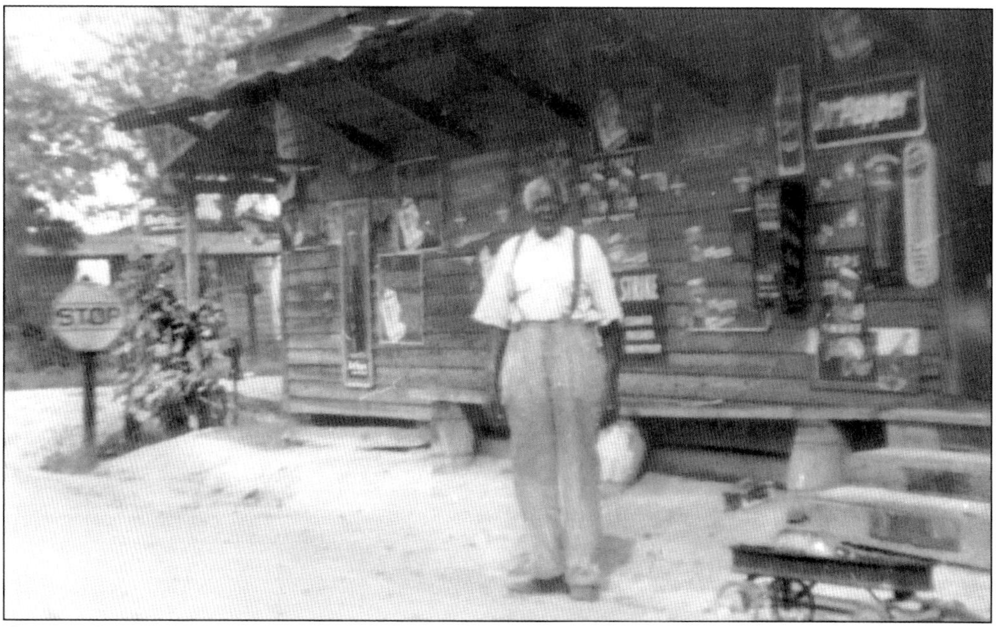

George Palmer's Store, c. 1950. Palmer's store was the main shopping center in La Grange's African American community. He was an excellent businessman who was held in high regard by all of the town's merchants. Palmer's store carried clothing, meats, cheeses, vegetables, homemade beverages, hunting supplies, fish supplies, and heating oil. In 2011, George Palmer was honored by the La Grange Historical Society. (Courtesy of Murthis Wooten.)

Four

Athletics

Athletics have been a part of La Grange society since the early 1900s, when horse races were held at Parks ball field. The horse shows were popular with the town's folks for several decades. La Grange has had state champions in basketball (1960–1961, E.B. Frink High School) and baseball (North Lenoir High School). Many students have gone on to play college and professional sports, such as North Lenoir alumnus Carter Capps. He is currently a middle relief pitcher for the Seattle Mariners.

The town has a faithful following in high school sports and recreation ball. In the past, La Grange had adult baseball, which Spot Fields played well into his 40s. This baseball league would play the neighboring cities of Kinston and Goldsboro. The town also had a softball league, which played on the Railroad Street ball field. From the days of clay basketball courts and bare fields without goalposts, sports have always been a uniting staple in the community.

The La Grange Speedway was another social event for townspeople. The speedway had a hobby class, two heat races, and a main event. At times, it also held a powder puff derby, when the girls would have their opportunity to race. Some former drivers remember that, on Sundays after church, the whole town would come to the races.

The people of La Grange also enjoy hunting and fishing. There are hunting and fishing clubs that meet regularly and have a great time during the season. Town businesses sponsor many of the athletic teams, and residents enjoy the closeness that athletics brings.

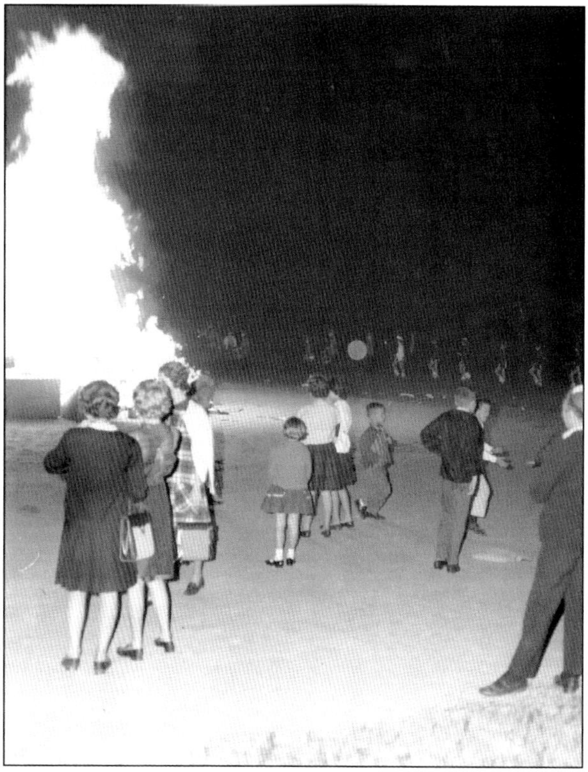

LA GRANGE HIGH SCHOOL BONFIRE, 1963. Bonfires are a tradition for many high schools, and La Grange is no exception. Here, students participate in the last bonfire to be held at La Grange High School before the school was relocated. Generally, the football team, band, and cheerleaders all attended. (Courtesy of Sonny Herring.)

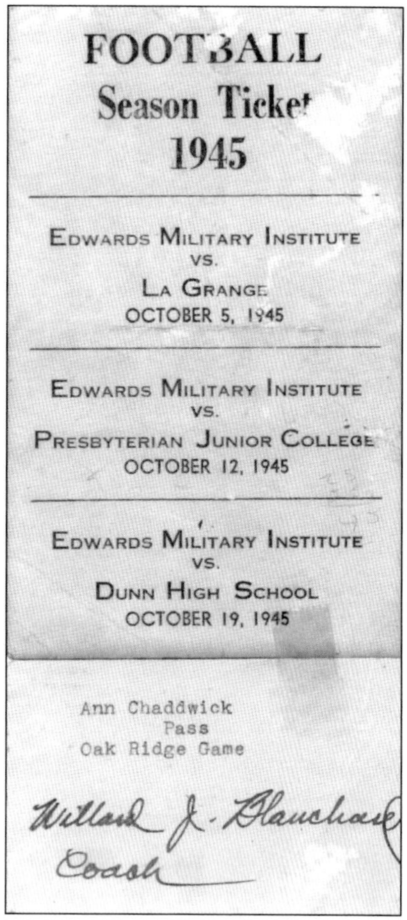

FOOTBALL TICKET, 1945. Ann Chadwick was the daughter of John Chadwick Sr. This pass was for a game not written on the ticket. Willard J. Blauchard was the head football coach in 1945. Edwards Military Institute, located in Salemburg, North Carolina, was founded by Methodist minister Anderson Edwards. In 1965, Edwards Military Institute and Pineland College merged to become Southwood College. (Courtesy of Ann Cashwell and Penny Chadwick Dawson.)

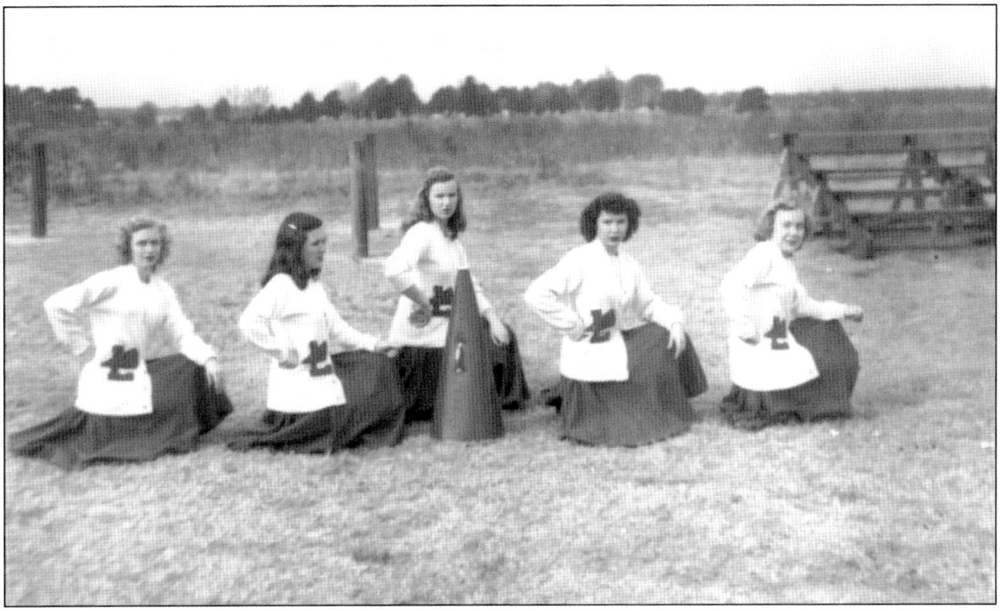

La Grange Cheerleaders, 1945. These are the La Grange High School Bulldog cheerleaders. Joyce Abbot is second from right. Ann Chadwick is at far right. This photograph was taken at the old school grounds on Railroad Street. The football field is now a part of La Grange Elementary School's baseball field and playground. (Courtesy of Sonny Herring.)

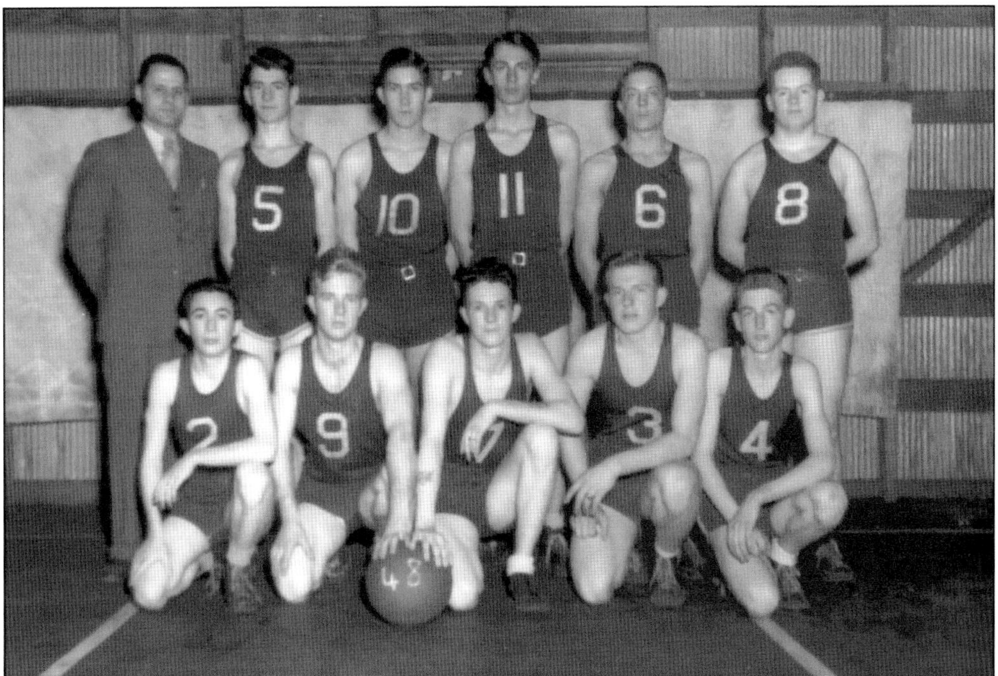

Boys' Basketball Team, 1948. The La Grange High Schools boys' team poses in the new gymnasium. Prior to 1948, the team played outdoors and on a clay surface. The ground was pressed hard as cement. Cecil Burke Jr. was the team's manager. (Courtesy of Sonny Herring.)

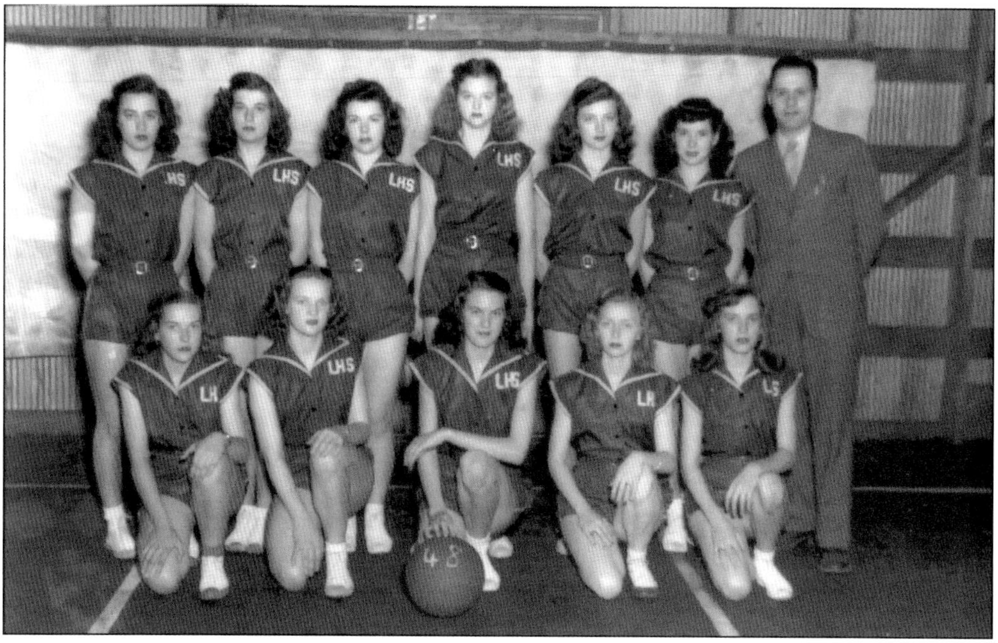

Girls' Basketball Team, 1948. A longtime tradition in La Grange High School history is girls' basketball. It was common to have the same coach for the girls' and boys' teams. Prior to the gymnasium's construction, the La Grange High School girls also played their basketball games outside. (Courtesy of Sonny Herring.)

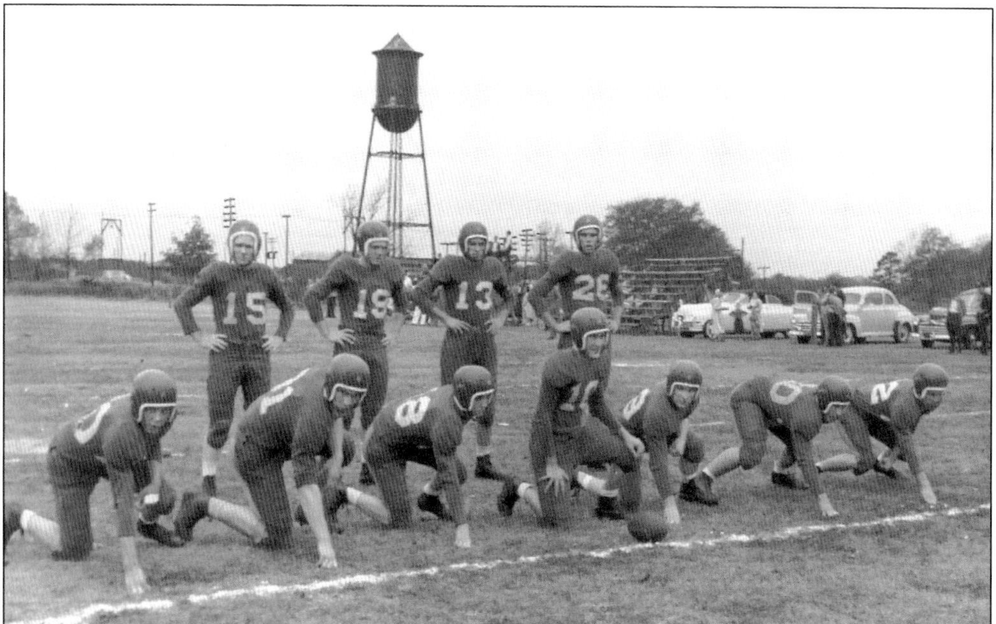

La Grange Football Team, 1942–1943. Robert "Bob" Rouse was the center. At quarterback was Jack Crews. After World War II, Rouse attended Campbell University and played football for the school. Campbell recently reintroduced football into its athletic program. (Courtesy of Grace Burke.)

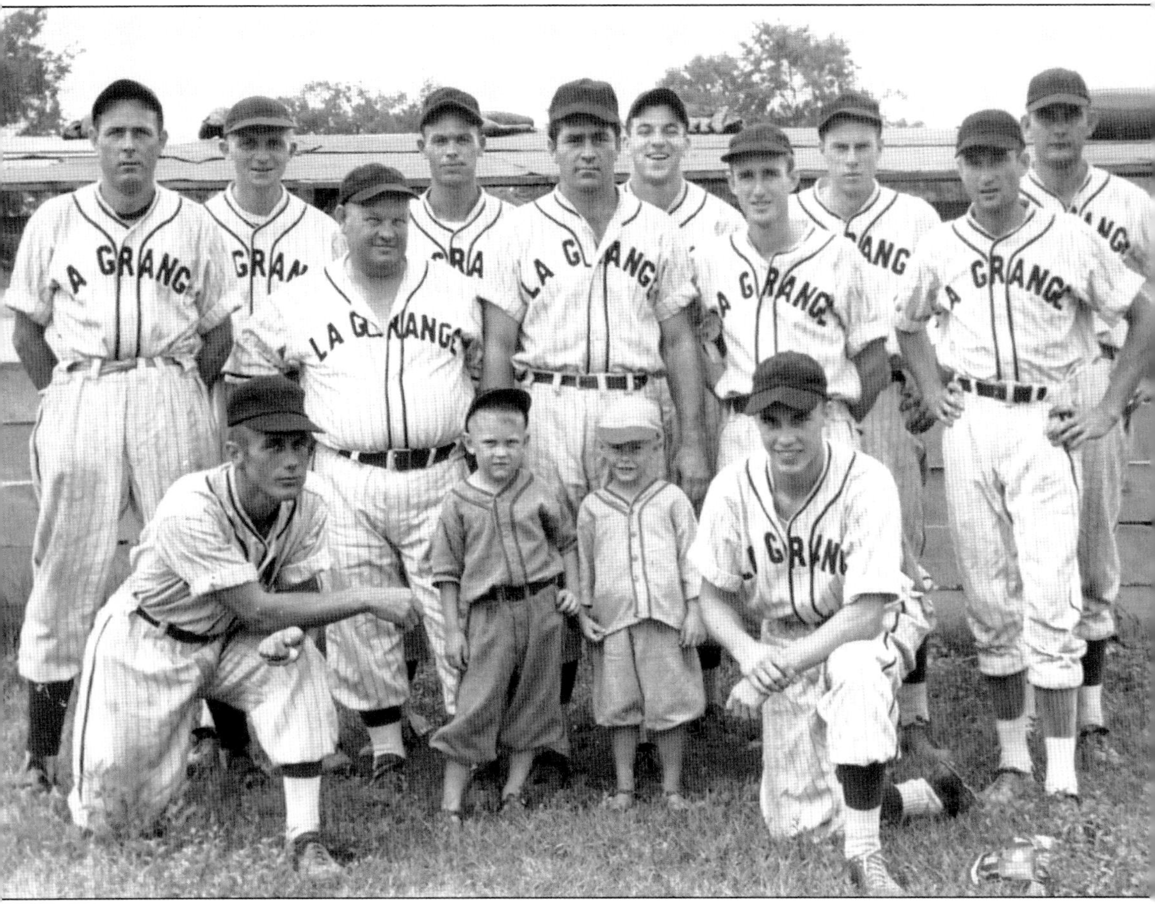

La Grange Town Baseball Team, 1948. This league would play nearby towns, such as Goldsboro and Kinston, to name only a few. Shown here are, from left to right, (first row) T.R. Vick, Joe Kinsey, Dickie Hardy, and Carlton Frederich; (second row) Roger Uzzell, manager Earl Kinsey, ? Price, D.S. Wood, and Jessie Coltrain; (third row) "Tuck" Crocker, Berry Jones, ? Carraway, Hardy Baker, and ? Newsome. Baseball was, and is today, a popular sport in La Grange. (Courtesy of Grace Burke.)

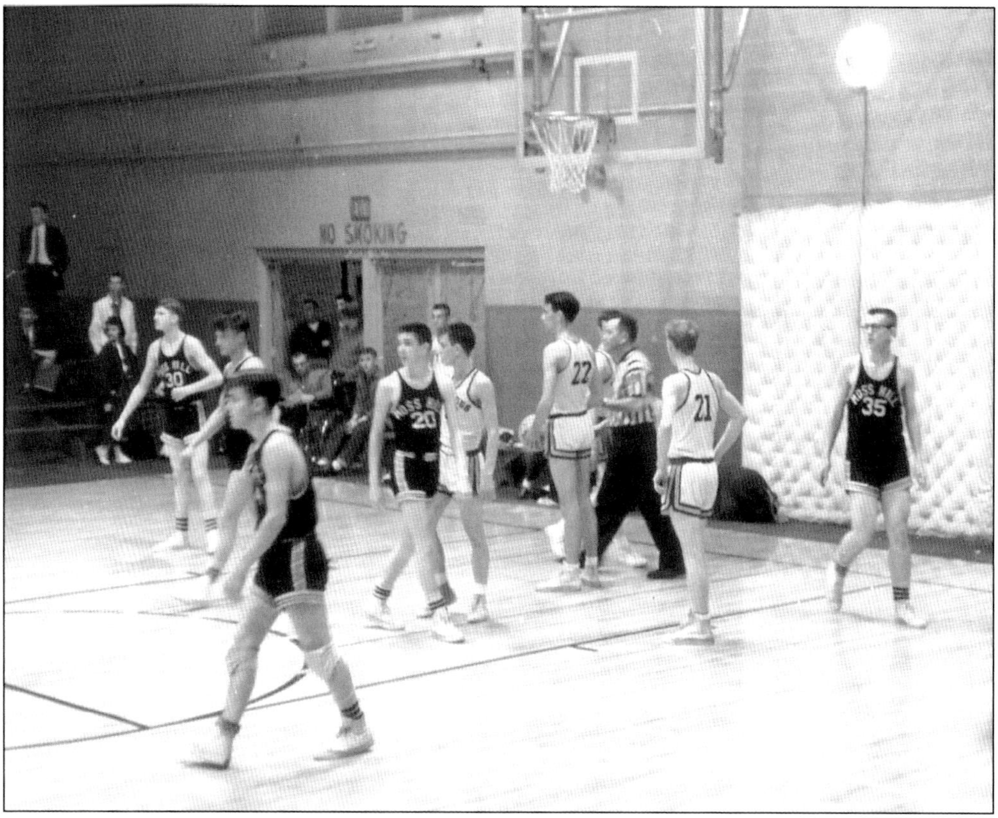

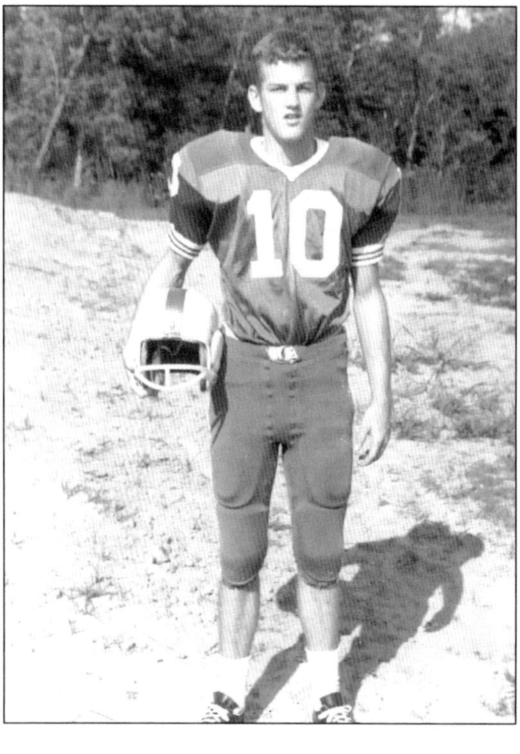

NORTH LENOIR BOYS' BASKETBALL, 1965. This photograph depicts a game between North Lenoir and Moss Hill High School. The gymnasium is still in use today at North Lenoir High School. Eventually, Moss Hill and North Lenoir were consolidated. Visible in the doorway is Paul Barwick, owner of the *Weekly Gazette*. (Courtesy of Sonny Herring.)

NORTH LENOIR FOOTBALL PLAYER, 1960S. This photograph shows the typical North Lenoir football uniform of the time. At the time of this photograph, the football helmet face mask had only been in use for a little under 10 years. This was the first year of North Lenoir football. The uniforms were green and black, and the mascot name was changed from Bulldogs to Hawks. (Courtesy of Sonny Herring.)

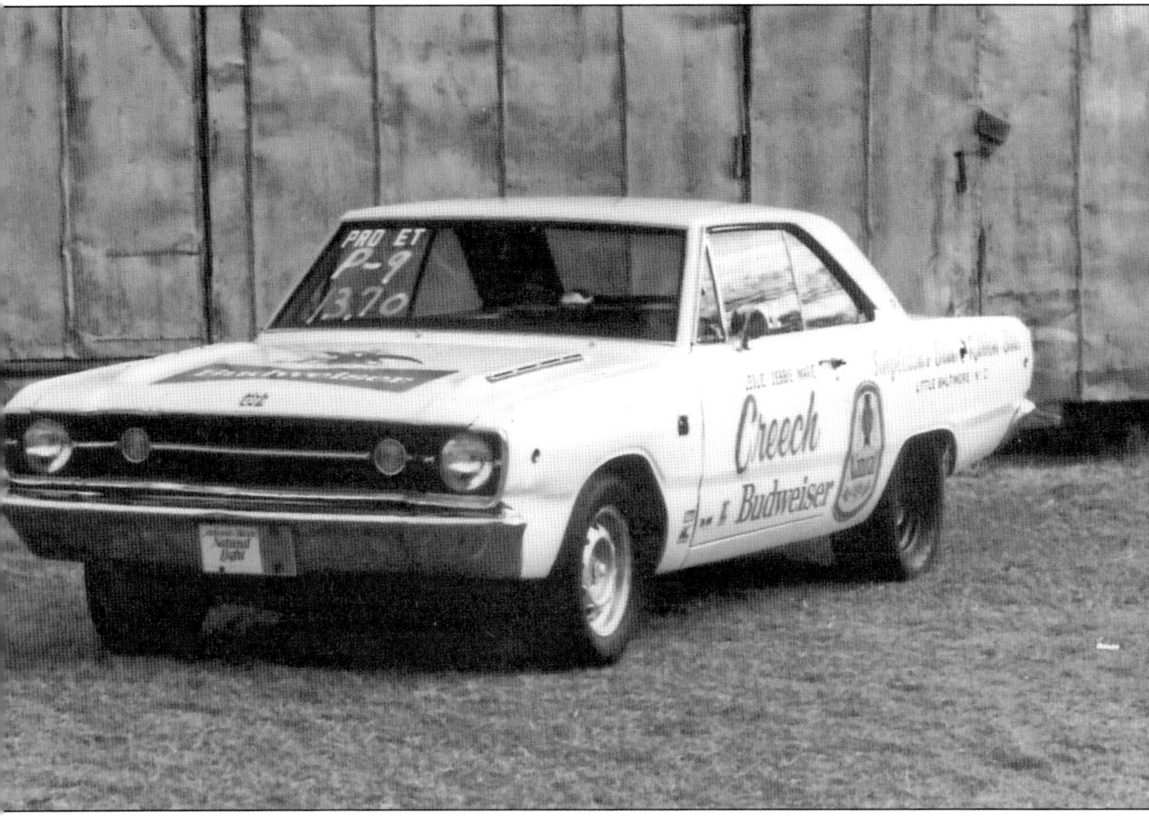

DRAGSTER, 1980. Shown here is Leslie Creech's car. His brother-in-law, Keith Bostick, helped to work on Creech's car. Leslie Creech raced from 1971 to 1984. He won races at neighboring Kinston Drag Strip and raced in the Pro-ET class. This class was derived from the fastest drivers with the best elapsed times. The Pro-ET class always had a monetary prize. At Kinston, this class was competitive. Creech stated that, "Alvin Aycock from La Grange was a topped-notched racer, as well as Jesse Vinson from Kinston and Buddy Sasser." Danny Waters was another well-known racer in the area. Danny's son, Danny Waters Jr., was a drag-racing champion of the International Hot Rod Association (IHRA) in 1998 and finished second in 2007. Creech also raced in Jacksonville and Bridgeton. The Kinston Drag Strip opened in 1960, and it is still in operation today. (Courtesy of Leslie Creech.)

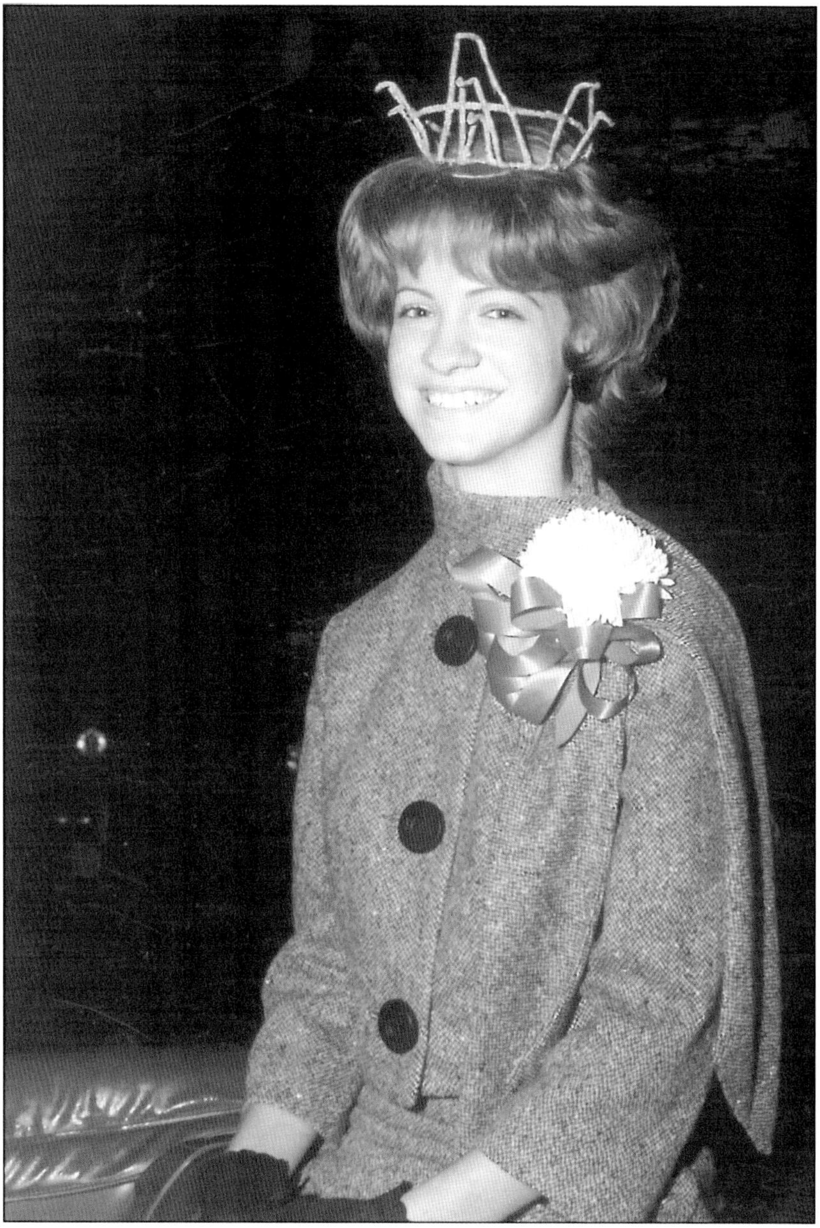

THE QUEEN, 1962. This is the 1962 homecoming queen, Mattie Kate Harrison. The ceremony was conducted on the field. Harrison was formerly crowned by one of the tri-captains of the football team, senior Corky Smith. Serving in that year's queen's court were Hope Denmark, Sharon Gilmore, Cleo Singleton, Sandra Sutton, and Nancy Jo Denmark. That same year, Harrison was also recognized as one of the most talented students in the graduating class. She was also involved with the school's chorus group and was the chief cheerleader for the Bulldogs. Serving as La Grange High School's last group of cheerleaders were Alice Harrison, Vicky Wallace, Sharon Gilmore, Janice Wetherington, Judy Foss, Kaye Dawson, and Hope Denmark. In 1962, school activities included the annual Halloween Carnival, the Glee Club, the Beta Club, Future Homemakers of America (FHA), Future Farmers of America (FFA), the Roman Holiday Junior Senior Banquet, and the school paper, the *Bulldog-Barker*. (Courtesy of Sonny Herring.)

THE MAJORETTE, 1962. This is one of the many lovely La Grange Bulldog majorettes, Linda Rhodes. She is getting a helping hand adjusting her majorette boots from Chris Wooten (left) and Lindsey Stallings. In 1962, majorettes were chosen based on their "beauty, poise" and it "was a very coveted honor at the school." (Courtesy of Sonny Herring.)

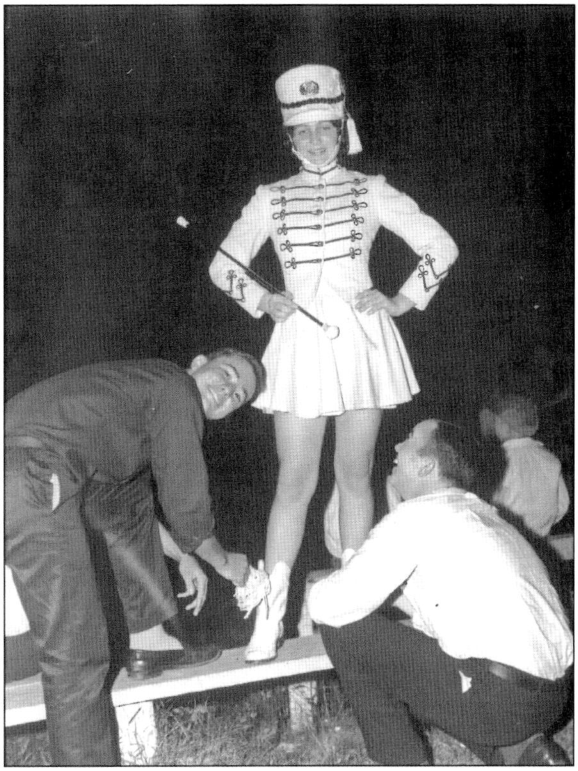

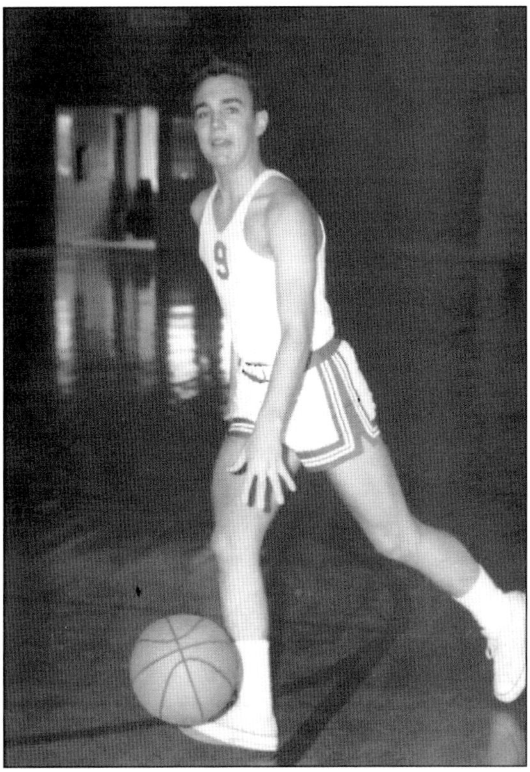

BOB WALKER, C. 1965. Here is North Lenoir High School basketball star Bob Walker. Notice the Converse shoe, which was very popular in the 1950s and 1960s. They were created in 1908 by Marquis Mills Converse. The Chuck Taylor brand was added in 1932. Charles "Chuck" H. Taylor was a former basketball player and later a salesman for Converse. (Courtesy of Sonny Herring.)

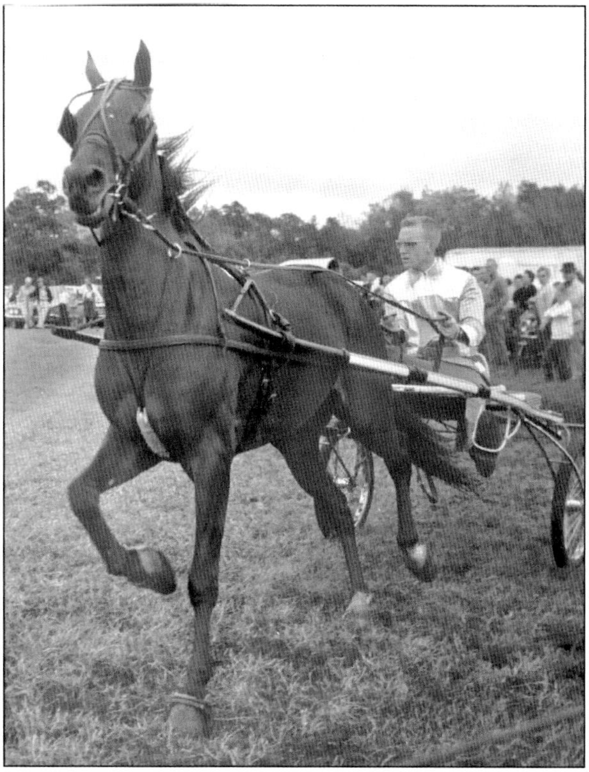

Harness Racing, 1963–1965. This was a well-attended event by locals. The show had Tennessee Walkers and various other ponies and horse breeds participating. At the shows, competing horses would run the barrels, and harness competitions were held as well. The horse shows and contests took place behind the old Freewill Baptist Church on Caswell Street. (Courtesy of Sonny Herring.)

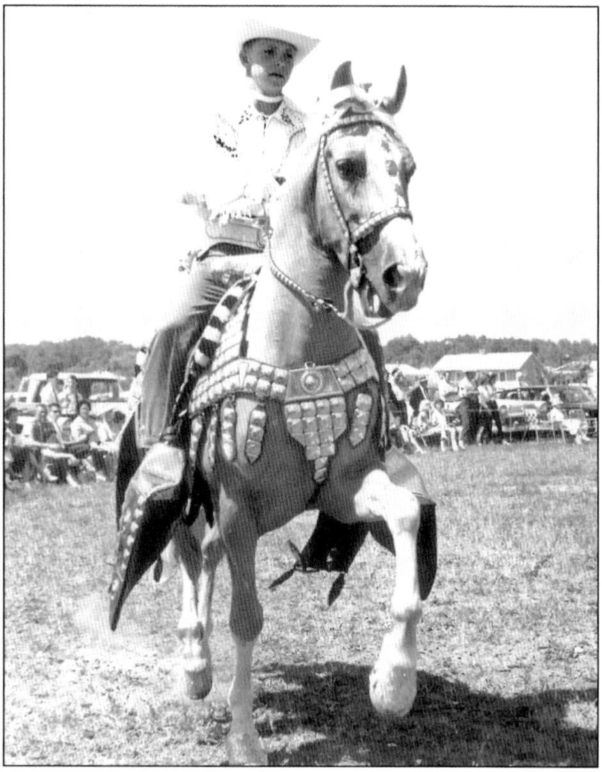

Horse Show, Late 1950s. Horse shows were held on Caswell Street, behind the old location of the Freewill Baptist Church, in an open field. Shows were also held in Bethel. Y.Z. Foss and his daughter Gail were big supporters and contributors to these shows. Foss, a World War II veteran, also owned a Chevrolet dealership where the library is today. (Courtesy of Sonny Herring.)

Five

Surrounding Neighbors

There are three main cities neighboring La Grange: Goldsboro, Kinston, and Greenville. Goldsboro was founded in the late 1700s and incorporated in 1847. The town took its name from the assistant chief engineer, Matthew T. Goldsborough. The town changed its name in 1869 to Goldsboro. In 1993, this neighbor of La Grange was recognized as a Top Ten City by *Money* magazine. Goldsboro is also proudly the home to Seymour Johnson Air Force Base (4th Fighter Wing).

Kinston, founded in 1762, is one of the oldest towns in North Carolina and has always been Lenoir County's seat. The town's original name, "Kingston," was instituted in honor of King George III. In 1784, the name was changed to its current spelling, to disavow any allegiance to the king. During the Civil War, the town was attacked twice, during the Battle of Kinston, on December 14, 1862, and the Battle of Wyse Fork, March 7–10, 1865. After the war, the town's population reached almost 2,000. Kinston, like La Grange, became successful in the tobacco industry. Kinston has enjoyed its local popularity and is home to several corporations, such as West Pharmaceuticals, Dupont, and Sanderson Farms.

Greenville, located about 40 minutes away, has had a great relationship with the citizens of La Grange. Many from La Grange have attended East Carolina University. The East Carolina Joyner Library is named after La Grange citizen J.Y. Joyner. Most of the people of La Grange support the East Carolina athletic programs, especially football, baseball, and basketball. During the 1800s, Greenville was a major point of interest for some of La Grange's most well-known families.

These towns have always been and always will be neighbors. The people of La Grange travel there for lunch, sporting events, and shopping. They are where physicians practice, teachers teach, and lawyers practice law. These three towns feel like an extension of La Grange.

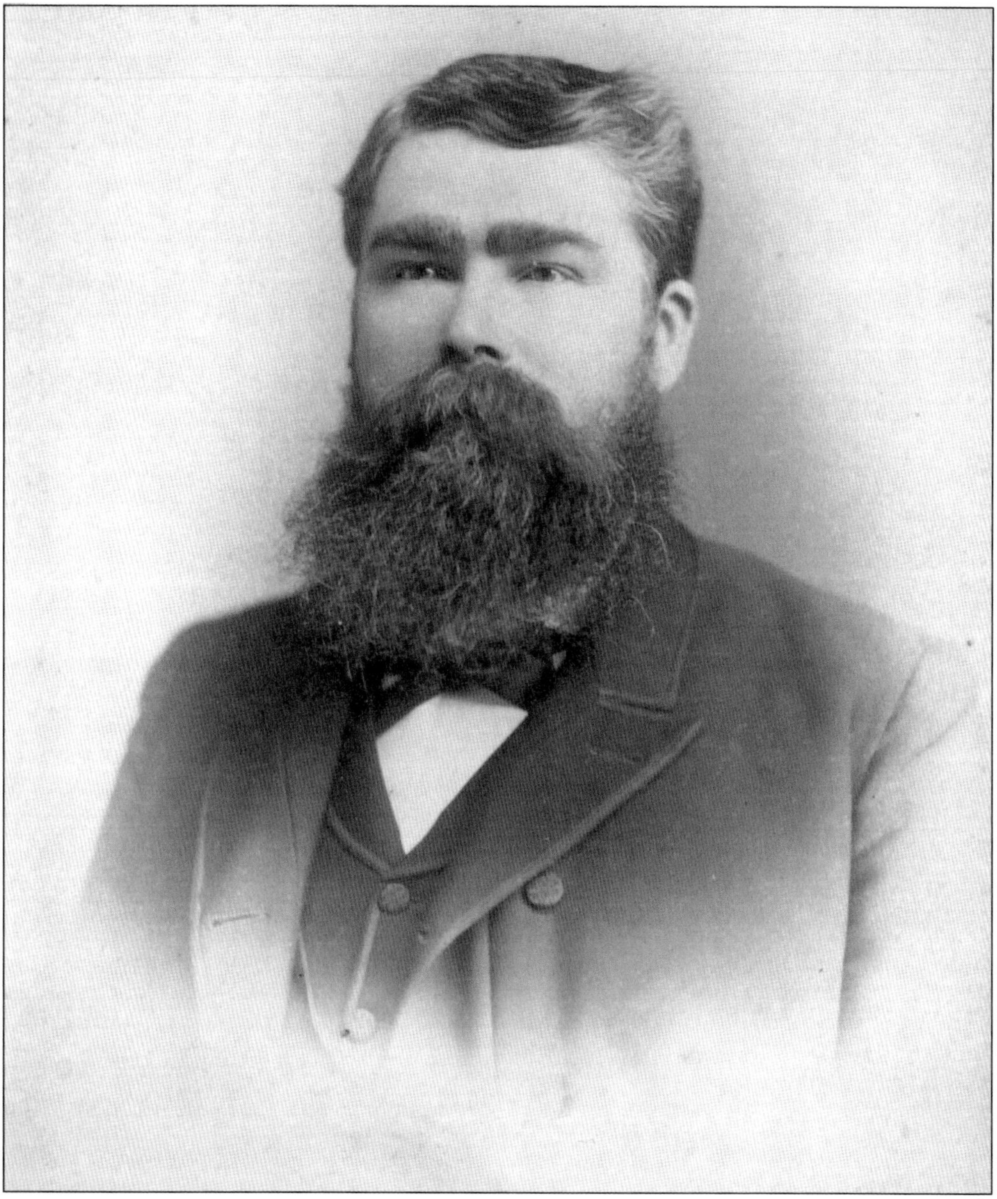

CAPT. WILLIAM LAFAYETTE KENNEDY, C. 1888. This photograph was taken by Cyrus P. Wharton, a well-known photographer from Greensboro. He had his studio in Greensboro from 1883 to 1886. In 1887, he moved to Raleigh and opened Wharton Photography. His studio was active from 1887 until 1906. He took on a partner, Manly W. Tyree, in 1909. By 1911, he was bought out, but the company kept the name Wharton & Tyree. The business was finally sold in 1919. William Kennedy was a former Confederate captain. He and his wife were the founders of the Kennedy Memorial Home, today called simply the Kennedy Home. In 1912, the family gave 1,240 acres of its Cedar Dell Plantation to the Baptist's Children's Home of North Carolina. "Captain," as he was called, purchased the plantation from his father in 1876. In the 1880s, Kennedy was an owner of the Coahoma gristmill as well as being a director of several banks in Kinston. The Kennedys regularly vacationed on North Carolina beaches. (Courtesy of East Carolina University, Joyner Library Digital Collections.)

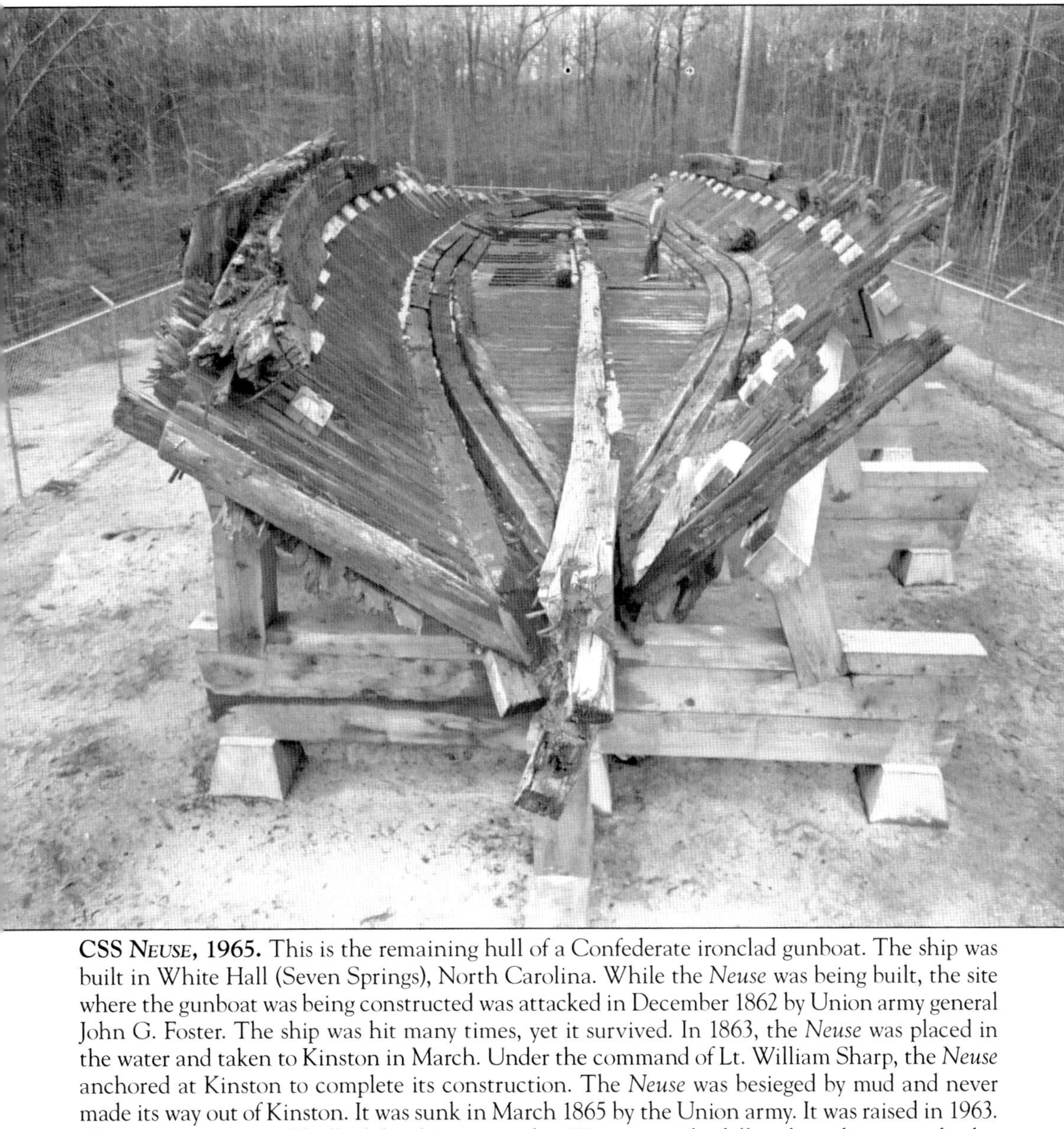

CSS *Neuse*, 1965. This is the remaining hull of a Confederate ironclad gunboat. The ship was built in White Hall (Seven Springs), North Carolina. While the *Neuse* was being built, the site where the gunboat was being constructed was attacked in December 1862 by Union army general John G. Foster. The ship was hit many times, yet it survived. In 1863, the *Neuse* was placed in the water and taken to Kinston in March. Under the command of Lt. William Sharp, the *Neuse* anchored at Kinston to complete its construction. The *Neuse* was besieged by mud and never made its way out of Kinston. It was sunk in March 1865 by the Union army. It was raised in 1963. The surviving original hull of the ship is stored in Kinston, and a full-scale replica is on display in the downtown area by the Neuse River. (Courtesy of East Carolina University, Joyner Library Digital Collections.)

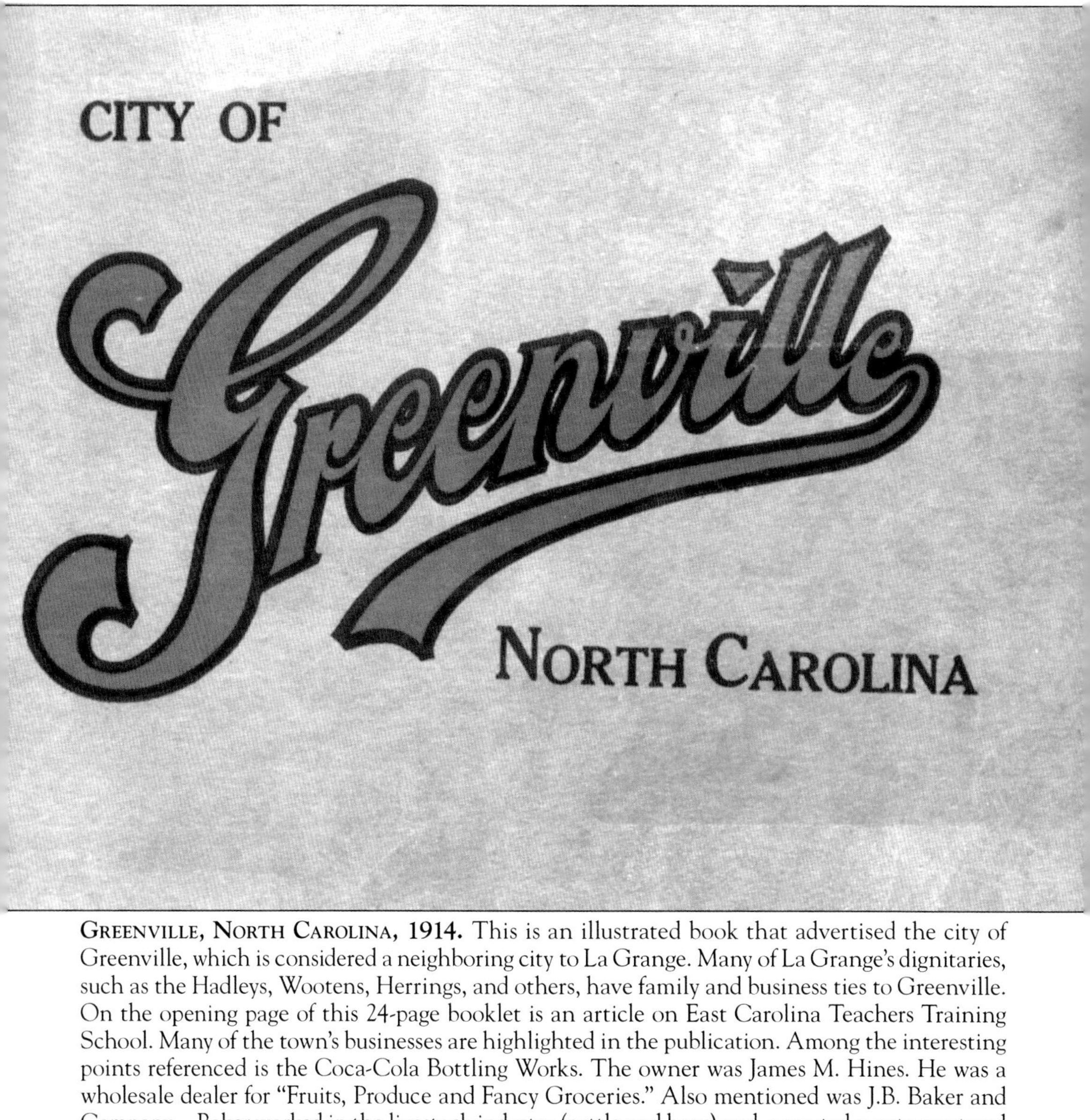

GREENVILLE, NORTH CAROLINA, 1914. This is an illustrated book that advertised the city of Greenville, which is considered a neighboring city to La Grange. Many of La Grange's dignitaries, such as the Hadleys, Wootens, Herrings, and others, have family and business ties to Greenville. On the opening page of this 24-page booklet is an article on East Carolina Teachers Training School. Many of the town's businesses are highlighted in the publication. Among the interesting points referenced is the Coca-Cola Bottling Works. The owner was James M. Hines. He was a wholesale dealer for "Fruits, Produce and Fancy Groceries." Also mentioned was J.B. Baker and Company—Baker worked in the livestock industry (cattle and hogs) and operated a restaurant and barbeque stand—and another business of note, the Hotel Bertha, which touted its up-to-date modern equipment which included "steam, hot and cold running water and call bells." The Hotel Bertha had 50 rooms. (Courtesy of East Carolina University, Joyner Library Digital Collections.)

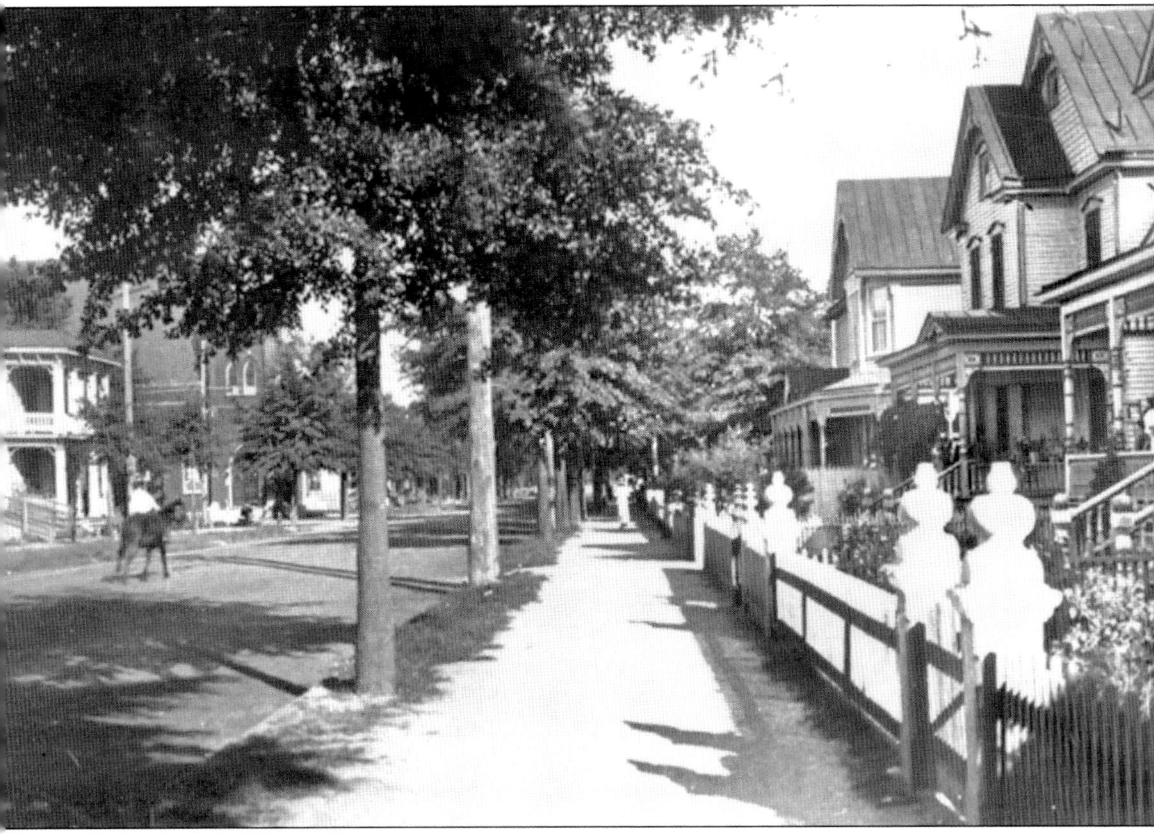

KINSTON, EARLY 1900S. Kinston was virtually destroyed during the Civil War, however, recovery is apparent in this photograph. The street is adorned with flowers and is neatly manicured. The rider of the pony appears to be a small boy. The popularity of the automobile would change the makeup of the city's streets and sidewalks. Kinston in the early 1900s became very progressive. The city built roads, beginning with Queen Street in 1906. It had a major newspaper, the *Free Press*, and it welcomed the automobile. Between 1915 and 1919, the town once again adopted a road-building program and established a solid public schools system. The predecessor for higher education was the well-known Kinston College, which began in 1871. Future North Carolina governor Charles B. Aycock attended the college, which lasted from 1871 to 1894. (Courtesy of the Heritage Place, Lenoir Community College.)

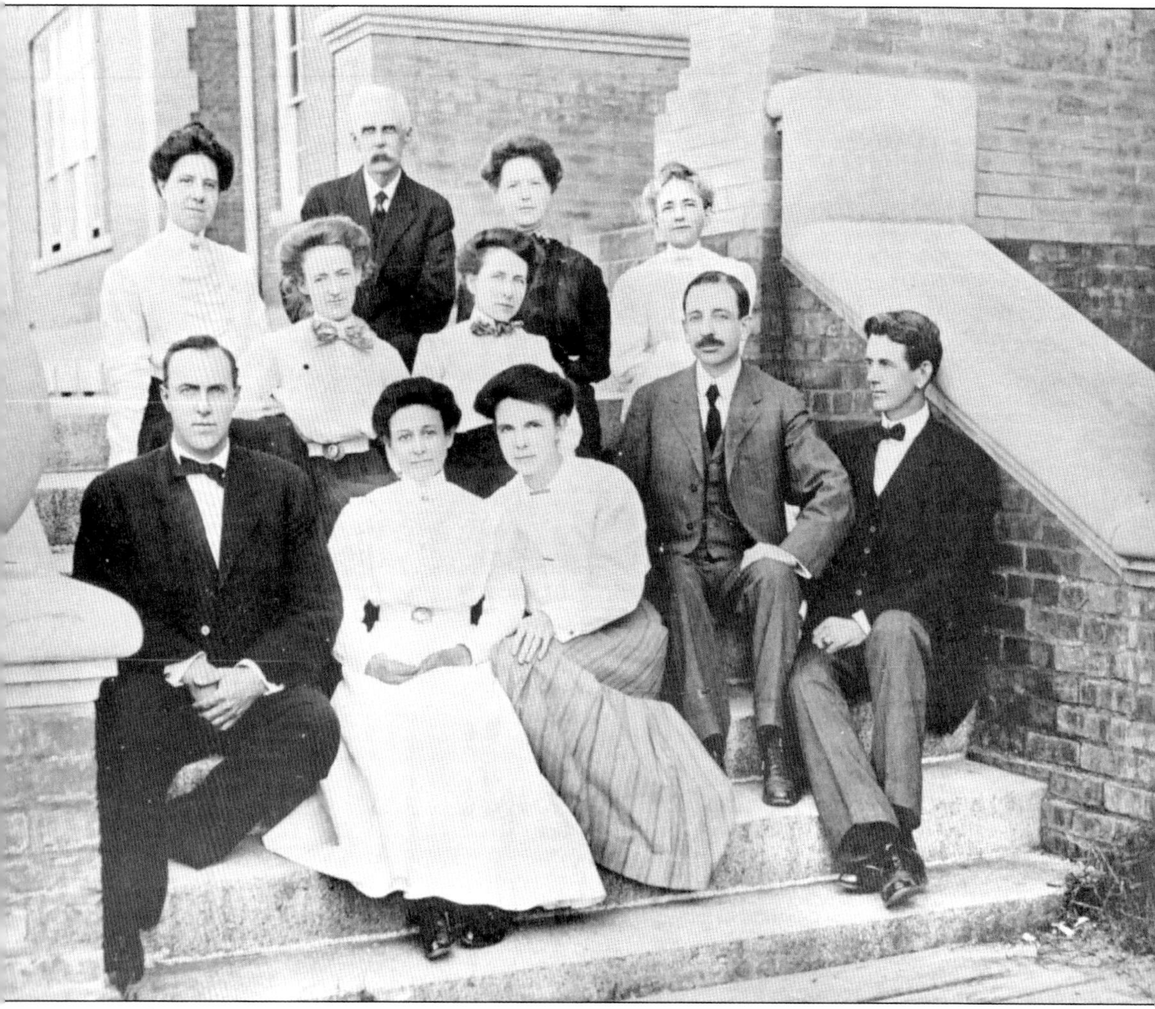

EAST CAROLINA TEACHERS TRAINING SCHOOL, 1909. The school began in 1907 after Pitt County offered the state 243 acres and the willingness to pay $100,000 for a school-building program. Robert Herring Wright was the training school's first president (1909 to 1934). The Wright Building is named in his honor. Among his major contributions is his bringing about the schools' first four-year curriculum in 1920. In 1927, the school adopted its master of arts program. The school grew exponentially from the early 1960s to about 1980. This photograph shows the original faculty, identified by ECU University Archives as follows: "first faculty of East Carolina Teachers Training School on steps of Austin Building. Kate W. Lewis, William Henry Ragsdale, Birdie McKinney, Sallie Joyner Davis, Maria D. Graham, Mamie E. Jenkins, Claude W. Wilson, Jennie M. Ogden, Fannie Bishop, Herbert E. Austin, Robert H. Wright." (Courtesy of East Carolina University, Joyner Library Digital Collections.)

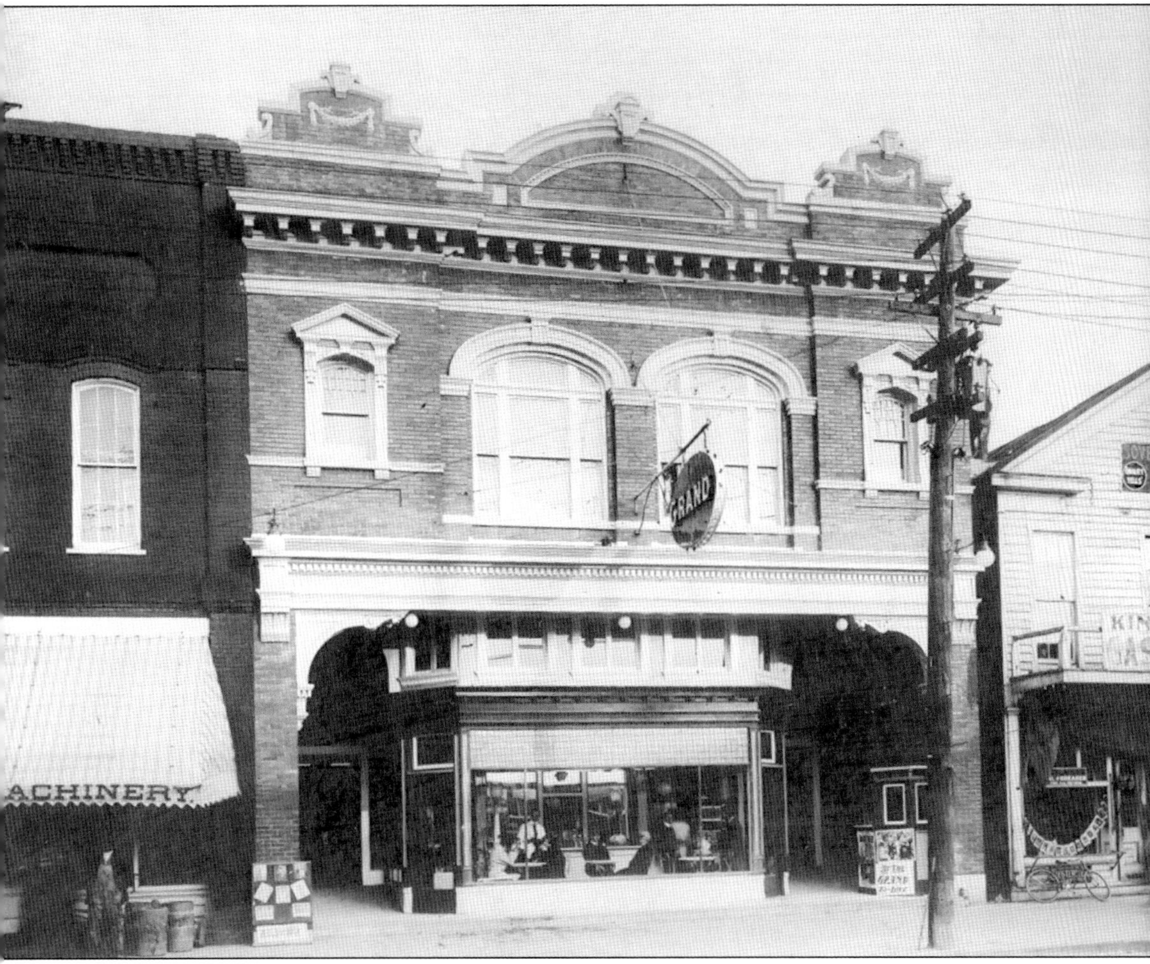

GRAND THEATER, C. 1928. The Grand Theater opened in 1915. It was renovated in the early 1930s and renamed Paramount Theater, after the Paramount Picture chain. The theater was damaged by a fire in the 1940s and renovated again. The theater was run by Wilby-Kincey Theaters, a subsidiary of Paramount Pictures, Inc. Wilby-Kincey operated in a few states in the South. By late 1968, the Wilby-Kincey Service Corporation only serviced a few states. During the Depression, the company renovated many theaters across the South. It is unknown who redesigned the Paramount, or who the architect was. It is believed that in North Carolina, Erle Stilwell, famous for designing the Carolina Theater in Durham, may have been one of those involved in planning the renovation. When Paramount took over the Grand and renovated it, Stilwell may have been involved. (Courtesy of the Heritage Place, Lenoir Community College.)

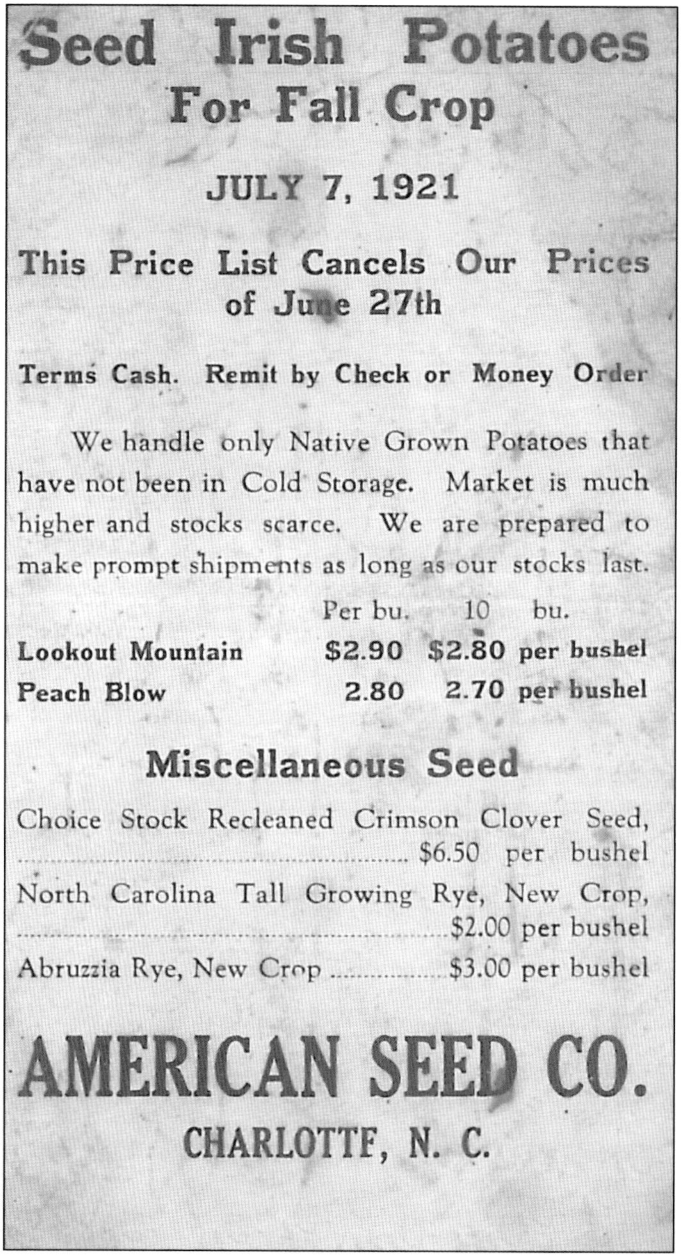

Seed Irish Potatoes
For Fall Crop

JULY 7, 1921

This Price List Cancels Our Prices of June 27th

Terms Cash. Remit by Check or Money Order

We handle only Native Grown Potatoes that have not been in Cold Storage. Market is much higher and stocks scarce. We are prepared to make prompt shipments as long as our stocks last.

	Per bu.	10 bu.	
Lookout Mountain	**$2.90**	**$2.80**	**per bushel**
Peach Blow	**2.80**	**2.70**	**per bushel**

Miscellaneous Seed

Choice Stock Recleaned Crimson Clover Seed, ... $6.50 per bushel

North Carolina Tall Growing Rye, New Crop, ... $2.00 per bushel

Abruzzia Rye, New Crnp .... $3.00 per bushel

AMERICAN SEED CO.

CHARLOTTF, N. C.

Seed Irish Potatoes, 1921. Many farmers would buy their seeds, fertilizer, and other crop goods from local merchants in La Grange. As can be seen in this 1921 advertisement postcard, the prices were very low in comparison with today's farm prices. This postcard was sent to local farmer/merchant A.T. Rouse. In 1921, the mail would come to La Grange with simply the person's name and the town's name, for example: "A.T. Rouse, La Grange, North Carolina." At this time, there were no zip codes. The post office personnel knew the people of the town and would notify them if they had mail. The company listed on this postcard is the American Seed Company, based out of Charlotte, North Carolina. The company, it is believed, was absorbed by the Clifton Seed Company in 1928, or it went out of business. The farmer's supply business in North Carolina in the 1920s was fiercely competitive. (Courtesy of Grace Burke.)

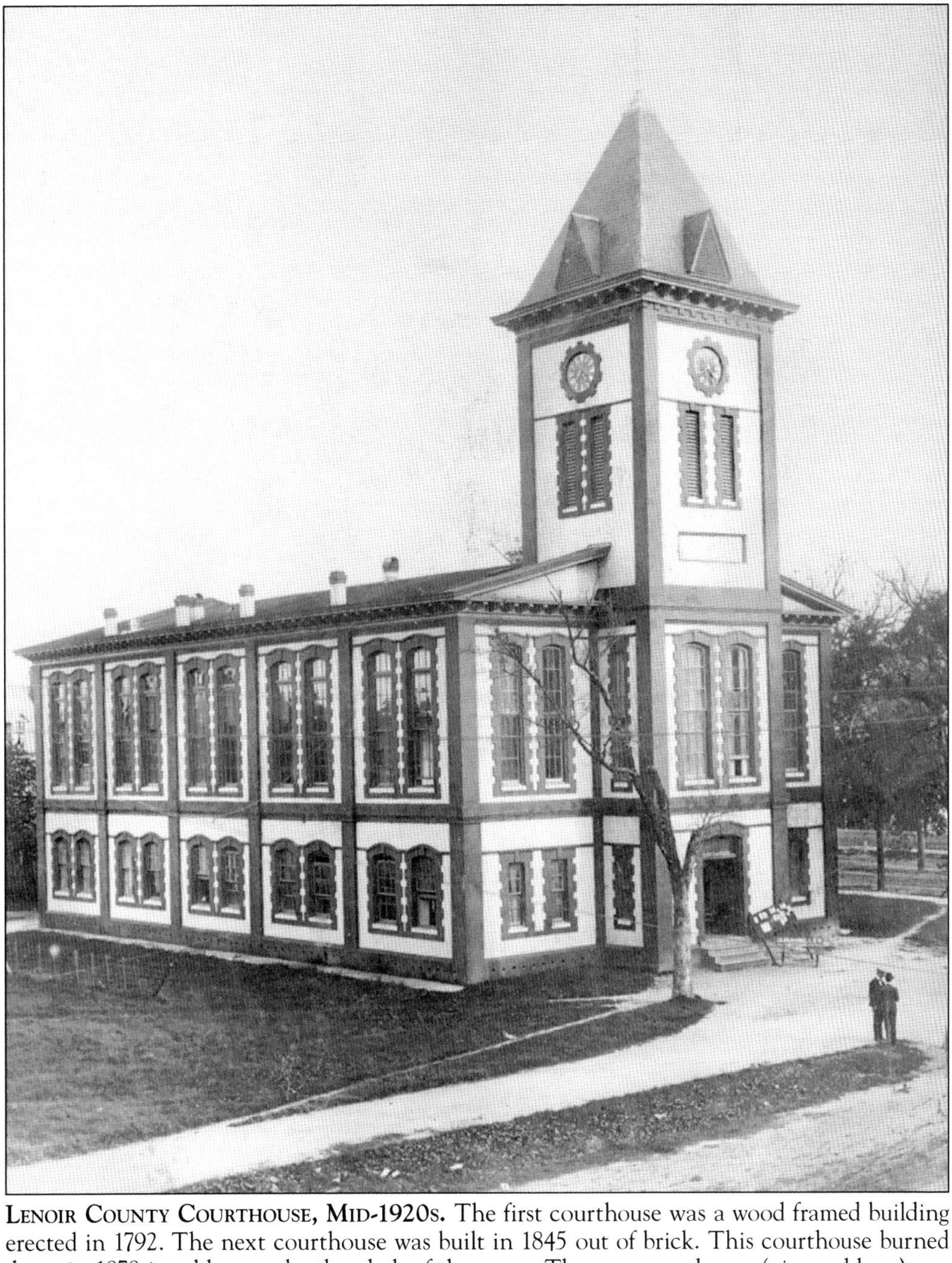

Lenoir County Courthouse, Mid-1920s. The first courthouse was a wood framed building erected in 1792. The next courthouse was built in 1845 out of brick. This courthouse burned down in 1878 in a blaze set by the clerk of the court. The new courthouse (pictured here) was built from stone and lasted until it was rebuilt in 1937–1938. The dedication ceremony was held in 1939. The structure was built by local architects A. Mitchell Wooten and John J. Roland. The courthouse was built by T.A. Loving & Company General Contractors. It is also believed by the Lenoir County Historical Association that world-renowned architect Edward Durell Stone was an advisor during the building. At this time, North Carolina allowed special superior court judges to preside anywhere in the state. Much of the decor of this courthouse maintains its original appearance. (Courtesy of the Heritage Place, Lenoir Community College.)

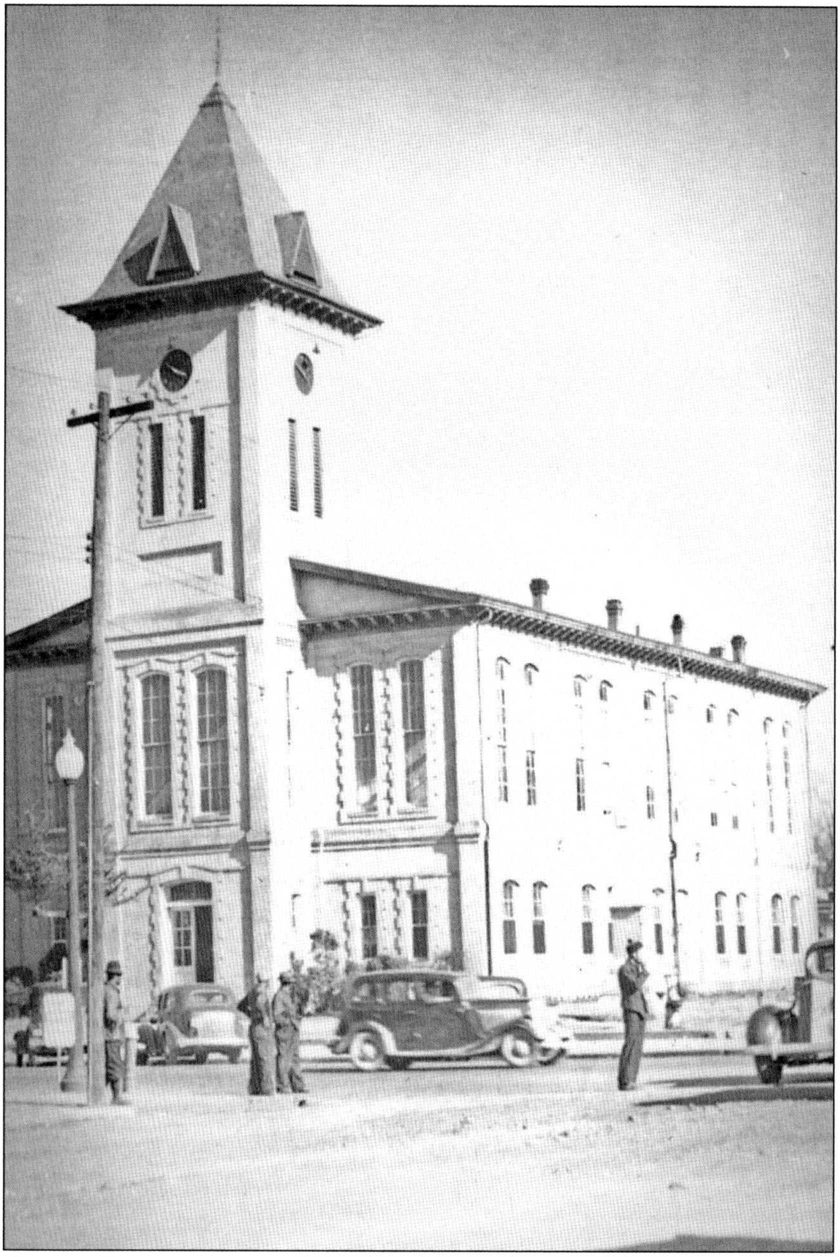

LENOIR COUNTY COURTHOUSE, C. 1943. When the courthouse burned down, most of the county records burned with it, including those pertaining to La Grange. The original records, including land deeds, marriage licenses, and other writs of importance were forever lost. The few records that survive and pertain to Lenoir County come from Wayne and Greene County courthouses. The local lore concerning the burning in 1878 tells that someone tried to break into the courthouse and steal some legal documents that would have incriminated him. He could not find the document and then burned the courthouse down. In the 1800s, the courthouse in Kinston held court once a month with a circuit judge. The town would make that a festive occasion. This occasion was popular with young people because they would get to meet others of the opposite sex. Hence the term "courting." (Courtesy of the Heritage Place, Lenoir Community College.)

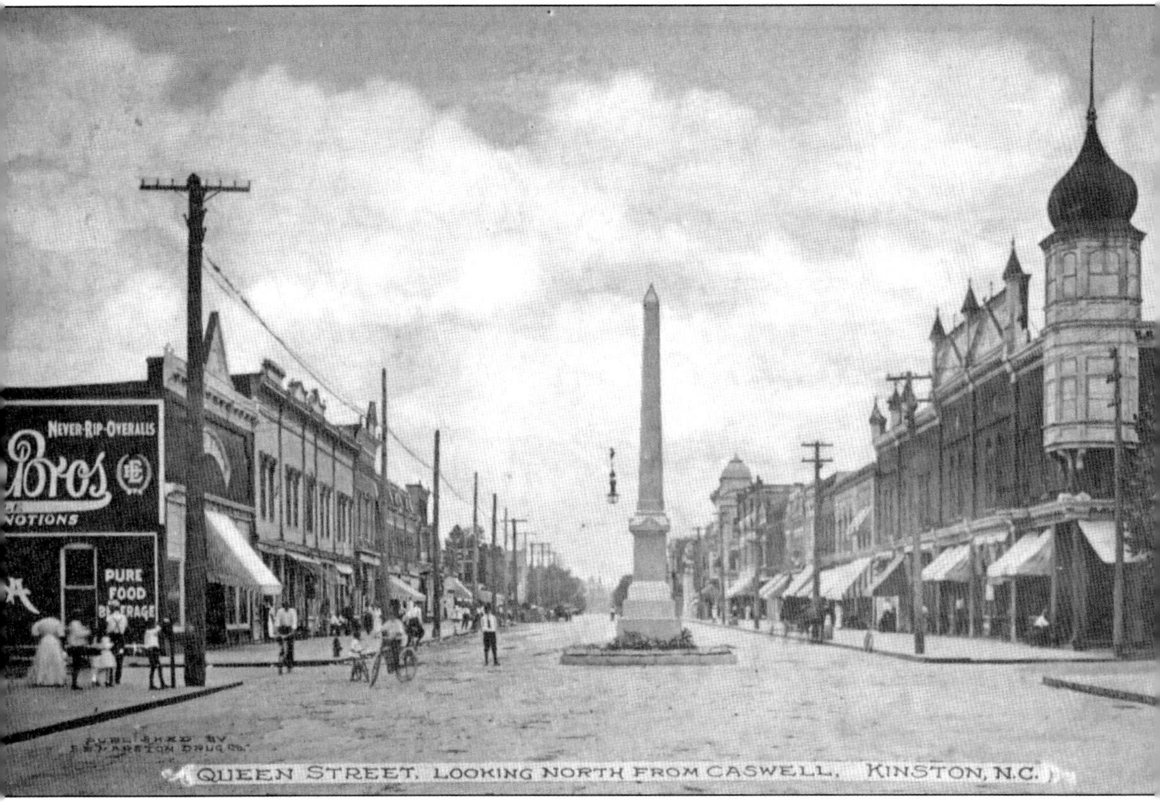

DOWNTOWN KINSTON, 1910. In 1906, King Street was paved, and soon, paving took place citywide. The progressive city voted in 1903 to add a $150,000 enhancement plan. This included a new sewage system, drilling deeper wells, and adding a new electrical system. In 1904, Kinston added the Caswell Fire Department. The automobile had yet to gain popularity. Carriages and wagons were still the dominant modes of transportation. Queen Street no longer has the monument downtown. This was, and still is, the main street in Kinston, the county seat for Lenoir County. There was an attempt to have the name of the city changed permanently in 1833 to Caswell, in honor of Richard Caswell. Many of the townspeople were not in favor of the name change, and the name reverted back to Kinston in 1834. (Courtesy of East Carolina University, Joyner Library Digital Collections.)

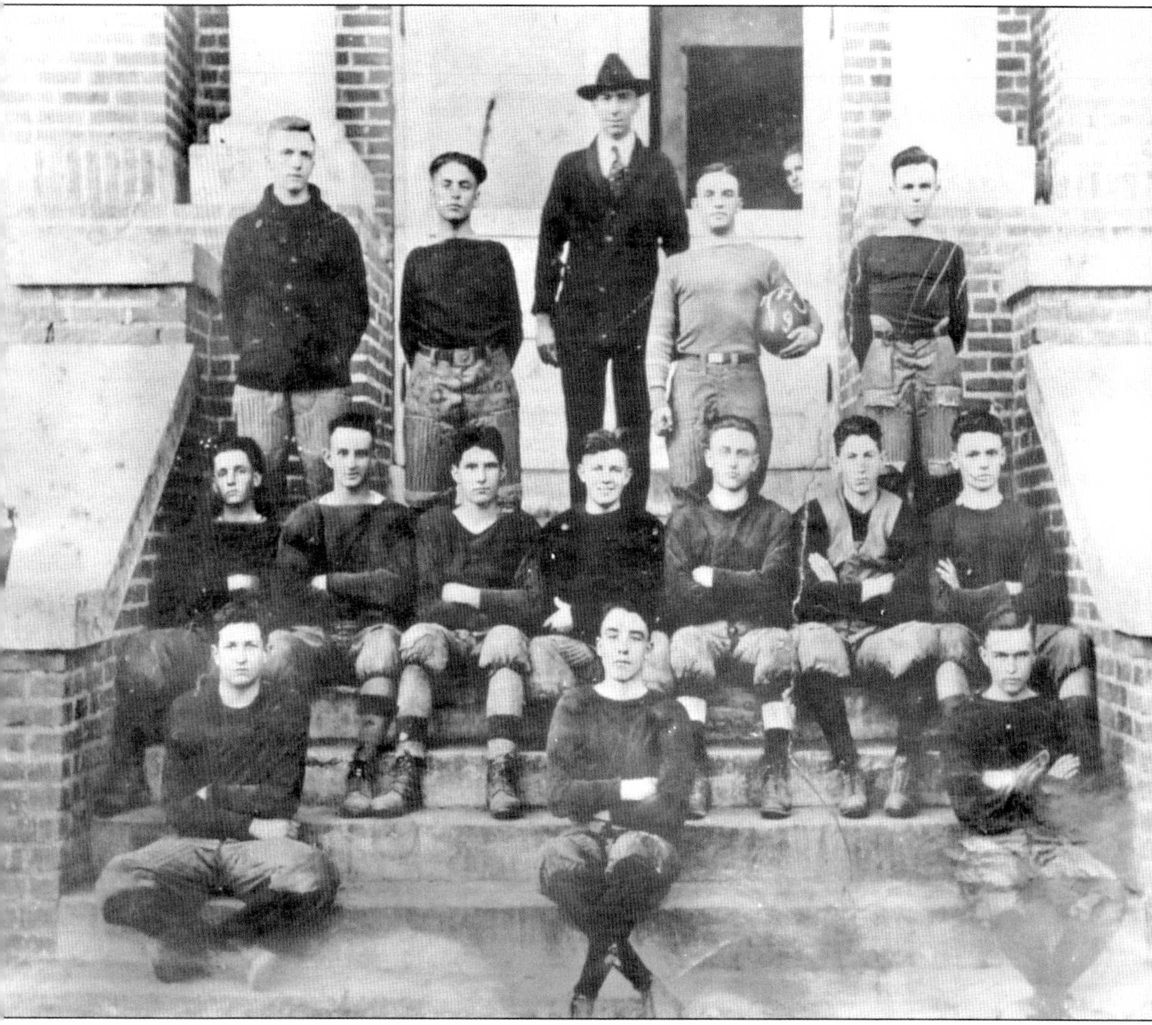

Kinston High School Football Team, 1919. This is a rare photograph of the 1919 Kinston football team. Prior to 1919, the only schools in Kinston were privately run institutions. Kinston's first schools consisted of a grammar school and a high school (pictured here.) The town also had an African American grammar and high school. The Kinston High School originally was on Lenoir Street. The first high school burned down in 1924. The next high school was Grainger High School, which is on Park Avenue. This school was built in 1926. According to the *Heritage of Lenoir County* book, those shown here are, from left to right, (first row) Thomas Mewborn, E.R. "Buck" Wooten, and Mike Lee; (second row) George Nensmask, Richard Tyndall, Guy Gooding, Roland Blow, Clarence Clark, David Pearson, and Randolph Spear; (third row) Charles B. McNairy, Ellis Simon, principal Dr. E.C. Carroll, Gene Surnell, and Herbert ?. The person peeping out of the window is Eroll Dixon. (Courtesy of Sonny Herring.)

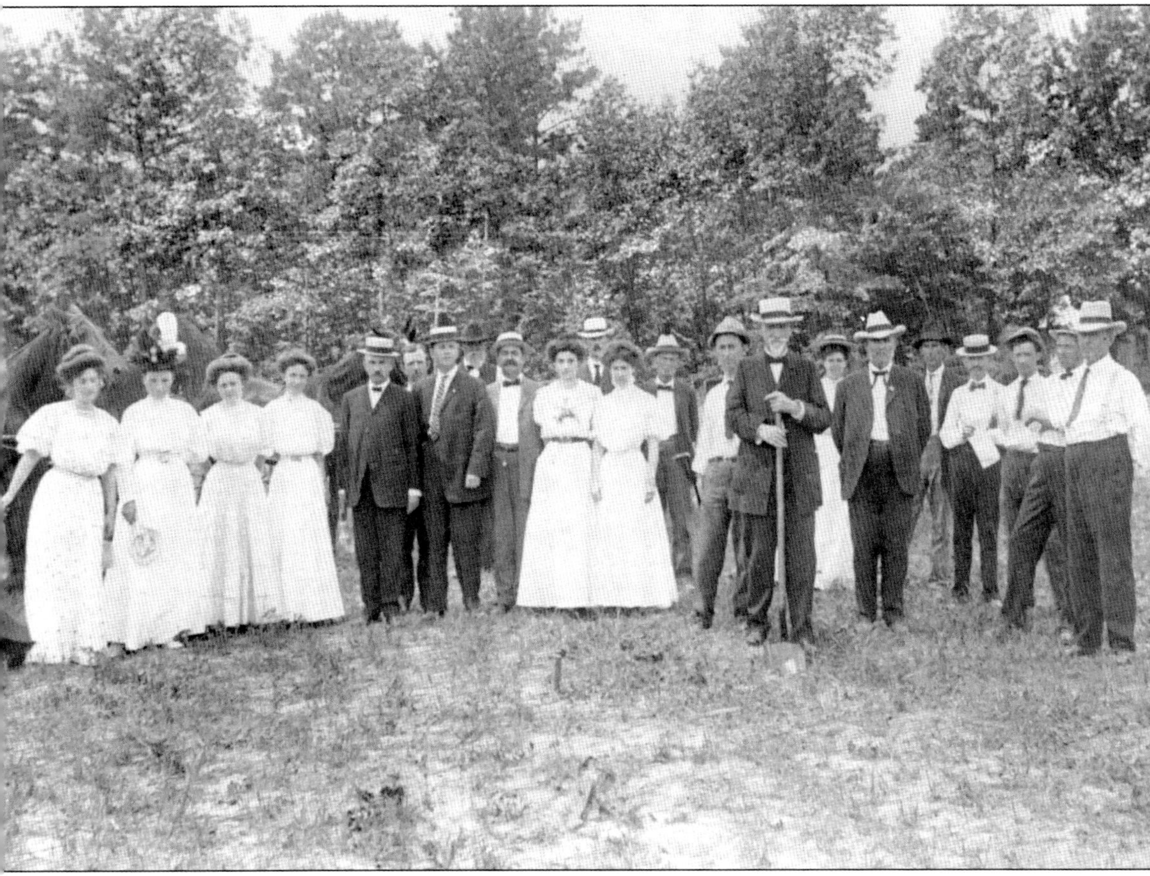

Ground Breaking of East Carolina Teachers Training School, 1907. This school would eventually become East Carolina University. In 1907, the state board of education nearly awarded the school to Kinston. The school originally had six buildings, including two dormitories, a power plant, an administration building, and an infirmary. There were 10 faculty members in 1907. Originally, there was no tuition for those promising to teach for two years. The school's name was changed to East Carolina University (ECU) in 1967. According to ECU archives, those present are, from left to right, Mary B. Dail, Mary W. Jarvis, Mary (James) Lipscomb, Jennie White, Fernando Godfrey "Dink" James, Herbert A. White, Robert D. Harrington, William A. Harrington, Jesse Speight, Nell (Skinner) Moseley, Bennett W. Moseley, Irma (Cobb) Dunn, Richard A. Tyson, Haywood Dail, Thomas Jordan Jarvis, Celeste Evans, Richard King, Ed Evans, David Jordan Whichard, Cecil Cobb, Charles V. York, and Robert J. Cobb. (Courtesy of East Carolina University, Joyner Library Digital Collections.)